Tales out of School

Real adventures at the chalk face

Stuart Newton

authorHOUSE®

For Julia +V.
Best wishes
Stuart X X X
April – 2018

AuthorHouse™ UK Ltd.
500 Avebury Boulevard
Central Milton Keynes, MK9 2BE
www.authorhouse.co.uk
Phone: 08001974150

First published by AuthorHouse 11/30/2009

ISBN: 978-1-4490-0870-3 (sc)

This book is printed on acid-free paper.

This book is for -- Jim Henderson, Ray Mooney, Charles Gallagher and John Stockbury -- colleagues and friends

Foreword

Scott Hilliard Robinson is my 'alter ego' – he came from America/Canada after college, lived in West London between 1980-2000 and taught in schools all round the metropolis; recounting endless tales of kids in school, teachers at work and diversions in the city. It was a full life of work, friends and family; altogether demanding to be expiated, eventually, to be set out for reflection.

I already wrote a full book of poems: 'Londinium Poeta' (2004), which relates the same life in London; but without the schools and from a different perspective. Scott's special stories still needed to be told; not just for teachers and their pupils, though this might be a big enough audience. They are for anybody who went to school, or lived in a big city just before the millennium; also for parents and anyone interested in public education.

The events/scenes in the stories are mostly true and real, because they had to be; the same with the characters (the schools also real). However, no story or part thereof, is intended to harm/insult or embarrass any person or any particular place.

I never thought, never intended, to write about teaching in schools; though it was my livelihood for over thirty years and devoured all my time and energy. But eventually the kids and the teachers, together with various themes, haunted me for years to come. I knew no better way to help myself, than write out the stories fully as possible; hopefully to benefit others as well.

Only recently, Frank McCourt wrote of his teaching in New York City – 'Teacher Man' (2005). I found it entertaining, informative and thoughtful; a valuable book, on a subject not usually presented so honestly and so fully. In fact, there are very few books dealing with teaching/education, directly from an experienced classroom practitioner. Unfortunately, there is so much ignorance/misunderstanding within the general public (including the parents) about the work/role of an ordinary class teacher; adding up to a very unsatisfactory state of affairs. I wish my own book will compliment his New York stories; his very much an American experience and mine a British one.

For years I have been reading James Herriot's

stories (1970's) about a Yorkshire vet; marveling at his mastery of character and detail. He has been an inspiration for me, because I knew him at work on the farms, when myself a farm-boy in Yorkshire all those years ago; noticing how he was quiet and diffident, observant. Later I read how his family came from my own hometown; the very same district near to the north docks on Wearside. My stories are not the same as his, they are different characters in very different situations; though he sought to present an overlooked area of society in a new rewarding way. Like I tried myself; to justify the ordinary school teacher and his pupils in school.

Lastly, I must mention F. Scott Fitzgerald's 'The Pat Hobby Stories' (1939); seventeen stories about a studio 'hack' in Hollywood USA. My own stories are a tribute to an author who gave so much joy from excellent writing; to read his uncanny observations with a sense of humanity in fullest colour. I owe much to Fitzgerald, since I first stumbled upon his books as a young student in England, to change my own vocation/ livelihood.

Scott Robinson, in school, is a full account of people in circumstances not of their own making. To see them triumph and fail, to impact on those around them and ultimately upon the reader too. Short stories are meant to be the wealth of 'human nature', that is rich in diversity and great in need, strong in spirit but weak in the flesh; ever changing and enlarging. Scott's stories are where we see the vagrancies of a working life; where you can find lots of 'canny' individuals at work-an-play, in full voice with humour, candor and hope...

An Easter Break

There is lots of flaccid emotion in a teaching career, much heartache and regret, many disappointments and misgivings. Yet teachers are a special breed who do not stay down, they keep coming back for another try; no one knows quite why they do this, even teachers themselves can't say why. Scott Robinson was at a particularly bad patch, but managing to hang-in. He was on the telephone this time, at a small hotel and trying hard to connect -- "How yuh doing baby, how are you"?

"-- not talking to you".

"That was last week; come on Kay"!

"You promised an ice-cream and didn't come on Saturday. I waited on Sunday as well".

Scott was between jobs; doing the rounds. Today

he was standing between reception and dirty wallpaper in the lobby; trying to pass this hurdle without falling --

"What about school; what's your favourite lesson"?

"I told you it's still Art and colouring-in".

"Well, who is your best friend now"?

"And I'm not a baby"!

Scott rubbed a tired face to notice new stains and wear upon his outfit. He wasn't doing so well this year; forty-something and divorced, in genteel poverty, with college degree but no school work. In fact he was painting for a while, decorating with Pat the Irishman; London Irish and trying to make two hundred pounds this week minus materials, minus Pat's share.

It was late afternoon for his monthly phone-call, agreed by the court; to speak to his estranged daughter, who lived down in Chelsea and Scott still in the family home above the park at Nottinghill. After a few more difficult minutes he managed a good exit, good-byes and so on, then gently hung-up. He was flexing his shoulders a bit as he went out the hotel and down the road to meet his man, his Irishman, about the next job and payments. But it was spring coming-up so he detoured at the park entrance, to go past the sand-pit of memories, the swings and slides. He always took the chance to go by memory-lane park; where he and his girl spent every evening in the safe noise of other children and parents, birds and squirrels with their families too. No pain, no torture really like some suggested, like they tried to warn him; in fact it was a comfort; happy memories of family and child did not distress him like it was supposed to. Two boys were taking their swings up very high and nannies were scurrying after their wayward toddlers – these were familiar dramas for him.

As he turned into his street the sun was weakening, but wind reviving with dust from the corner and Pat further down at the door with his kit and coat.

"Hey Hils, what's up; oh yeah --

Not too long; just got here ten minutes ago".

Scott gladly had some good news -- "we got a big flat upstairs to do; complete redecorating and money up-front, a hundred pounds"!

"Sounds alright; yeah, okay" Pat said as they left the street, got through the door and entered a small studio flat – silly small and a squeeze all round. They spread out with glasses of orange-aid and rolled on about the job and money; then went upstairs to see a young Russian lady tenured in another flat. She opened up to them in a loose house coat and lop-sided hair-do; but she was young so they were friendly and peered round everywhere. They were keen to see all the angles,

3

all the concerns of a young lady of-th-town at home to rest and re-charge. When she went out Pat spilled the beans about the new foreigners and Scott added his bit, his inside info from the house; till they had it figured out and how they were on the outside looking in again. Pat lost his contract job at a hostel years before and now searched the city residences for new paying work. He liked a tickle in the ribs and quickly got into a happy mood fit to cope with any trade job even if it be drains and hands on. By afternoon his residual aches re-appeared and he was haring to be off; off home to another rat's hole-inth-wall in west-by-west London. But all day it was paint and sweep, or sweep first then gloss over, brush up high and bites of bakery bits with black tea. At the same time thousands of Irish were re-decorating London, or feeding it from counters, building places and cleaning them; a noble tribe in front of a breakfast mess every day. It was no coincidence Scott had contact with those other Irish too and their diverse dealings, except for love/romance; when wit was not the bait, when blarney got in the way. Because the city also had lots of exotica, lots of new people/women arriving from faraway lands.

Like his own child -- she was a new kind of girl, a new mix; her mother from the East and Scott an old style 'wasp' from middle America. The child was fair but lots of her mother in the cheeks, the sharp retorts. He was proud of this mix, but not the marriage. East can meet West on maps and such but not join up, not mix-up. He could see that in the child who smiled from the photo across the studio room to overview Scott's daily heroics, his coping. The photo was from school with a uniform, a nice pose for teacher/camera and best ribbon in tidy hair; on an open shelf to invite suggestions of attention each day.

Sometimes Scott was quiet for an evening and thinking how they used to be in the family residence, for a few hours if he dared. Then he remembered the Easter gift; he had to go out and get something and deliver to school; find a nice chocolate egg and a card with note. Because he was still struggling, still trying to have it on with a child far away; taken away from his influence, though only three miles distant. Obviously the 'in-laws' were now looming large and the school, the Catholic culture and all the distractions for a child -- adding up to no-daddy, daddy-faraway, daddy-gone!

A sudden reminder made Scott stand up to find his summer shorts, because Spring-coming was strong. He tried them on, to fit and went out the door. He paraded on the pavement in front to catch the air; then thought to go upstairs again and find the Russian gal, to get some funds and last minute instructions. She was home but no money yet; maybe tomorrow.

But tomorrow he had an interview, a job interview; then it would be down to Chelsea with his egg gift. He had a chance at employment again and another middle-income. The job was humanities teacher at a High school towards Heathrow; lots of greenspace and correct behaviour from a lower-middle intake. He was to appear at late morning; then straight back into town to Kay's school by the afternoon. Before sleeping, clean stuff was set out and his case re-packed with shoe-shine, papers and fruit; the Easter gifts were separate.

By ten o'clock next day he was ready to make a quick break to the station and sitting on the first train going west, he tried to go through a check-list; to find he left his bank cards and route-map on a window shelf at home. The carriage was empty this time of day except for a young student at his book, right opposite; he kept silent but often glanced up at Scott, looking right into his gaze. The hollow train scored and screeched along the dark-blue diagram; checked at each stop-mark by Scott as he broke from his own reading, school bumph and the nervous student. By the time the student left his seat Scott too was nervous and worried about a timely showing at school.

Mr.Arnie Rineholt was Headteacher; heavy and compressed in a long-life jacket over button-down collar shirt and gold-style cuff links. Ms.Angie Longhurst, head of Humanities, wore silver power earrings and a polo-neck sweater, next to Mr.Hubbard from the Education department on her left. One more person; but Scott didn't recognize him as he sat square with the chair, Mr.Rineholt and fingered into his brief-case.

The preliminaries were shy and quiet; names and rank round the table, tight smiles and some eye contact. Then it was straight into the deep-end after Scott was given notice of more applicants that same day --

"What makes a good humanities teacher", followed by "what's your best lesson" and Mr.Rineholt took it further about blue reports, book plans and scores. It was overwhelming for a solitary teacher on the receiving end, when Scott knew honesty was naive; he had to say what they wanted to hear, but also disguise this. His responses were only standard text, so he distracted their attention to the department man with quick comments about his past, as seen on the CV papers -- "Yes, I enjoyed the wilderness; great material for teachers in class – between lessons", with laughs all round. It appeared to work in his favour. But he shouldn't have mentioned forests or Canada because Scott was suddenly back there, twenty-five years ago; when he was quick and slim, life was clear and straight with money and no bills, work and no stress, family and fun.

But the questions did not go away -- "are schools the same as here; what could be highlighted, in view of…" But his day-dream continued into California and the fabled sandy playgrounds, sun and youth, youth and health. Scott was a volunteer in a small-town High school; first time in school on the staff side. All the co-eds were blonde or wanted to be and boys wrestled fairly, studied quietly and ate ice-cream at lunch. Scott skirted the halls and grounds as a fly-uponth-wall; he learned to find the sub-text, eat with plastics and finish early every day --

"About the new curriculum, urhmm, what works for you…" Scott heard someone say.

-- The next school for him was in the Salinas area, a Catholic grade school, opposite the big breakfast centre in town. The school were all Hispanics; but the lunch cook very Irish, Chicago Irish; proudly forcing tortillas onto Scott or tamale pie, burritos, into his fledgling constitution. The classes were near forty or more, double language hellions; with penguin nuns in charge, in charge of Scott even. Two eggs over-easy he kept getting across the street; 'hash-browns', he called out and spied his big chrome sedan at the kerb as his first true set of wheels, first big chance for action.

"Doctor Hubbard, would like to ask of Special

Needs and nuclear-fission families, as part of the urban sprawl/spawn…" Scott was becoming confused and dizzy with the intake, as his dream strengthened.

-- The schools in Canada were large square blocks, with straight kids; more grades and hurdles than ever, more strain less summer; more money less fun, more people less movement. Lots of school work by then; an inevitable route to his 'career'; but full of turns and cross junctions, going down hill fast: back-to-back college, school, jobs and weekend alcohol.

"Now your employment record Mister, urhmm, Mister Robinson. Can we turn… I see that…"

Scott could see -- see very well the fixed eyes infront of him, thin face signals and short laughter; the service coffee-tray with plain biscuits. He always could see those things and no changes, no chances, no gaps and no job. Likely Scott could also see himself at these times, see himself in others; glance his hidden image by conventions he mirrors to the panel. He might see the shadows in his complexion, the slack limbs and bits of gray.

"We made big strides planning on tiered strategies, to oversight our targets… so that pupils own a share of learning – what d'you think Mister erhmm Robinson – cultures too, multi-abilities and mixed-organisms from Doctor Hubbard over there…" By now Scott was bewildered as well as scruffy; not too difficult in this stagnant enclosure. He barely knew if his answers were coherent.

But what he said to the panel was contrary to his own experience, he dared not even admit to himself -- to be beaten with feathers, a truly terrible process; they and the kids were trying to beat him to death like this, lay him low with a million-an-one airy blows from paper tigers and miniature harpies; like Gulliver in Lilliput, like a bear in baiting. It truly was a new heroic; like Samson against columns of words. It was more than words from the temple but nets upon the weak, lashes upon the guilty – because these were professional types drawn to their end vocation, they were profiled to such direction. Scott didn't perform in front of the panel so much as paddle along in the soup, or tread water to remain upright.

Time for the coffee. They all did partake at an invisible cue left and remade the familiar china clinking, the Pavlov sounds of gratifying fluids. Each take an equal share, same strength and equal bites of rapport between swallows. By this time the air outside is wakening up to light and sound, but nothing awakening inside. Outside somewhere Pat was warming up to the wood preparation at a skirting, in the corners on his haunches, glancing round the details of a lady's flat in fastest London. He would be thinking of the painting and then clean-up. Next wondering what ladies do with two phones, four jars of cream and three toothbrushes – and think of his earnings.

Scott was also thinking of his pay as Mr.Rineholt went over the salary rates and increments. He had it divided into hundreds per week – a flat 500 say, or 400 with hols, lunch, travel pass and of course pension at 10 a week. Kids always asked what he earned, usually the bold one up front; the boy first to ask his name, as a friend he thought. Scott always made the wrong friends; like young teachers who were touchy and competitive, or the dinner lady alarmed when she heard he was divorced. No good to be friends with the Head either when it meant unequal power.

"When could you start, what's the earliest; should we ask, could offer you this position, job --?

I see, alright then".

"Maybe Friday Mr.Robinson or Monday; Monday at the latest".

"Yes we write and phone first, see if you accept – erhmm Mister – erhmm but we have four more candidates; we must prioritize… Right, any questions for us"?

The hour was near one o'clock; with little time left before getting to Chelsea. Because the light had gone up outside, thick shadows came into the room, over to the right mainly; resulting in a painful glare mid-window and across the table. The panel were beginning to silhouette against a magnolia wall, with a dust halo joining each head – very ominous; it was time for Scott to go before he feinted or such like. But he managed a sensible concern/question which always worked well:

"Mizz erhmm, sorry Mizz Longhurst, about the intake; what is the intake projection/ targets…"?

He was exiting in the best tradition of a beleaguered teacher; anxious to go the limit and be completely squeezed for the Chelsea appointment. There was no denying the profile type, no escaping the copy syndrome, no chance with professional archetypes. He finally scrambled out the room with embarrassing anxiety, babbling pleasantries over his shoulder, as they stood to watch him leave.

The return train was full, full in his compartment with sixteen German college students; or was it eleven Swedish tourists and some Danes. He tried to reckon his diary entries beginning the Sunday before, looking for asterisks and finally gave up not having a pen to mark the entries. Must be more items for today; why can't he rely on his jacket pocket office. The Danes were happy with a running chat, lounging on the hand-rails. The Germans, or Swedes, looked overheated and very red round the jowls; maybe been drinking at lunch, or just in London first time. The Danes got off together at Earls Court as the door snapped open to the platform; quickly but unsteadily they stepped onto a fixed platform with people moving everywhere. The Swedes seemed to follow Scott through to Gloucester Road and remained enroute; as he scurried to exit clutching gift, card, bag and a ticket. Finally he was marching along the last road to the school, checking his buttons, fingering his belt; a sweep of the hair and poke to his sore eyes. No turning back now when he saw the iron gates ahead and a small blue intercom box at shoulder height. He leaned forward to speak: "Mister Robinson here.

I mean, Scott Robinson, to see –

Thankyou!" After a low hum of electric drone from the box the gate-door gave way, into school via the school yard. Scott followed the signs as if they meant only for him: 'Reception This Way', 'Happy to see you -- welcome', 'Go up and Left'… 'You can come again'. He wanted reassuring signs, omens of luck for his first visit to the new habitat of his child. He could not help entering that day, feeling as if he were going to school the first time and to see his child the first time like a parent not a teacher, like his child was first time entry -- all these together inside the brick-walled building and empty corridors with lots of green paint and sharp echoes.

He had a gift today because it was Easter next week and school closed for Spring break, so it had to be today; a big chocolate egg, not too big, with two small baby eggs pushed into the box at front to fill out the gift. The card was mostly yellow with rabbits and grass. The bag was sweaty in his hand, heavy with the excitement.

A tall lady loomed before him: "Mister Robinson, I'm Misses Hobby, headteacher… sit down please".

His knees bent easily as he crouched in a chair opposite, hoping not to look overly concerned like he really was, trying not to give the game away.

"I am practising Anglican; but sympathetic to Catholics and really like the new Pope" he thought to volunteer.

"Does she – that's good" he chimed-in later, after hearing more details from the opposing side. But underneath Scott was anxious and agitated.

"I know, me too. Yes every weekend and holidays. I can't do this tomorrow" – Scott was joining in best as he could with his own silly pleasantries.

Mrs. Hobby was not nervous but listened for relevant information -- "Twenty, almost twenty years in schools; but mostly secondary. I started in America, where my parents are, Kay's grandparents – and over here for ten years.

Just an egg – the card in there; so no letter next week, just to spare your office a small chore. But a great kindness to me; in fact the first…"

Mrs.Hobby was sitting straight and letting it all go by, like he was a parent not another teacher; fairly and evenly. She was talking and looking at him without favour without surprise -- while Scott was busy being polite/informative and thankful. He was glad to stop, glad to keep quiet, when she stopped smiling and lowered her voice to become more serious.

"I saw the correspondence you sent and like I said on the telephone, I thought it better to actually see you today; I also rang her mother this morning. So can tell you, we will read your letters here in my office; is that alright? Good. Let's say once a week".

All this in the midst of a nice clutter; school clutter of paper in piles, toy things in boxes, pen things in jars, chairs and cushions, books in stacks. These items could have put Scott at ease if he chose to notice how they were very still and important, how they were silent yet effective. His just showing-up might be enough for her. He tried to relax and say more before Mrs.Hobby started to move ahead.

Mr.Rineholt and Ms.Longhurst had forgotten

about him now and onto candidate 'D'. But Scott did not forget so quickly, when suddenly seeing them here in the room; they appeared to have followed him into this school and were sounding their influence, nodding over to Mrs.Hobby. Two headteachers were too much in one day; because they were never discussing without intent, never frank to anyone exclusively, never polite for long. Scott's wheels were turning, he was functioning; but in deep sand, wet sand, where he was trapped and exposed.

The egg box was upright on the table facing between them; the card set against and showing up his handwriting to be very average very nondescript. There was no disguising the script this time; it was hurried, uncertain and unsure. How can a failed father write evenly, play fairly or lose carelessly? The sun was heading to tea-time in April, turning down to the left window corner from the small world outside. Birds and such knew to pack-up for the day, to leave a graying light by three-thirty; another sad end to a short afternoon for a long cool evening beginning.

He was keen somehow to show he knew his cue for the scene's end. No more answers today for Scott; nothing given away directly about handling his gift or the card-note. But lots of 'shop talk', role-playing, school noise and clever manners. He really needed a drink, any kind of drink, if he could think of one --

Scott had to cross the playground again before leaving and now the kids were out of class, outside. He could not look at individual children in case he saw her; he simply looked ahead as if he had more on his mind. But he did listen to the excitement, the loud calling and for Kay's voice; as he went past at a firm pace back to the gate, then the street. There were lots of young voices and any one could be hers; they all sounded so much alike, happy and free. How could a child break your heart like this, he thought. He was a grown man with assets; intros, success even. What kind of love was this; that always had a melancholy seed within, always a lot of fragility; like holding onto an injured bird fallen from above.

By the time he reached the station again, he was shaking and dry-inth-mouth as if he just left an exam room, or got fired from a job, or nearly hit by a bus. But not forgetting the painting job; he still had other matters to attend today -- not so important and not so difficult.

It was good to get back to Pat at the door, like he said, without excuses or manners. He took the fifty pounds, then his tea at the door and made like a young Irishman just over to London first time. Scott still needed a drink if he could think of one, or food, or a long walk out if he could think of somewhere to go. Anyway he was breathing deep now after some laughing – that was Pat's real job in London to make people laugh and good value too. Scott hadn't got a real career anymore; bits of work, bits of money, but no job he could call his own; he needed someone to cheer him. Inside, the flat was quick to darken, so he stayed at the door sitting down on the top step with Pat; both looking over to big plane trees along the street. The council men came by last week to trim the branches and Scott looked at the clean cuts above to marvel at dangerous work. He was listening for birds, to see if they were nesting; because it was Easter for them too, with lots of eggs and chicks.

"Those damn pigeons; the council can't stop them, nets can't, nor saw-cutting" said Pat and he was right in this way, easily right. Scott continued, "next month the new canopy green will cover everything, just like before". As if he were looking at something entirely different, seeing something new; trying to hear the noise of young chicks that might fall from above and be hurt, some undoubtedly would when he was not there.

SCOTT on the MOVE

Scott Robinson was an ordinary teacher but had a full life, because West London was not a backwater; definitely not the 'boonies' as they would say in Minnesota, over in the mid west of America. It was the centre of so many things, government, commerce and theatre; with lots of favoured sites hosting a new breed of people. Scott even had relatives in town, first and second cousins; those who were equally distant for one reason or another. London had a big turnover of residents each year, though the nation was very small; which meant that all kinds of unlikely aliens came to reside in the metropolis sooner or later. One such cousin to Scott was a bit of a high flyer, with his brand new MBA from an exclusive alumni; got him straight into a Bayswater section, in an up-market abode. Soon enough, Scott got an obligatory invite and firm date set for introductions the next weekend --

It was Coburg Court, the address read; his new pad was just off Queensway, facing Kensington Gardens. Scott passed the block of flats often, on the way to tube trains or going west to Shepherds Bush. It was a large building with brick facing, made to look Victorian; but probably built more recently. The façade was ornate and intricate, with a lot of cornices and shapes; presenting sash windows as bay windows to reception rooms and clever sky-lights fitted into odd sections of the roof. Obviously the apartments were spacious inside and expensive.

Scott got to the door by eleven-am as arranged the night before. He wanted to give his relative good clearance on Saturday morning; in case he had a tough week or a late Friday night. But he must visit before lunch, before he intruded on the day's main activity; so eleven seemed like a good time to call.

He rang the door-bell at the flat and eventually an eye appeared at the spy-hole to check on the visitor. The door swung open to reveal a scruffy resident, complete with old style dressing gown and rumpled socks appearing from the bottom edge. The man was young but looking worn, still tired and drowsy. Scott was fully awake after a good breakfast at his place round the corner; it was his habit to rise early on Saturday, to get a full day ahead. The difference in composure was awkward at first; so Scott only made polite noises, nothing to surprise or confuse his host. Apparently there was a lady somewhere; likely still in the bedroom out of sight, thought Scott.

He had visited before and never seen the lady, but did hear her call out one time; something domestic and muffled, possibly about serving Scott some refreshment. In fact, Scott always hoped for some warm coffee by then, but was never able to achieve this –

"Do you have any coffee, Graham"?

"Let's see, what I can find" he grumbled.

Yet nothing happened, no coffee was found or served. This same scene was played out in a similar vein, two or three times – but to no avail. Scott began wondering if he was welcome at such times, or welcome at all; altogether an ambivalent attitude from the host, which was tempting material for Scott.

Unknown to Graham, Scott was full of rude fun on weekends; arising from his time with hundreds of teens during the week. They were full of wicked mischief and dangerous pranks; enough to influence any teacher away from plain dealings with people. The kids were changing him, into a playful prankster.

This same morning, Scott politely requested

coffee and saw the host scratch his head and rub his face again. He said something about looking in the kitchen without much hope and made a few steps in that direction; then returned to a position at centre of the fireplace in his gown and grubby socks. Scott was thinking of some Whitehall theatre at that moment, popular domestic farce, along with stock caricatures and silly scenes.

It was now time for him to play his part, when seeing his cue with the scratching and mumbling. He already had the props from a nearby convenience store; a paper-cup full of coffee, with milk and sugar together inside a small brown paper-bag. It was sitting out of sight, on the floor beside his chair. Scott said – "No coffee again; you can't find anything! Not to worry; I brought my own" --

Whereupon he reached for the paper bag and took out the contents; pouring milk sachets into the cup and adding a bit of sugar. He even had a small plastic stick to stir with a flourish and proceeded to enjoy. 'It was good' he gestured and sat back, holding the drink in his lap to sip at pleasure, at will.

His host seemed to be unmoved and carried on with the usual banal conversation, while his guest purred over his warm beverage and listened to the jumbled chat. Not to overplay his hand, Scott soon straightened-up and put the coffee away; to make a considerate exit, a prompt departure. He took his coat and the bag and said a perfectly normal goodbye, as if nothing extraordinary had happened, nothing unusual from the last visit.

But he did not see his cousin again, though he visited one more time on Saturday morning, a whole month later. After ringing at the door, a figure inside came to the spy-hole and looked out; but the door never opened and no one replied to Scott that time. It was a nice tidy outcome, a very neat end game, more favourable to Scott.

He had no time to dwell on his performance that morning because school business was the priority and more pressing. It was the main event in his life for years to come. Everything else had to be held within strict limits, routinely partitioned from his school duty, as major discipline of the profession. His third year classes were top of this apex he ascended every day, along with quirky office staff he had to contend with. Miss Joan Johnson was difficult as the kids, insolent and cheeky, way out of line with her authority. He just hoped she would not align herself with other classes against him. That would be unfair, too much for a middle salary man. He had to be quick-witted and sure-footed when starting to slip and slide upon his conical apex --

"Right Three-B; I must get this copied at the office; I will only be a few minutes". Scott ran out with a page to copy; it was 'suffixes and prefixes', set to occupy the class for two periods while he sorted out a test for them.

"No one move, no one out of the room – okay"!

The office was only down the hall, where the copier sat; along with the secretaries, registers and the Head's office. One of the ladies was on the telephone, a big black bakelite thing from the Nineteen-Fifties; heavy duty and reliable in case kids had to use them. The other lady was sipping tea at her desk; showing a kind of rank and long service record in her demeanor. Clearly she deemed years at her desk and close proximity to the admin to equate as real professional status --

"Yes, Mister Robinson, what is it now"?

"I need copies please, Joan".

"Shouldn't you be teaching; I hope you haven't left them alone"!

"A good group this period; no problem for a few minutes".

"You got some copying this morning; wasn't that enough for you"?

"That's next week – I need this one today".

"Alright, just this once; how many in the class

then"?

"Thirty-two. But make it ninety-six copies please; okay, good, thanks"!

"What ever for? You said thirty-two in the class! Why three copies each, what's the big idea"?

"One copy for class, one to take home and one to fly round the room – you know, make a paper airplane. Thankyou, great"!

"Oh no, get out of here! You can have thirty and that's your lot today. We have a quota on the machine, for each department – we're going to, starting next Monday. I let you off lightly Mister Robinson; now scarper or else the Head will know about this"!

But Scott was already out the door and away down the corridor, with the paper sheets flapping in the draught he created in his run back to the room.

The kids were beginning to get loud, but still in their places, with nothing wrecked and no one injured. This was the top set of Year-9 and they went through good material very fast. He ran out of lesson material today, forgetting he would see them in the afternoon. It was an oversight from fatigue and confusion; after the Head re-shuffled the timetable to accommodate the police talk on Friday – 'Health and Safety', or 'drugs and petty crime' as teachers read the topic, circulated in pigeon holes at Monday morning.

When they began the 'suffix' exercise he had a thought toward the coming test and vowed not to make the same mistake as last term; when he quickly made a test for them, without thinking ahead. After the test, he gathered in the answer pages and took them home; to find he had masses of marking and a complex grading task to award a mark out of one hundred. It had been a nightmare for the week, he dare not mention to colleagues or friends; very upsetting the way he had to slave through the night a few times, before managing to turn in lists of marks for the department Head. This time it would be different – no more late nights and headaches, no more panic and hardship. This time the class would be working hard in the exam room and he would grade their efforts more easily; with some new tricks, like checking over the best pupil first and the worst pupil second. To see the scope, how much difference in the answers, to account for grades and failures.

Nightmares, headaches and panic, eventually meant illness or chronic ailments peculiar to teaching. Scott was not long into his London job after leaving America on sudden impulse and the new kind of schools took his constitution by storm; causing sudden bouts of flu, laryngitis or digestion problems. Later in his career different maladies appeared; after a long period in between when a surge of recovering strength won out for a while.   But first weeks into London he took a sore beating from the fractious kids, from a change in location and the new pace of city life. There was a medical clinic within reasonable distance for him, on Garway Road behind Queensway and he got an early appointment one day --

"Come in Mister Robinson and have a seat". Scott sat before the doctor and related all his ailments. Lots of minor things, but working together to put him out of action, to keep him away from school.

"So, you off work again, I hear; let's take a look". He got out his stethoscope, a tongue depressant and thermometer, to start thumping the chest at different places.   The doctor continued, looking into all the orifices and trying a reflex hammer and the pulse. Then he paced the room, humming a little tune, obviously thinking things over. Scott was very still and quiet, to give the doctor lots of unhurried space.

"Well Mister Robinson, basically you are fine; just a bit run-down, that's all. How long you been in London"?

"About three months".

"And your job, your work is --"?

"School teacher".

"– that's from America, correct"?

"Yes".

Obviously this was all leading somewhere. Doctor Green was getting closer to his prognosis and at the same time closer to Scott as persona; because he said a lot about Scott's profession and his raw exposure to the vagrancies of London life, the onslaught of a threatening environment.

"It takes time, but your resistance will strengthen; rest this weekend and lots of fluids. Try to scale back after-school jaunts; you sound like a one-man band out there on Queensway".

"Thankyou doctor", said Scott quietly.

"Come back in a month, for a chat if you like, I still get paid".

Scott had sound advice which set him up for the next few years in the city. He went out to buy some lemon powders and straight back to his room where he poured hot water into a glass and tried his new medicine – on the way to a good cure. Doctor Green had been funny too; if also a bit outrageous with some outlandish comments in the surgery.

"When do I retire" he once cried out, after sticking the thermometer into Scott's mouth and rushing over to the wall. "Let's see", scanning a big picture calendar hanging on the wall, "I just can't wait"!

"Doctor, not infront of the patient, surely", the nurse

said entering the room; an older woman with middle looks and middle values. Clearly she was shocked and alarmed at the lack of professional decorum.

"Oh what does he care" he rallied, guessing how Scott might react to such outbursts; sensing he would also find it amusing. Scott grinned towards the doctor; a signal of fraternity, recognition and confirmation.

Scott did not consult the retiring doctor after that appointment; he went onto a different tack for good advantage, but always looked out for him round the surgery premises and failing that asked about him at the reception desk. The doctor was very Scottish, very terrier like; brisk and up-beat with his patients and the staff. Scott was not surprised to hear he had been associated with the late Doctor A.J.Cronin, another Scot and successful doctor as author. Photos were framed round the waiting room, presenting scenes from his books made into movies, for the benefit of patients and staff alike; a source of pride and tonic. For Scott it was the partnership that healed him and sent him on his way: Doctors Cronin and Green, pushing and pulling, testing and teasing, leading and learning.

Scott did get more rest and fresh air that same weekend. He took a power nap on the Friday evening; got under a top blanket after taking off his sweater and kicking his shoes to the corner. He even decided against quiet reading and curled up for two long hours after dinner. On Saturday, he got to the park at late morning and began walking towards Westminster. Tourists milled in front of Buckingham Palace and at the Embankment, but Scott continued undeterred right down to the river, chewing some apples he bought from a street vendor --

On Monday he was fit and full of fun again, ready for his London hellions; this time it was the Junior team. Scott was out in the school yard at break, in a supervisory role, after his name appeared on the duty roster. But he had some coffee and biscuits, wandering across the asphalt in cool sunlight, enjoying fresh air and light duty. The kids were playing an amazing array of games; some of them a hundred years old, like 'London Bridge is falling down' and skipping-rope rhymes, 'one-two, buckle my shoe'. Usually the boys played football with a small tennis ball, kicking it from one side of the playground to the other and goal posts were vertical chalk marks made on the brick walls.

Scott was circling round the lower grounds, making a leisurely pace, not to interfere with their gamesmanship. When suddenly infront of him, one of his favourite girls was walking upon a yellow painted line. Her friends had concocted a new game, involving the lines painted on the asphalt and some kind of balancing act. There were four girls together, with one walking a straight line, going all the way across the yard. She was stepping very slowly on the middle and balancing her arms out to the sides with school bag steady over her shoulders. It seemed to be going well, but she scowled at Scott when realizing he was watching, because it was a serious endeavour for her. Scott was at one end of the line and keeping still, not to distract her. Finally he could not resist the temptation to tease, after he suddenly thought of a clever line, to amuse them and himself –

"Okay, Susie, that's enough; I declare you to be stone cold sober, you can stop now" he said!

The girl looked up at him quickly, in real surprise. But Scott did not stay to see what happened; to watch her possibly lose balance and step off the line. He turned away smartly to head towards the building, swinging an empty cup in his fingers. No need to gloat upon the fray; it was time to go and round them up for form entry. He had his fun and might have to pay for this at a later time; they sometimes complained about their teacher man as 'off the rails'.

By Friday Scott was feeling decidedly dizzy, after a whole week of kids and kids things; he was unbalanced, out-of-sorts and not himself. The weekend was meant to reconstruct his adult persona, or at least begin this process. But maybe it was too late, he slipping back imperceptibly; because at the slightest provocation he might revert to type to misbehave in childish ways and alcohol would facilitate this regression --

Friday evening, it was time for a quiet drink of beer across the road; a hotel bar made for this kind of premier venue. Scott managed to persuade a young student to join him, at Farmers Ale and packets of nibbles. They sat quietly in the theatre bar on Inverness Terrace; where thick pile carpet covered the floor and everyone paid extra for peace and quiet, cut glass tankards and a mock fireplace. Apparently the hotel once belonged to Lily Langtry, King Edward's mistress and she created a small theatre in the back to entertain select friends, which became the lounge bar. Part of the flooring was raised up in one corner and heavy maroon curtains, complete with cords and tassels, hung at the sides; inferring something that once was, a private stage for the lady's amusement.

Scott and his companion were happy to be out but saving their energy, their grand plans, for the next night. Another couple, maybe man and wife, occupied centre floor and the man gently nodded over to Scott to be polite. Just then two gals from a local student hostel entered, a bit too loud not to notice.

Immediately Scott recognized the young ladies

as a hardened pair, out of favour with him and his retinue, from a long while back. Though they lost no opportunity to be cheeky with Scott and insensitive to the restrained proceedings –

"Hey Scott, funny seeing you here"!

"Get us a drink, will you, we're broke" said the other.

"Beer would be great, same as what you have".

"Thanks" they chorused!

Scott hardly had a chance to talk, let alone respond properly. It stung; the way they pounced upon him unfairly, taking advantage of the 'man's prerogative' and rubbing it in too. But they kept moving and landed in the other corner at a small round table, facing each other to reinforce themselves. Scott could see them babbling and giggling after their quick 'coup'. But he was not bested yet – not completely.

"Who are those two, Scott"?

"Minnie and Mousie – two small stage mice, escaped from the hotel cat"!

"What you going to do, give them the beer, or what"?

"I'm going to do something, not sure yet".

The bar-keeper, Ty, was taking no notice and wiping his cloth round the glass counter infront of him. He was quiet and surly and foreign. Either he did not understand or chose to ignore the fuss.

"Wait here" said Scott; an idea gradually dawned on him, to restore his position and satisfy his bruised ego.

He went up to Ty and ordered one more Farmers pint and asked that he deliver it to the ladies, after Scott paid. Ty placed it on a silver tray and headed over, but stopped by Scott at the last minute, when he placed two drinking straws beside the beer glass and said: "Here Ty, take these straws to the girls, one for each; so they can share the drink. Thanks"! Scott resumed full attention towards his pal and chose to ignore what ensued behind; it was daring and decisive for him and had to be embarrassing for them.

Saturday evening was a more standard event; a mixed foursome down to Leicester Square for dinner and wander towards the Soho district for a desert café. Sunday observance followed for the salary man as rest-an-recreation. And Monday was a complete reversal of fortune for Scott, back to the call of duty, for the remains of the term --

Everything was going well; the class were into an exercise on 'Idioms'. A lesson he created himself, separate from the text books; not for job credit, but the subject interested him and was worthy of extra time for himself and the kids. There was humour in it too.

They were looking for the meaning in idioms and using these in a sentence: valuable language stuff alongside writing practise. Taking a tour of the desks Scott could see they were enjoying new material for a while and chatting about the work, quietly in co-operation. Everything was going fine; untill Scott got to the back rows by the window. He saw a cell-phone up at a girl's ear, looking like she was talking on it --

"Monica -- what you doing"?

"Talking to my friend".

"You must know, they are against school rules; really, right in the lesson too"!

"Sorry Sir, I'll put it away".

"I should confiscate it and send you to the office – you know that".

"I said sorry, Sir"!

"Alright, just hide it away out of sight – thankyou"!

Scott was ready to move on and instruct the class together, to consolidate the learning; see if they were on the right track with their answers. But he was curious about the phone call and thought it useful to follow-up --

"Just a moment Monica, a question for you".

"Yes Sir".

"You don't mind me asking; who were you talking

to"?

"My best friend".

"And where might they be"?

"In school".

"What, this school"?!

"Yeah, she's in History".

"You mean in a lesson"!

"Yeah".

"Really Monica, that's outrageous – you both have work to do, real school work. Heaven knows who's paying for the phones, but don't tell me. One last thing. What on earth are you talking about; the day has hardly started"?

"About her lesson" --

"What"?!

"I mean, what they're doing in History".

"And you are –"?

"I told her about the 'Idioms' and all that".

"You mean, she is telling about a History lesson and you are telling her our lesson – is that correct"?!

"Yes Sir".

"Extraordinary really; well, carry on please; thankyou"!

But he could not continue; Scott was totally stumped. Thankfully the class were still happily occupied and taking no notice: just not interested in

Scott's new conundrum or the girls misdemeanor. He never saw the girl call again and no more phones in his classes; though the kids, girls mostly, were immediately calling someone after school at the gates or in the yard at lunch. They were a new fangled phenomena; becoming as familiar and popular as the new 'ball-point' pens were to his generation. Amazing, Monica retelling his lesson to her friend and vice versa; so they each had the benefit of two lessons at the same time. It was not idle gossip they proffered, but real lesson material. In this case Scott could hardly object strongly, could not condemn outright. There was a modicum of sense in the idea, enough for Scott to leave alone, to let others decide about rules with such new technology. Clearly it was a generation gap, the way kids utilized them without compunction, whilst there were none in the staffroom yet.

"Scott you big softie, looks like your baby was crying all night, are you alright"?

Scott was an ordinary teacher but in extraordinary times. He had 'new age' kids, upwardly mobile cousins and daring doctors within one precinct and within one term. Everyone in town seemed to be breaking their bounds, tearing down walls or jumping the traces. But Scott was from America, at a distinct disadvantage with his conservative core of mid-west values. Within such a context of conformity, rebels and eccentrics were easily identified and marginalized. But in London everyone and their kids seemed to be firing-up new individuality, to hold high aloft, like placards at a massed marching rally.

"Yeah, fine; I just need more coffee and less sweetener. Thanks"!

SCOTT on the LOOSE

Someone once said to Scott Robinson: 'you can teach anywhere with your certificate; you are free to travel'. Maybe it was Scott's own father, who always dreamed of faraway places and more things to learn. Scott turned out the same, because 'the apple does not fall far from the tree', he remembered. He did teach all over the place and was set to learn lots of good things on top of fewer bad things. That's the way it turned out for him; he was a teacher on the payroll alright, but also exposed along the way to an incomparable journey. Scott began working close to his own college, so he could go home to his father's house on weekends. They would talk together about school and about men's work; it was illuminating and a new kind of interest for them --

'Parents Night' in Scott's first posting was back in Minnesota. It was late October, mid-semester and he stayed in his classroom for the evening, to await the parental influence. Scott remained in school after the kids left, because a buffet was provided by the admin, to encourage teachers and soften them up. He was young and always hungry, to concentrate on sausage rolls and potato salad, before getting back into his room upstairs; to tidy the effects and stack the exercise books in order, for easy reference. By seven-thirty there was a trickle of nervous parents finding his room and knocking on the door. Only about half his parents came to visit and most arrived together around eight o'clock. He was thinking of the TV schedule that night, to keep people at home, or conflicting events in the town.

Scott remembered a lot of shy talk and muted responses to his comments. Many parents had been to college and keen to compare this with Scott and their spouse; then talk about education in general and this particular school, finally before departing they would remark on their own child. It was almost too late for Scott to reply; he simply produced anecdotes and suggestions, before they shook hands several times to say good-bye. This was fitting, because he never saw then again for six months or more; the Principal preferred written reports sent out to their homes or interviews with counselors.

Many parents were surprised with young Scott; they looked him over cautiously and were hesitant to approach directly. They saw a slim young man, looking studious and reserved, well mannered and restrained. After more parents showed a similar reaction, it occurred to him how they were looking for another person; someone the kids described; a teacher their child railed against at home after school when lumbered with homework, reports and test warnings. The parents were expecting a modern kind of monster, a dragon of the classroom, angry pundit, a mean spirited academic – and were shocked to see what they found, nothing like that. Of course it was a new experience for a novice teacher and older colleagues enjoyed spoofing him the next day, when hearing cross comments from everyone in the staffroom.

Not surprising, it was not long before Scott got restless in the small town and by summer's end he reserved a flight out of state to New York. But friends told him he could not get hired in the 'big apple' and to try the 'big smoke' instead. They were correct; he quickly got a new post in West London, satisfactory digs and new things to do. The theatre was his first interest; every Saturday, in the West End; nothing like TV or movies he watched at home. After the New

Year, he went out a lot; he hit all the hot spots in town, after finding Leicester Square --

Scott went down Piccadilly to the Haymarket theatre, for a 'Sherlock Holmes' production. It was Saturday evening and he changed into runners and casuals, then started to jog through Kensington Gardens. It was Spring break in May and a lovely evening of warm air, sun and light. After a relaxing day of loafing near the Round Pond with sandwiches and new book, he was ready to exert himself and prove he still young and keeping-up with the big vibrant city; his newly adopted address. He was from middle America, flush with youth and college diploma; relocated to Europe into an old-world city.

Next leg of the run went across Hyde Park; he was warming-up and striding out well alongside the Serpentine Lake, dodging the tourists ambling along in the opposite direction. He finally got to a large flower garden at the far corner, near the Duke of Wellington's old home. There were masses of tall tulips waving in the breeze and old people sat on benches near them, reflecting in their colours and their scents.

But Scott had an objective; this was not an idle excursion, he could not divert his route or his schedule. Crossing the road junction he had to follow trail signs and descend to the underpass tunnels, to reach Green

Park. He knew the route from before and enjoyed running down-hill under the street levels. He emerged into a smaller grassy area, with simple landscape of plane trees following the pathways and from there he found an exit leading down Pall Mall to the theatre. It was a mere forty minutes on the run and he landed at the box-office in good time for a cancellation ticket, because it was only seven o'clock.

He bought a seat for the Upper Circle and waited for the curtain to rise. He was hot and flushed after the exertion, but happy to spread out in a good viewing position. There were only about a dozen people in this section and well spaced apart at their places. Suddenly the play began with a burst of sound and light, as the house lights went very low, to entrance Scott with the special stage magic London was famous for. After two or three scenes of such arresting form, Scott turned to other spectators to see their re-action. It was the same, everyone was bowled-over with the production; they began shouting across and waving to each other. So much, that first chance they got, everyone moved to sit closer together; the whole of the Upper Circle became like new friends; all the excitement had to be shared around.

During the intermission Scott retreated to the theater bar with his new found pals, he grabbed a pricey beverage and silly nibbles.

"How is your school", someone asked him?

"How d'you know that"?

"Everyone here is a teacher" she said. "Who else has a week off in May"!

"Conan Doyle does us proud, eh! A bit of History served-up as entertainment and old Londinium cleaned-up to be made mysterious for us" he said.

"Yeah, I love this Victorian stuff; reminds me of my grandparents".

"Listen, it's the buzzer" Scott declared! "We have to return".

"Have a good week everybody and a great term ahead"!

"You too, thanks and take care" they called out.

"Cheers"!

In fact the city tempo infused Scott with a certain amount of élan, some bravado and new zest for risk. He let school slip away quickly after hours and preened himself as gay bachelor without harm or hindrance. He was plugging into the juice of the metropolis and enjoying close proximity to the glitterati, the glamour of major players. A host of 'Sloane Rangers' sped past him every day by the fast lane to encourage him, distract him, on their way to the high life.

Every Saturday morning, towards noon, Scott

watched Marie on TV doing a short fashion show; he was hooked for thirty minutes each week. He also noticed her in advertising, magazine shows and about town with the rich-an-famous. No surprise; she was a stunning new beauty on the London scene and in her prime at thirty-something. By the third week Scott went to Kensington library to borrow her book, photos by her husband and he was hardly disappointed. Another volume added some biography of early life in Hawaii and a sister. Altogether she was an exotic dish in London, whose time had come; a definite move away from the 'English rose' of Jean Simmons or Shirley Eaton. Marie was of mixed blood and brought a welcome flavour to post-modern Britain.

Finally, he sent her a book of poems, he had to act; it was after all London, where like the 'Puss-an-Boots' story, a cat can look at a queen. Summer was coming to Kensington; the fauna was blooming, pollen blowing everywhere; ladies wear exchanged for skimpy outfits and men took off their shirts in the royal parks. He enclosed a note with the book, declaring himself as school teacher and inviting her out to tea – it seemed perfectly respectful. He asked if she had any teacher friends, man teacher friends and if not, then she should.

Scott was bold enough that summer to mention

this to his student teacher; but was reprimanded by the young man. When a reply came, soon after, in the form of note on studio photo; the student recanted to exude awe and wonder. The glossy card-note landed in his scrap book and for several days he left it open at the page; laying on his desk at home above piles of books to be marked. But there was nothing about a 'tea date'. So he dropped another quick note, care of the same newspaper, to beg the question.

The next week everything collapsed; his fanciful balloon had burst and fallen to the floor as hopeless torn elastic. One evening as he took an early nap, because school term was not quite over, the phone rang and a man spoke to Scott. He sounded of middle years, tall and strong; with straight no nonsense questions; letting Scott talk to expose himself as gentleman teacher, genuine person and harmless admirer. The man finally hung-up firmly, convinced Scott was no threat to any lady, that it was not a cruel hoax or a press stunt. Of course no 'tea party' arrangements were made, though he was still hopeful for the next few weeks.

But the parents still wanted to see him, the very next week. True, they were not glamorous or photogenic; they were anxious, shy and confused. Scott had used up his special kind of fling as foolish-free bachelor; but was not of independent means, he still a wage earner and slave to the system.

It was 'Parents Night' for Year-8. Scott did not go off home after school, this day; he quickly went round the corner to a sandwich shop and ate in the staffroom with a large brew. It was another hour or so before parents were due to arrive, to hear a review of their child's progress; a general overview without marks or serious exam concerns, meant to be informal and informative.

There were small tables set out in the hall, with subject teachers sitting behind them. In front of each position were two chairs together to invite parents sit and discuss. Scott counted ten teachers in the hall and knew a few more were in the gym at a similar set-up. Their names were printed on cards and stuck to the front edge of their desks, so that parents could browse and locate a target teacher person.

Scott brought some papers to check-over at his place, in case no one showed-up for him. Anyway, it looked good for the Head for a teacher to appear studious and might avert some nuisance; because suddenly he wanted to be left alone, to day-dream about the weekend coming or a nice hot whisky drink before bed. School paled into distraction for him by four o'clock, because he was not always a teacher, it was not the only life he knew.

Scott thought them a ragged lot, every shape and size of adult, in every sort of dress, wandered round the hall; yet not really in earnest like they should, for the review was only twice a year. They were ambling and shuffling across the floor in odd looking pairs; looking lost, confused and a bit over-awed at the mock academics on display. His own department head hovered somewhere near, after posting-up various sign cards for the visitors and catchy phrases written with felt pens on coloured paper; like it was a political event and they council members of the local town hall. But not so, teachers were meant to be honest and serious at their fiduciary duties with such young charges --

"Mister Robinson, hello! We are Mister and Misses Towbridge; Annie's parents".

"Okay, I know Annie; she has good marks so far and is great to teach".

"Thankyou, we know about that, but good to hear. No, it's the homework"!

"The what"?

"She gets too much…" Misses Towbridge also butted in: "Yes, she is up till midnight every time and us too with worry. It's not natural for a young girl to do so much every night"!

"Hey, I only give homework once a week, very little, hardly any at all. I prefer they work hard in class, makes

48

my life easier"…

"Yes, that's correct" they said.

"…don't believe in much homework, it turns the kids off school – you know what I mean"!

"Well, it's History", he said.

"And French too, Mister Robinson", she said.

"Yes, but I teach English"?

"Yeah, we know that" they nodded.

"No, she gets too much French and too much History – it's terrible" she insisted!

"Every night, every week – terrible" he concluded!

The parents were beginning to flush and breathe hard, obviously in close union over this matter and glad to talk about it. They both paused together, at intervals, catching their breath and catching-up on the problem; looking for more consideration from another teacher.

"I know, many girls can never do my homework because of other demands. I mean they do History and French first, then go to bed, leaving my work to cram into the lunchtime next day". Scott was divulging his own frustrations, "have you talked to Miss Wirrell and Misses Arniston"?

"No, not yet".

"You don't have a problem with my assignments; so you must talk to Annie's History teacher and her French teacher. They are here tonight, somewhere in school; I glimpsed them together a while ago".

"No, we can't".

"I don't understand"?

"Oh yes, we can talk to you, that's easy, our girl too. But --"

"Go on, please".

"But, we can't talk to Miss Wirrell or Misses Arniston", she said.

"Why not; you have the right to speak for your own child. I will find them for you, right now". Scott stood up and moved away from his desk.

"No don't, please"!

"Why, what's wrong"?

"Well -- we are afraid; not afraid of you Mister Robinson, of course not".

"What's that"?

"Our girl is scared of these two teachers; a lot of girls are. So we came to you; because everybody said you would listen", he said.

"Well thankyou. Maybe we can help each other. I mean, if History and French back off a little, I might just see more of my stuff done for a change"!

Scott was good as his word and next day sought out his department head to retell the story of Mister and Misses Towbridge. But the lady did not respond kindly, she was not sympathetic to his plea and vague about approaching History or French. Clearly he entered murky waters, school politics; though petty for Scott, it was real and important to main players in the school. His story was honest and genuine, but Scott's position in school was lowly and weak; because careers were not based on good teaching or working with difficult kids; careers were based on reputations and influence. Not surprising his head of department did not confer with Scott again and she seemed to be fending him off the next week or so. Of course he never saw the parents again and was spared relaying a disappointing result for them. But their images came back to him, whenever Annie appeared in his class and he wanted to resolve something of their plight. Yet as she continued to busy herself with books and friends, it was easy for him to let things slide away. Once or twice, in the staffroom, Scott saw Miss Wirrell and Misses Arniston at coffee or chatting idly and thought to take some initiative. At the same time he also sighted his own Head in the room and saw her like before, tense and tired, hurried and serious. He deferred to caution and prudence, for once, but made-up his mind about the two teacher cronies, as unfair adversaries; he resolved to steer clear and keep them at bay.

It seems a major conflict had been uncovered for Scott; not uncommon when he stayed in one school a long time. Of course the problem was already in place, well lodged in the system before he arrived; but not apparent to him till he ran into a silly dispute like homework and went to clear it away. Sooner or later beginners luck ran out and he stumbled onto bigger issues, tripped over serious faults in the school and nobody warned him. All the while silly details were important too, things like proper dress or overall appearance and it was an every-day thing, a continual chore.

Scott got a new pair of pants for school use, on the weekend. He tried them out on Sunday evening before wearing on Monday morning and found them too long. But he had an idea and looked for a small stapler among his desk jumble. He folded the material on each leg, turned the length up to shorten by two inches and used staples to hold in place; until he went to find a repair shop.

Next day he rode the tube to school, as usual and checked his deportment on the way; like he normally did on the morning journey. He would finger his tie knot to see if it was tidy, check his jacket for lint, try his belt tension and so on, down to his shoes; re-tying the laces if he managed to sit before arriving at his destination. He finally checked his complete appearance in the glass reflection opposite at the doorway, before stepping down to the platform. It was a tried routine and seemed to work, all the years he worked in London schools and traveling by underground train. Good impressions from all sides were important in school. No doubt, other commuters had their routine, their own wardrobe checks and exacting standards.

Today he also checked the staples at bottom of his trousers, which seemed to be holding well and delighted in his ingenuity and the success of it. He thought no more about this by the time he reached the school gates; because he was suddenly onth-double to his duties for the rest of the day, barely catching his breath till lunch time. Teaching was not a genteel occupation anymore; now the kids were in charge, setting a frantic pace and intolerant to any staff short comings.

Scott was at English in the annex classrooms across the playground and settling into a new text, 'The Old Man and the Sea'; American prose at its strongest. He got to the room before the kids and wrote some theme headlines on the black-board; straightened chairs and opened one or two windows so they would not notice. He was keen on light and air for himself, despite an early chill of the morning and it wakened the kids. But he knew how they did not like to be roused and stirred at first lesson. After about twenty minutes he sat in his chair behind the main desk and glanced at papers for next period, as his class began their own task into note books –

"Hey, Mister Robinson, Sir"!

"Yes, Sharon". She sat in the very front row, right infront of Scott.

"What's wrong with your trousers"?

"There's nothing's wrong"!

"Why turn-up the bottoms like that; what are the staples for"?

He was dumbfounded; how could she see over the top of her desk, when his legs and feet were hidden behind his own desk; the staples were so small and only two in each leg. But they were tiny bits of steel and might shine out in the right light.

"They look new Sir; is that it"?

"Are you finished, Sharon; what page are you doing"?

"Page ten now; I just did page nine".

"That's good, well done; please continue" --

"Thankyou Sir, alright; I'll just keep going then".

Scott was caught in the minions of school life; he became tangled in a bramble patch, where prickly leaves were soft and green, but difficult to extricate from. Getting close and personal with pupils was essential; but it also entailed some nasty scratches or sharp stings. But he saw next week would be different, when glancing at the notice board, about a day excursion coming up; how he would be safely among friendly staff at arms length from the kids.

The train was leaving Victoria Station before 9-am; going out to Margate for the day with the whole of Year-Nine, before summer term ended. After a few stops in the Medway towns, Scott saw another school outing on the same train, for a full day of recreation. It was midweek, so no other passengers on board. He knew the train would have been full of city commuters going the other way into Victoria a half-hour ago. Now only school kids journeyed out of London, to catch some sun and fun in a Kentish seaside resort.

Scott hunkered down with science teachers, in full view of the kids, as a kind of nominal supervision. The science department were good travelers, amiable and humorous. He often covered their lessons for absences and found them to be generous and lacking any guile. They were sharing fruit with each other and relating funny stories about a recent set of tests they delivered to Year-Ten.

"You been to Margate before, Scott"?

"No, never – is it alright"?

"I prefer Ramsgate, further away from the 'great unwashed'"!

"I love the beach huts. My aunt rented one every

summer, when I was a boy, so we could boil the water for our tea and hide from the adults".

"The promenade lights-up at night, to help our carousing, chasing after the local talent".

"Hey, that's my wife you're talking about"!

"Sorry, I thought she was from East Ham"!

The countryside was not showing at its best from a speeding train and railway cuttings occurred at regular intervals blocking the view, to make window gazing unrewarding and frustrating. Pastoral scenes quickly slipped by as the train sped eastwards to the north Kent coast at the far end; where a small town sat on a sandy bay, with a 'fair ground' sighted behind the rows of whitened cottages. Old Victorian houses lined the front cliffs; looking like most of them had been turned into comfy bed-an-breakfast accommodation.

It was late morning when Scott followed his science chums off the train to a café for coffee and croissants. The kids were spreading out in small groups to amuse themselves freely before lunch; when they would gather together at the sea-wall and hear suggestions and time plans for the rest of the day, from senior staff. Scott took to the beach after eating and explored the harbour from one end to the other. He was alone for a while and enjoying familiar territory from boyhood days. He traced the water's edge as it lapped the shore line and crept up the beach towards high ground; the tide was imperceptibly rising and no one else noticed, no one thought it important. But Scott was always a sea-salt in the making; so he easily forgot about school, city kids and jolly science people. Seagulls called out to him, sea spray blew onto his face and wavelets chased after his footsteps. The water was playful today, welcoming and friendly, with its silver-blue sheen reaching towards the long horizon ahead.

One of Scott's friends had said he wanted to try drama, to be a professional actor after college. 'You can be anything you want' he said; 'I get to experience all kinds of things, many different characters'. Scott thought it an appealing idea and visited his pal in dramatic productions. But Scott went into education and found teachers were acting in school too; they were never really angry, never really foolish or funny. It was an act, they said; because a teacher must have self-control, to ensure safety and not be exhausted. Unlike his friend in the theatre, Scott also knew he had to be 'himself' in a special new way and set to discover this truth all through school years with lots of unexpected help.

SCOTT on DUTY

School can be a strange place, where grown men can find themselves in ridiculous scenes and some of these situations can be very risky, for any teacher left alone in a forgotten classroom. Scott Robinson was never one to dodge difficult duty, but no teacher ever got used to the 'unexpected' from school kids --

"Sir, Sir; you have to kiss her"!

"Now my lady, all is well", Scott delivered over to a thin blonde with freckles and scarlet blush.

"Sir you must do it. You promised us"!

"Lancelot, you are gallant; a brave knight I'm told"...

"And bold with it -- come on Sir"!

Scott needed an aspirin, if he had one and a quick

way out of the mediocre melodrama --

"We cannot return to Camelot my lady", he gasped out from under the folds of a coloured tunic; then gathered up his kit and shield to ease an exit left, from scene two Act one. What a talent he showed that day to Year Nine's on the dinner-hall stage, what a real thespian.

Lady Guinevere was indeed a fresh young spirit for a lapsed humanities teacher in deepest London. She really looked the part of a court femme from the Middle Ages in a Kensington High school. Scott had the voice to carry it off; he had the experience of treading the boards on a thousand classroom stages -- and it showed, weak knees and dry throat. It was well past confidence; it was weariness and heartache.

"Ready to carry me Mister Robinson. Our last scene together".

"Ready", he lied. He adjusted his outfit and belt, re-tied a shoe lace and suddenly dropped Rosie onto his white arms for scene four, past the lifting curtain and up-stage.

"Yeah and neah, mi-lady. You must go; but I wish you to stay".

"Kind Sir, I must be off to a nunnery -- I pray".

"With a bun-inthe-oven", came from the back row.

"You got a girl into trouble, again. Nice one, Sir", from the front row this time.

His patience fluxed like a spiteful woman between nine-to-five; yet after school he was a different person, if they let him and if he could remember what he was. He kept thinking of Errol Flynn in the swash-buckling movies he once saw, kept trying to be effortless like him and glib.

At home he took off his jacket and put the kettle on; his tie came off picking up the post and his shoes were unlashed as he got the lights on -- to finally sit infront of the TV with tea and quiet, seeing only two bills for payment. He yawned and drank, sighed and sipped, for a full thirty minutes in front of news and gossip; then tried a nap because he was off to Earls Court late evening to drink at a hotel bar, with Ray and Charles, two more lonesome teachers. He got under a duvet on the couch with no shoes and small light, till the next evening news. When awaken he re-dressed in civvies gear and made off through Kensington village, to a mansion house rendezvous with two Irish teachers and a simple plan -- drink-talk-sit, same as last week and the next week.

By the second pint of bitter ale Scott repaired to the bowl of chips they had, then olives, whilst they paraphrased last week's events and tried a few jokes on each other. It was very tame bar chat but comfortable and reassuring. Charles was a Dubliner (post Joycean) and Ray a Belfast man (post haste); rubbing up against Scott's Irish side for the easiest few hours of the week; a good way to both end and begin a week in post modern West London.

He knew Earls Court by day too and knew how it was the rump-end of South Kensington and the red-light zone off Hammersmith: with street people, busy nights and train outlet to the exhibition centre. Ray lived on the Kensington side of the red-lights and had a set piece garden to be snobbish about. Up the same street were private-house hotels and food outlets, traffic and noise, dust and neglect. Every day the station exited new foreign visitors to stay in London, not as tourists, but long stay visitors and students; so that Earls Court was always young and awake.

Scott was moving home that Easter; moving from Nottinghill to Hammersmith because he had fallen-out with the landlord, a Chinese lady and had too many years with no family, no Kay; it was now a hollow nest. He got more space in Hammersmith, two bedrooms and balcony over a rear view garden. Ray called in to see him first week, then demanded they go to lunch at the church. It was a church/council effort to provide for the homeless at Earls Court; top end of the homeless market, instead of the real homeless who never came. Ray, Scott and local oddments sat in front of chicken curry, then prunes in custard. Scott shied off and settled for tea and biscuits next to a fat lady who liked to talk about her neighbours at the council housing. Ray sulked over two helpings of prunes, because of a scratched face made by his kitten. Scott was enjoying shortbread biscuits and big tea as he gazed into the future of a new flat with no Kay, new area and no family. They all sat opposite one another in lines, infront of canteen utensils, nodding to late entrants and letting them squeeze into a place at the common table.

The homeless also appeared at Bayswater next to Nottinghill and they begged a lunch centre -- so no surprise that same month Scott was stopped three times by a tramp on Saint Petersburgh Place as he hurried to church on Sunday. Twice he handed over his collection coins, the third time managed to lie about money and handed over a concerned attitude instead. There was a fair share of street people in Bayswater, but this one meant embarrassing recognition, which required some greeting and polite words. Scott appealed to the world and one town beggar how he too was of lowly status, suffering and undeserved; how he only ate once a day, yet managed it every day. Not to mention he was happy though, very happy to be meeting with Kay after the service and it was dry and warm enough to do anything they wished.

Scott beamed and bowed at attendants of the congregation stationed at the door, the aisle and side pews. He was last minute again at sound of first bars in the processional hymn. Such a time, such a place, in Paris years before, he did not dodge a beggar as easily. The French beggar-man had prostrated himself in the empty church, at the altar, with Scott watching quietly. But the man stood up and saw him with picnic stuff for a day on the move, for a teacher holiday at mid-term and he gestured clearly to the food. Scott struggled to hurriedly divide the fruit/bread/cheese; when he suddenly changed his mind and pushed all to the man who held out one empty hand. How could he measure off a correct portion to such an appeal; he felt better straight away after he pushed all the food towards the need. But the beggar took only a small part; he left the remaining food to Scott and went away without talking; Scott did not even have to show his weak French.

His French was weak, as was his faith in facing the real need in London, in his part of town; by end of service his beggar was en-route to Moscow Road and other churches. It was still dry enough, early enough, to do anything they wished after morning worship. So that Scott decided upon Oxford for a day; to see the sights and soak up the erudite ethos of a fabled town all Americans learn about same as London town. He settled down in an express bus with Kay next seat and they had a satisfying munch of fruit on the way. He also chose to ask a few fair questions about the country fields they passed, like any good teacher-parent would --

"What animals are they", as they passed brown and white beasts on the pasture and "what are fences for"?

"To keep people off the animals and they are cows that get white milk from green grass".

Scott was duly impressed.

"And scared of the farmer-man, because he only has two legs"!

In a good hour they were into the old town and heading up High Street to Pembroke College, where Scott spent a summer for English courses many years ago. Kay was attempting to keep up as she swung a lunch box in one hand and held his hand with the other, sporting questions all the while, about new things they saw.

"Is it far? Is this Doxford"? By now she started making up a walk-an-skip stride.

"Yes, we're here now".

"Do cows live here, Daddy"?

"What"!

"People are lying down on the grass; do they eat it"?

"No, of course not".

"How d'you know that"?

"Daddy was here before, many years ago; before you were born even". No answer to that one as she faced the long road ahead inclining upward. No more queries as she started to rely on his hand clasp, pull on it and Scott knew he needed to organize the day to the strengths of a four-year old, which meant treats and stops along the way.

"Where we going to", when they stopped at road's end?

"Daddy needs coffee".

"I want a drink".

"Okay Sunshine; over here. Daddy always came here before, when he was young and thin, happy and free".

"Orange. I want an orange drink". Kay sat down while he went to the counter for attention, swaggering like it was a date with a big girl -- but he was no less proud no less lovesick. Next stop was a bookstore past Carfax and they picked up the first of their load into the rucksacks. Kay was an amazing talking walker, but she could not carry much.

Scott got to the shop and thumbed through some stories by Hemingway and Hardy; new Penguin editions while Kay looked around for Rupert Bear albums. The Nick Adams stories were his favourites, then Saroyan and Damion Runyan. He bought a new edition of Saroyan and went to look for Kay, past the Enid Blyton sets and big floor cushions, to see her trying to get onto a rocking horse in the play area. It was a lovely stained-wood model with leather fittings and good rocking rails. Scott lifted her on and said ten minutes to ride, because they had places to go and people to see, miles to go before she sleeps. Kay agreed to nothing; then really set the hinges creaking for near twenty minutes, till Scott bribed her off the steed with small promises and small coloured candy.

She released his hand later when taking her ice-cream cone. She stood before him in the open sun to joyfully lick her cone without instruction and swapped hands every few minutes, while Scott wondered if this one would crash to the ground -- none had so far. She knew how to enjoy herself and she also cared to see Scott enjoying himself, once or twice looking over to his face/eyes. Not that Kay could know why he was happy: nothing to do with ice-cream, drinks, or getting a bus-ride to buy a book. She would not see how he enjoyed her happiness, how could she? It became a complete memory for them both, when she licked her prize in front of him that day at Easter at the Carfax in Oxford.

He got a Japanese tourist to take their photos in front of the Bodleian library and kept saying that Daddy had his own book inside. Though Kay heard him she never understood and would not consider Scott important or clever; she considered him ordinary and friendly. He wanted to be important and clever at school also with his book, but not on a day like this.

This was nothing like college at home in America; with the fraternities, letter-men and prom-queens. Nothing in Oxford like English-200 in Minnesota, where hundreds of students filled the classes with their Norton anthologies. Instead, Oxford had cozy tutorials in college rooms and tea-shops for the undergrads. He usually had toasted tea-cakes and Indian tea at four-pm with two class-mates from New York, when they heaved with laughter at their own conundrum as Yanks in Oxford. It was still there; the blue tea-shop behind Broad Street and the lawn quad where he met new friends to sit in the sun by May term.

Kay was now having her own thoughts as she sat in the Cathedral Lady Chapel and fingered her lunch box; she enjoyed new places and wanted to be with her father like she remembered from before. His hand was soft and warm as she paraded with him all day among different kinds of people. She insisted on MacDonalds next and a new toy, but then accepted some more walk for his idea to sight-see memory lane.

Down to the river was a short walk to a longer past and a slimmer Scott who was more lazy than happy, less money with less trouble. He was in classes then with the poetry of Pope and dramatists of the eighteenth century; English writers -- after producing a thesis at Minnesota U. on American Lit, Longfellow and Twain. He wanted a literature experience in England because he loved the language; even though he was mostly Irish, Irish and Swedish parents. After five years in Junior High School teaching outside Minneapolis, he went to England for a summer term at an old town college with a colleague from school. He did not intend to stay in teaching, but his alternatives were vague and ill-supported; always tormented by the whim of another career; ambiguous feelings of a career mistake. The next moment proudly telling anyone he was a teacher; there were no solutions and no resolution to his own trial. Though lots more teachers admitted this same double interest, it did not help how he went through contradictory feelings/opinions each and every day at his job.

He managed some rowing on the river, then tennis

on Sunday and wrote a folio of poems in his last course. Chester, his room-mate from Staten Island, took Scott to Wessex country in the autumn term and to Stratford-upon-Avon at Spring break; they made the college rounds in grand ole style. Today, it was going to be a short circuit to Exeter College and back to Christchurch meadow; with a little girl now apprehensive at her sights, both tired and curious by late afternoon. Kay was ready to return, she had enough. Scott would also be tired that night, as he had preparation at home which could not be put off, for an appearance next day at the Royal Courts of Justice.

Scott got to the Strand twenty minutes early and went to sit in passageways with his papers. He was quickly caught up in dialogue with the opposing lawyers, as the mother got behind them to enjoy watching then listening; no lawyers for Scott now, not after the first half-dozen hearings. He went smartly to his chair at the call and spent the next ninety minutes in a tough set of cross comments from the bench and counselors at the table. It was not a long hearing or a short one -- it was a difficult session; with extra time afterwards at the elbow of the welfare officer, a blue-stocking Hampstead lady of high tones. Everyone was lavish with the esoterics, the lawspeak and enjoying performances of those appearing that morning; many strong greetings and up-straight conduct.

"The applicant father, one statement, directions hearing..."

"Your Honour, I'm confused, unclear about petitions at next undertaking of this court..."

Someone, not the judge, kept repeating, "directions" and "not relevant", to Scott's appeal. But there was much anger and frustration underneath all the formality. The table they sat at was long and straight, easy to interject. A clerk came in and out of the chamber four times to a desk behind Scott and a tree branch brushed across the middle window when Scott looked up. Distractions seemed to become important when tensions rose and arguments failed. He took small comfort with personal observations, which may have been exclusive for him, when all the issues he raised were made oblique or vexatious.

Outside he needed a coffee drink, if he could find one and some company if they agreed. But they said it was improper to appear friendly, when Scott proposed it to the welfare lady and/or her counsel -- he took a wide apology and tried to head from the scene like he was well. Not so, he was in considerable flux by the time he found his way down to a basement den among lots of legal bodies, with a china cup and biscuit plate. He had stumbled into a quasi sanctuary for the lawyers upstairs; the offering was plain fare, yet it was full of talkative advocates in their short black gowns. He placed a briefcase near his feet and tried to decide if he was going to listen to the legal chat around him, or go into his own papers again. Suddenly a body loomed towards him, then a voice --

"Scott, what you doing here"!

"Same for you Eamonn. Is it half-term already"?

"No education and not my hols; on a legal practise course. I am quitting teaching. You must have heard"!

"We thought you were in the ascendant to headship? Sit down, tell me about it"!

"I hear you moved schools again"?

"You don't appear at Family Courts after a job sacking; unless your wife is third-party to the action".

"Third party action is their forte, Hils"!

"I was litigant-in-person today; for two years appearances. Top marks eh"!

"Middle-ranking top marks; but very civic minded. Are you sparing the tax-payer or messing about with the respondent's brief? Answer without thinking okay".

"But you're on my side, right".

"On your side if you plead; after you sport me coffee and share your papers".

An unparalleled hour followed; loads of professional cross-over banter with equal slurping over the table items. Of course it was the decompression chamber after the upstairs proceedings and eventually Scott was ready to emerge into the Strand concourse again, by noon; where he found new light and air and decided on a longer route back to the station. He walked past more chambers, more clerks and the Inns of Court where cloisters were occupied by VDUs on every window table and mean little lights spoiling the cornice ceilings; the impingements of legal labour into medieval residences. The garden fragments were as is: a few roses and dusty shrubs leading to a fountain pond at Pump Court; where Scott deliberated on a bench facing the water and started tearing up letters with notices he checked over.

He passed an old haunt, the Tate Gallery and remembered years before he was married; he was with a new lady-friend with extra pocket-change and new school position. They went directly to giant canvases in the far rooms and tried cafeteria teas, then more picture gazing; before a quiet stroll along the river embankment when light was breaking up for early night; it was first year in London and a fresh start. He went to all the galleries and theatres by years end; charged into the metropolis with his American verve, like he just got out of High School and trying to catch-up something he was not conscious of. That first half-term in the job he met lots of other teachers at cut-price events and matinée afternoons around Leicester Square.

His lady down at the Tate was a London girl but new to the gallery, so they shared some surprises and the whacking great landscapes, to make a happy event; always good for romance except this romance. Like so many other attachments it twinkled and faded away, like distant stars above the night city. But he still had his job and a room near to Kensington Gardens for the summer to come. So it went before he married -- prospects were good and love looked like a big cherry pie, sweet and not sticky, red and not dangerous.

A subsequent Monday back at school, Scott lost his open period before morning break and had to fill in for French Year-Nine. After a preliminary fluster and flutter round the teacher's desk he gathered them in for his intro --

"Sorry, I'm not a French teacher".

"What then", came of disappointment?

"Humanities really or English and I like History".

"Useless stuff, very boring", signaled anger and disruption!

"I don't know any French except for 'Bonjour' and 'Au revoir' -- sounds like a love story, doesn't it"?

"Oh Sir; it's too late for you. Forget it"!

"Alright, maybe not -- Anyway; what page you doing last lesson"?

"Page forty-five".

"And, how old are you, Sir" came from the girls side?

"Let's turn to page forty-six, for today. Now get on with it; thankyou"!

A standard quiet passed for an additional thirty minutes, before the first of a series of upsets set his metabolism racing for break/toilet/caffeine; a raisin tea-bun and glance at Miss Raeburn now with Eamonn on the big cushion seating. But not before --

"Any homework, Sir"?

"Oh shut-up", came from the boys' side.

"Yes of course, I almost forgot, let's try page forty-seven"! Scott responded loudly and quickly before an indignant haste to the door, at sound of the bell.

"Are you forty-seven, Sir"?

"Mister Robinson, we did it already; I finished the chapter last week".

"Well do it again. Properly this time".

"Hey, you're not our real French teacher"!

Scott did it properly this time too; back in the staffroom he had a very quick drink, one bun and glare at the winded occupants. Then off to the Strand again, for another hearing at the High Court; to stand to the duty of love where it took him this day -- away from the surface away from the light, down into cloisters and chambers of a medieval fortress. He had to go down and back and not know how far or how long, because it was for love. By now at middle-age all he had was love; he had no money, no success, no career, no status. Only love -- as much a part of him as the breath he drew; though it had no reason and no reward, no promise. It was for him, both termination and salvation; like the fish that love the sea with no escape and no intent -- endless depths without direction under the glinting mirror surface.

But there was hate too, there was hate in the room he headed for; that special kind between women and men, now men had no war and the women had no need. But he was duty bound to head towards the hate and conquer it without weapons, without comrades, with no training for such inglorious conflict. He wanted to finish this hate and survive as whole and unmarked. He knew how no one else had done this so far. But he put this fact out of his head, as he grabbed a bag and clutched his eye-glasses, found his pen and pushed through the doorway with no hands. Already he was succeeding at the impossible and set to face the incomparable --

Scott In Clover

Eating in London was not like America; you could never be sure what you would get or what you might pay. It was not a uniform service, because every place was so different. Scott was unsure what to expect, so he stayed home or ate at school. In Minnesota you could find several kinds of fruit pie: apple, blueberry, boysenberry, pumpkin or cherry, with or without whipped-cream/ ice-cream. But it was the same pie everywhere, probably from the same pie factory. There were also steak houses, Italian diners and Chinese take-aways. But it was the same in every city, you knew what to expect, how much to pay and what to enjoy.

Here in London, every cafe was a world apart. Each place wrote a new chapter in eating; from high cuisine in Mayfair all the way down to the local 'greasy spoon'. All had special charms for Scott and as working teacher he tended to frequent the low-cost outlets; his favourite was a bacon sandwich with big mug of warm tea to watch the patrons come and go. In summer term he would sit outside the doorway, with his lunch-time repast at the front tables, to see the locals at their daily doings; endlessly distracting and entertaining, like watching people at a beach-front.

That was yesterday; today he still had work to do before heading off round the corner to the High street. The full face of another teacher appeared before him, head on, to get his rapt attention --

"Scott, please, can you mark these"?

"What's that"!

"These projects, on the heart, from class 3-B" and to strengthen his request Mr.Chai laid a pile of folders on the table at Scott's elbow.

"You know I'm not a science teacher".

Scott was partaking of morning coffee, in the science prep room, because he enjoyed the staff; they made him comfortable and he could express himself freely – no correct behaviour to be concerned about.

"They did a great job with this homework, really enjoyed the subject; most of them producing more pages than asked for, with diagrams and colours, everything"!

"I see" –

"I'm away to a conference this week. It would be a big favour"...

"Another thing I must tell you" Scott declared; "3-B and I are not getting on well this term, we got off to a bad start in September".

"Yes I heard something, but"... he was not to be deterred.

"Use a letter grade, not a mark out of ten, with lots of comments; nothing negative because they are a weak class and need encouragement".

"Okay Sir, you talked me into it" and Scott took twenty-six assignments home with him that evening to begin screening their best efforts.

After supper he got them out again and saw lots of red; red for the blood and blue colour for the veins. They all had an elaborate cover sheet -- name, form and fancy title; the more ambitious ones including a contents page. Mr.Chai was correct, even the poorest student tried hard to impress and deserved worthy attention. In fact, Scott did not grade anything less than B- that evening; before putting them to one side for more comments at another evening. He had an idea this may be a turning point in their relationship; they might come-round to Scott if he gave good feed back; it was worth going the extra mile for them.

The next evening Scott took out his own red pen and began to trawl through each assignment; with the idea of helpful comments upon the drawings, the text, or anything trying to be innovative and original. It had to look like the teacher/marker was paying a lot of attention to their work, was glad to receive it, liked the ideas and wanted to reward them fairly. Scott would be lucky if he could reverse his fortunes with this class, by simply marking one set of homework, but he had to try.

Almost one week later, the big day came, to return the projects; he wanted to keep them waiting, to build suspense, create anticipation and so on. On Friday, just before lunch, 3-B sat infront of Scott to hear his preamble about heart issues in general, then their own work in particular. They were delightfully quiet and patient, so he prolonged the event a little longer; for it would be neatly squeezed into the end of period, then straight into lunch break.

"Okay 3-B, the good news -- you did well, most of you did well; the rest of you did especially well, excellent really. There is no bad news".

He stalled; he played his highest trump card and waited to see how it would play out. Not to be disappointed, they all took a big gulp and sighed out loud; the atmosphere changed and some of the girls giggled or smiled towards him. For about ten minutes each student leafed through their pages and glanced at the comments; but most were too excited to read properly or digest Scott's suggestions and his rationale.

He did not find out till next lesson after the weekend how they would choose to respond – now he was in suspense and the one held waiting. Not to worry, it was to be a happy ending; on Monday they were in a great mood and sent out various signals to Scott, to announce a new beginning they wanted with their teacher. They quickly forgot about the heart and ploughed into a new chapter: 'asexual reproduction' -- close enough to the real thing for them. Sometimes we get what we deserve, thought Scott, as he schemed out the next lesson for them right on his feet.

But as was his calling and others too, food was more interesting than sex; always in closer proximity and more tempting. He liked to arrive at the canteen early; to enjoy the presentation, check out the colours and smells steaming away beneath glass covers. He was compelled to linger over new dishes for the day; a 'plat du jour' for the unaffected hungry --

"More potatoes, love" asked a lady on the other side?

"No, I must cut back, so I can enjoy the fruit

crumble today".

The dinner lady stood poised, with a ladle full of mashed potato and seemed hurt to hear Scott's protestation. It was like mother's love had been rejected and clearly the lady equated this imperative with feeding Scott well, albeit against his wishes.

"You are too thin, Mister Robinson; you're going to blow away, my love"!

It was a big effort to refuse the lady and apologize to her for his non-compliance. This same scene happened the next day and the next, till she finally accepted his position and deferred to his wishes. It seemed Scott was open to the kitchen staff in matters concerning self-interest and culinary success. Scott also fended off basic advice from the service staff regarding his health, his safety and his future: "Are you the boss yet, Mister Robinson? You will be if you keep mum and stand tall".

"Not this term Joe, but I keep trying, thankyou". He sought to understand their good intent and generosity, so tried to reciprocate with good manners and due respect.

In the staffroom, at first break, Scott was on his own and managed a correct measure of nutrients. He found a small savory to go with coffee; an egg roll with lettuce, cheese, or something warm. He needed food and taste, as well as stimulants – because it was a long day ahead, with many unseen troubles and demands.

More troubling was afternoon, when he was decidedly empty and tired and few schools offered refreshment at end of day. Except one, a church school, which served apples, biscuits and tea; for any staff that observed religious service by joining the headmaster after school in prayers. It was a fair concession and Scott was interested in the church; so every afternoon he knelt with a deputy head and others to sing and pray for thirty minutes, then repair to a reception area for assorted edibles. This thoughtful arrangement worked well for a few months, so that Scott could eat dinner at home at a late hour.

School, however, was the be-all and end-all for Scott at this time; because he was still low ranking, insecure in his position and therefore needing to excel. Sometimes in unexpected ways, his own life impacted on classroom duties in a surprising manner. Everything was going well, the morning lesson chugging along at a steady rate; he had the class on 'auto-pilot', as he might say, when a girl's voice suddenly piped up --

"Mister Robinson, Sir; Colleen is crying; she can't do her work"!

"Who's that"?

"The girl in the corner. It's her dad"! The whole

class watched to see what Scott would do, what he would say, sensing it was serious and important.

"Send her out to me, to the front, please". The girl was a thin waif, in Year-Six, looking vulnerable and sad. She stood infront of Scott at his desk, but he drew her to one side and sat with her in his corner; he sat on her left side to free-up his right hand/arm, if he wanted to animate the comments.

"Tell me what's wrong" Scott said, as he went down to a whisper – but she was unable to respond. She was listening and thinking, which was good, so he continued to gently coax her: "I have a daughter about your age, you can talk to me, I'm a dad too". The class were getting on with a math exercise by now and not paying any attention to Mr.Robinson or Colleen, allowing him to continue probing her.

"My dad has gone" and before she could say more, tears came again. She was heart-broken but very young, so Scott knew she could bounce back very quickly. Eventually, Scott heard how the father was on the road, driving long distance and not easily contacted. He also sensed there was trouble between her parents; she was frightened and confused. At the same time Scott remembered how he was separated from his own daughter of the same age – the coincidence was amazing, fortuitous and fortunate – because Scott could easily relate to her situation and quickly knew what to say, how to help.

"I'm sure your dad loves you very much". Scott thought how this would contrast with her mother's outbursts and the girl heard this clearly; she seemed to rally. "He must be thinking of you, driving his lorry and miss you a lot; I'm sure". This was definitely getting through to her – seems Scott hit the button right on the mark. "D'you love your daddy, yeah, of course you do"! Her tears had evaporated by now and she was looking up at him with a new face and brave stare; pointing her nose out and forward, ready to face the world and make friends with love again.

"Right, I want you to sit at this desk by me and write a letter to your dad; you can leave the maths till later. Just tell him what you're doing and how you think about him, okay. Take it home this afternoon and get your mother to send it on to him, alright, good"! Scott had all the ideas that day, he just couldn't miss.

Colleen promptly went to the front desk and began something on paper immediately, finding the words right away. He glanced across at her occasionally, when he paced between the rows of desks, to check the class progress with working fractions from the black-board. Everyone was well employed and ignoring the girl, giving her the privacy and space they knew she required. They were sensitive to her plight and left her alone for awhile, because they too fought with parents sometimes or got very upset about something.

For Scott, it was a terrible irony when he witnessed another family separation and he simply told the girl what he wanted to say to his own child; how he wanted her to write him a letter and make a happy ending for them all. It was healing and be healed, to give and receive, do unto others as...

Back home, Scott was glad he resided far from school. East Ham was off-putting to him after living in Kensington. West London offered a modicum of refinement, diversity and entrées for him like nowhere else. Scott never became acquainted with the East End; he never shopped there and never encountered any of their park outlets, as if they had none. Kensington had full recreation and his local park was a daily jaunt for him, with countless benefits.

If Scott wanted to impress a lady, he chose the Kensington Park Orangery first and prayed he got the opening hours correct, when he paraded down an avenue of plane trees from the gates at Nottinghill; to encounter a delightful landscape presented at front steps to the café. Stepping inside was entering the Regency period, like a romantic interlude was beckoning, like someone important was waiting with something good to happen. Inside, the high ceiling-roof created echoes and reverberations from sounds of conversation; trays rattling, spoons banging and chairs moving. It was like a cathedral roof, sheltering scores of glass windows and huge plant boxes for the incumbent lemon and lime trees inside. The café had once been an 'orangery' to the palace, to produce citrus fruits for the king's table. The same trees still resided on the site and traces of aristocratic connections showed in the stone sculptures and plaster moldings. It was a truly elegant service for the Kensington elite. Part of the café effect was its exit past large manicured greenery, lawns and rows of park benches, towards the private flower enclosure behind the palace proper. Scott could never visit at evening to exit into shadowy gardens; he had to visit for lunch-time coffee and exit to sunny walks alongside the Round Pond shimmering on his left, as if even better things were to come. The orangery was about more than eating; it was mood and location, style and history, architecture and surroundings. Scott was its number one fan; he was a happy repeat customer and registered no complaints.

But there was another orangery nearby; another old building designed to house citrus fruit trees; which had been refurbished into a smart café, continental style, serving French pastries along with loose-leaf teas. It was only a mile away, going the opposite direction to Bayswater past Nottinghill, to Holland Park Road. A small side lane, onway to Shepherds Bush Green, went left up a hill towards a different kind of garden park; with a lot less lawn and not so open. One day he had a rendezvous there, accepted at urging of the other party --

Scott waited almost a half-hour, but no one showed, so he went into the orangery at Holland Park. Charles his teacher friend, was usually reliable and prompt, but not today; so Scott decided to brave it alone and strolled into the café like nothing was wrong. He took a table upstairs and looked around to note anything or anyone of interest.

The interior was less imposing than the orangery at Kensington and the patrons more liberal; corduroy outfits with golfing jackets and lots of earnest conversations ensuing. He was against the wall at a quiet corner and took to observing, first the white décor and stone paving, then the waiters who appeared distinctly foreign. After a few mouthfuls of beans and potato, Scott rapidly lost interest in his surroundings and the food infront of him, because he was tilting heavily towards the Kensington café he knew so well. To compare the two was making no contest; in fact it was distasteful for him to remain any longer. He took a last nip off his plate and nodded to his waiter against ordering any desert. It had been a disappointing experience, even though he saw a showbiz star at lunch with his family. They occupied a big table near the kitchen and there was lots of fuss an-carry-on over the order and kids not settling at their places. David Essex had a lot of unruly curly hair and a bohemian jacket, which managed to set him apart; though there was no condescension, no servile attendance shown to him. London was still the big smoke, the great leveler.

But Scott had enough of everything and quickly went to pay his bill; to stand outside for a while in the cool open air that was favourable and free to anyone. He glanced back once, when walking off in the direction of the one small pond – 'Good-bye Mister Essex' he mouthed into the empty air, 'and good luck'.

As it turns out, it was also good-bye to Holland Park Orangery; he was not inclined to repeat the visit. Indeed the park itself never appealed to Scott, he found it moody and a bit stale, full of fringe elements making fools of themselves – altogether distracting from a good fresh air open walk he always needed. Because Scott's preference was for air and light, he tended to go left from Kensington towards Hyde Park, after a refreshing detour round the palace gardens. He usually aimed to walk a large circle course round Knightsbridge and Aspley House, to return by Bayswater pumping station; where water fountains splashed over flower beds and stone gargoyles, to attract more people with good moods.

One terrible wintry afternoon Scott found himself in Hyde Park, at the Marble Arch end, along with a lot of other odd sorts. It was 'speakers corner' at its best, or rather its worst, depending upon who you spoke to --

About a hundred oddments gathered round various speakers, older men mostly, standing on their own improvised box platforms. Often the same speakers each weekend and saying the same things/ideas, with exactly the same words spoken: "What did Winston Churchill do – he did this – not that", as the man poked two fingers into the air; firstly, palm to the front, then reverse of palm! The first signaled victory, defiance, triumph – the second was angry, rude and profane. It was meant as a kind of joke, in association with a popular figure, Prime Minster Churchill. The speaker was right out on the edge, getting a shocked response from his listeners, with the juxtaposition of good and bad together; a clever ploy for a pedestrian proletariat, out in inclement weather too.

Scott was amused with a British tradition made into a poster exhibit for the visitors. It was easy for him to become smug as an American, when seeing this ludicrous side-show of human rights, liberty and freedom from days of 'yore'. It was the olde country trying to be poignant and proud, but it was comical and eventually embarrassing; rather like a man might look upon his elderly mother as pathetic, unworthy, unlikely.

All the speakers were men, white and working class, or of dubious class; all except one – Doctor Donald Soper. Some of them railed against religion or foreigners, or against foreign religions. They might only have two or three listeners, but still they shouted out loud and clear, to thrust a pointed finger out in the cold damp air. Dr. Soper stood upon a real podium, in a corner on his own each Sunday afternoon and quickly gathered round him a swelling troupe. He was erudite, well spoken and respectable; the front of his podium read: 'West London Mission'. He was silver-haired; but fine looking, robust and engaging.

Scott always ended-up in front of Donald Soper and enjoyed hearing his feisty exchanges with individuals in the crowd. But he also learned something about the Methodists and British life. This day was cold and terribly windy, making for an assault upon the chest; which was specially difficult if you had to speak out loud, in full voice, for an hour or more. It was public speaking at its best, with a testy audience to contend with. He would notice Donald's chest filling-up and heaving with the effort to reach out, embrace, connect, persuade and confront –

"Yes, you are right, I am not God -- but am a pretty good friend of his", Scott heard. "Our friend over here wants to forget about God and concentrate on his wage packet – but that's like denying your parents after they handed out your pocket money"! The man over there was no 'friend'; it was a brave pleasantry, because the hecklers were usually hostile, cheeky and stupid too.

Marble Arch was not always fun and amusement for the tourists; only recently was it loud talk, argument and laughter. Long before all this it was much more ominous – it was the site of 'Tyburn gallows', where highway robbers were hung and before that Spanish priests came to be martyrs for the Pope after their famed executions. Scott could see the Tyburn nunnery across the road, nestled into the Bayswater housing, where the Roman church consecrated a convent and memorial. Altogether there was an underlying gravitas at the location, which eventually turned Scott away to seek afternoon refreshment and warm shelter; and he expected visitors for his weekend tea party. The occasion was hosted at home with suitable teacher friends and featuring his select raspberry jam, a sure success; a weekly calendar event he offered as alternative to going-out.

However the very next week a new staff colleague managed to change Scott's mind and get him out, right after school. Professional courtesy demanded he oblige the young lady and accompany her to a West London landmark store --

"Let's go together, just wait ten minutes, I'll be right back".

She had mentioned Harrods and going for 'high tea' after school. It was all the rage this year, finding a new place that served teas about four o'clock; starting with big name places like Harrods, the Ritz, the Savoy and Fortnum & Mason.

"We get the tube to Knightsbridge corner and easily walk from there. We need to be dressed, so that's okay; they don't accept jeans or runners" she instructed Scott. It was still cold and dark at evenings; so they dashed straight out from the staff-room replete with school bags and coats to follow a quick escape from dusty Fulham streets.

Miriam was new to the school and full of opinions and concerns, while Scott simply needed a companion for his new adventure. They hurried to the station and out the other end, to make a timely appearance on the fourth floor; where pink table-cloths were out in force and a short queue formed at the entrance.

At ten-past-four Scott and his colleague were shown towards a small square table, where they sat up-straight with ready made manners for the affair. Unexpectedly, the waitress was an Irish person of middle years and homely style –

"Yes my dears, what would you like"? But there was no choice; everyone paid the same price and helped themselves from a whole array of light recipes, followed by lashings of Earl Grey tea. The room was full of patrons, mostly people who had frequented the floors below in the afternoon, most likely tourists. Scott did not notice any other professional types at the event, so directed some fizzy chat towards his school friend in the opposing seat. He began with his stock thesis on the history of tea drinking in England; how Catherine of Braganza from Portugal married King Charles ll and brought her own secret 'stash' of tea from home, locked in an ornate 'caddy' box. No one seemed to know about this. If encouraged a little, he would continue with his theme from World War One, where hot tea with milk and sugar became a food substitute for soldiers and folks at home alike; ensuring it a special place in the public conscience.

The two class pundits took a full share of sustenance and tonic; in fact Scott decided he would forgo dinner at home, if he managed a round of pastries after his fill of cut sandwiches. The lady was more delicate with the servings; it appeared she had pre-planned sensible nutrients for her dinner and eventually said so.

It was soon time to be moving, but the Irish woman was sad to let them go, by now she had almost adopted them: "everything alright my dears, lovely to see you, bye for now". Miriam said 'cheerio' at the main door and sped off among a crowd of pedestrians, which were swelling in number at end of office hours. In return, Scott reckoned to attend more 'tea' sessions during the season and next time he presided at an unknown cafe down Queensway in Bayswater; where a host of Arab tea-shops also offered traditional English fare with more noise, more choice and less price.

Scott On Hol's

Teachers can be very organized during holidays, because they do this in their job, each and every day for their pupils. Summer holidays are the main opportunity in the year for them, not to be missed, not to be squandered. Scott Robinson lived nearest the South Coast and time on the beach, at the open sea, was a prize recreation he dreamed of since Easter.

He went to Brighton for one week at a touring centre, with pack and gear to unwind. To break away with sea and air, sky and sun; even if he be alone again, without his family or his daughter. The hostel was three miles from the waiting sea, a short bus ride to the salty edges of a busy shore-line; to find a royal promenade of candy-stores, ice cream and long stretches of iron railings. He had only a swimsuit for the week; no books, no money to waste, no letters to write and no alternatives.

Scott had endured enough that July, in a stuffy glass-box school north of Paddington. He was really an open-air type and needed to swim in summer, in the sea; because he had been a college swimmer. But now it was still school -- no holidays yet, no togs/towel; but jacket and tie, bag and papers and very sore hot feet. The sun was a June/July torture, to weaken the best resolve of daily employment in a 'Sixties' basic-bare block. He went to the window at a fain attempt to swallow a share of air and light; saw himself dipping into a glossy sea, smiling again, strong and tanned splashing out to the rocks.

Splashing and stroking from the rock pools -- school was far away and he was smiling to the sun, going to be strong again so quickly, so easily. He stormed out of the waves to the pebble-shore, like Adonis at the fountain bulging with energy. Two girls were in his path, in the sand with a castle, bucket and spades. One wore a spotted outfit, the other a two-piece costume with deep brown hair. She was the leader, or the child with the ideas and stopped Scott in his bare tracks; to get all his attention, because she could have been his daughter. The sun was full blast across their small shoulders and tender arms, all of about four years old; so fragile and busy, so small and fair. Scott sat a few feet away and tried to spot parents. He worried about them burning, worried about arguments, or the sand may be too dry to make a castle. He continued like this a half-hour, afraid to be noticed, afraid of parents; compelled to watch when he should be off to dress. Finally he fiddled with a match and toffee-paper he found and presto, made a flag, a sand-castle flag. He took it over to the girls and showed to one then the other, turning it round in his fingers; then placed on the castle tower and smartly strode away to make an impression.

The town was a tidy set of cafes/stores/cottages and sights he sought out, to tick off with college discipline; on his own with a diary, swimsuit, one book for a rainy-day, one set of foot-wear and one pen -- so effective, so alone, so prepared, so full and tight. By the week's end he was ready, ready to go, to face London again. His last day was to be a full list of activities; dinner on the promenade, stroll up the High Street and climb chalk heights to look across the endless sea like anyone else, like last year. Two trawlers were trying to fade away to the horizon and go unnoticed; but a sail-boat followed their course and seagulls went straight out from the cliffs to a sheet of big blue sky across the platform of deep blue sea, out to France and beyond. He could feel like he mattered, like anyone else; in this bigger setting he was same size as everyone else, same portion of happiness/ loss/ success and failings – at last equal portions all round.

Going along the upper promenade Scott heard a different kind of shouting, not happy voices, from a boy about ten years-old hitting another boy who had to be his brother. One called out, "Hey mister; can I have fifty pence please"?

Scott could see two boys getting very heated with each other; the older one bashing away at the other and there was terrible shouting.

"What's that"?

"My brother lost it, lost our bus money; please, we need a pound for the bus"!

He had run infront of Scott's steady course; left his brother to fold over at the rails and weep in confusion. Scott stepped towards the older one, to glance at the smaller boy and offered two pounds straight away. It was an amazing reversal of emotions for them; how quickly they cheered-up and recovered, to run off in the direction of a bus station nearby. They were even happy enough to grasp hands together, as the older boy helped his brother to cross over the roadway. Scott saw his own father in such distress, knowing how he too was impoverished at such an age, with scant resources and how a lot of kids in school today were still very disadvantaged.

Suddenly he was back to London, West London brick estates; endless blocks of angry red brick, battleship gray paving concrete; even the sky dark gray or light gray and dust always blowing from the gutters. Every shade of gray, every shade of anger; the people the same, lots of angry people with the gray people, one or the other. School was set in the midst of an oven-like area of more brick, galvanised fencing and asphalt. Boredom and unrest dripped from its very walls; as teachers bolted from one station to the next as if a target and kids scattered the buildings like bugs in a shed. But it was more than a hostile environment; the core was overheating and imploding. People were chewing their claws and turning on their families, their own children as victims, as progeny of degradation. These children were full of confusion and unsettling organisms, which swirled inside them, like acrid water fermenting in a pressure vessel. What could Scott do, forced to watch and clearly see the oldest obscenity; suffering children, like his own father spoke of --

But someone was waking him, nudging at his elbow: "Hils, come on your turn. Yes, your turn to buy. Two coffees and slice of ginger-cake for me".

"Hi Eamonn; yeah alright.

Hey; I hear you're getting out, leaving us this year – is that correct? How can you? What about loyalty and vocation, what about hols and pension"?

"Listen Hils, too old; you're too old and me too!"

It was morning break and very July in the city, in a stale box of a staff-room; lots of NQT's and management swirling around a coffee pot and then swirling round the staff 'umph-gal'. She was twenty-something in solid 'M-an-S' wear, expecting a good turn out at ten fifty-five-am; when she wore a 'fem-lit' top from college, slipped right down this summer term to reveal a dun chest and fresh shoulders. Her eyes were non-authoritarian hazel, to declare egalitarian interests; par equity, meritocracy and enjoyment.

"Judith, meet my friend, Hils. It's Scott really, but we call him Hils since it's Scott Hilliard".

She took him in at once; middle-income, middle America, middle-age teacher. She was both intrigued and repelled, like he was foreign food.

"Hiyah Hils, if that's your name; what's your subject"!?

But she left no time for a response, as she picked-up a bag and pile of books, starting to leave. "Listen, I gotta go; will see you all at lunch, till then, bye".

She quickly turned, off and away together, to be

safely out of reach. And Scott looked forward to the lunch encounter, coming after two more lessons in the room above, on the Humanities corridor. To shorten the process he snatched his gear from the floor and speeded to the door then to the stairways like he was important, like his work was important; but it was important to get to the room before the hellions got loose, before they trashed the place.

A few moments later he dragged out some work-sheets on 'The Crimean War: A New World emerges' and before he finished a standard prelim, they settled into a writing-chat-read session. This allowed him to go ahead with next lesson papers and info for the staff-do on Friday; when it would be green lights for food/drink and Ms Reaburn. In fact he had two tickets for Wimbledon-tennis on Sunday; maybe she could go with him, he had to find somebody.

Year-7 was next lesson, with the girls still in school ties and boys still in pairs at the door -- waiting. They came into the room and waited again. He reshuffled the same lesson sheets from last period and extended another prelim, 'The Crimean War: Anzacs arrive'. Of course they waited, to listen for the questions called out, like a Bingo session; favouring neither boy or girl, fat nor thin, quick or slow – good correct parity.

"My dad was in the Army," sang out from row two,

the plump boy with a canvas bag.

"This is his kit bag; he said I could bring it into school".

"Fascinating Tom, can we all take a look"?

"Yeah; thankyou Sir", as a royal blush overcame him right where he sat. Two girls looked at each other to giggle and gush; so that Scott felt he had to underscore its value –

"Can we pass it round the class, please"?

"My dad says the Navy was more important; that's what he was in", came from the back this time. But everyone was on Tom's side by now and Scott was building upon the sympathy, empathy, to extend the discussion and harden the reality of war.

"Right; who else brought things for us to see? Anymore"?

For the next twenty minutes it was show and tell, or talk and chalk; so Scott forgot the time and had to collect class exercises next period, had to register pupils later; a lot of mess at the end to indicate a good lesson, the ragged edges of good content.

Back to the staff-room Ms.Raeburn was between Geography and Maths; two department heads making their pitch about advancement, schedules and maybe something about Friday.

"Hils, over here; what you got? Still fighting the

battle of your bulge, eh! I can eat all the chips I want --
the ladies said so"! Eamonn was enjoying his advantage,
again, to the full. He also wanted to trample on Scott's
feelings, to spoil things --

"I see you moving on Mizz Judith; yeah, join the
queue. She probably won't show on Friday afternoon
anyway. She's saving herself for Mister Right or Mister
Opportunity. Besides you couldn't take the glitz ole
chap. Do yourself a favour, face it"!

"Face over here, yuh fool, she can hear you"!

"Who cares; these NQT's need their wings clipped
and learn to put a hand in their pockets. Listen I gotta
get outside after lunch; are you coming"?

"No Eamonn; not today. I have to finish a letter,
now, before pm lessons".

"Alright then".

It began -- 'Dear Kay: Happy Birthday! Your
school promised to hand over my gift this week. A
lovely story of songs from Denmark, I enjoyed myself,
when Daddy was a boy; have you got a video player?

Flowers are growing at the front again. I must
water them every day because it's hot this week -- isn't
it hot! Remember you helping me last summer? I
found your small watering-can that's blue and yellow
and use it myself – okay!

Next week I must clean the carpet, because Ray

spilled his drink on the floor last night. He says, Hello Kay -- remember him, how he used to make you laugh'!

He folded it with a leading edge and drew a face, before getting into a pocket quickly out of sight. Two more lessons in the afternoon; one exam prep, Year-11 and then another Year-7 when he was going to look at Alfred Noyes poem 'The Highwayman', out of sight of the department. It was hopelessly incorrect rhyme/meter verse; but Scott was incorrect, so were his views and his dress-sense. By three o'clock he was well away with:

"Bess, the landlord's daughter, plaiting a dark red love-knot into her long black hair.
Tlot–tlot, tlot–tlot; he came riding... over the purple moor, where the road was a ribbon of moonlight..."

"It's really nice," said Jaycee sighing into a grin.

"Really -- why, why is that"!?

"Don't know – we just like it," someone added. Scott was easily disguising his preferences, like it was a random choice – so he could continue without excuses:

"He came riding, riding, up to the old Inn door.
And he rode with a jewelled twinkle...
his rapier hilt a–twinkle, under the jewelled sky...
Her musket shattered the moonlight,
shattered her breast in the moonlight and warned him –"

Jaycee continued the reading; then someone else read in whispers:

"When the moon is a ghostly galleon tossed upon cloudy seas, a Highwayman comes riding... whistles a tune to the window..."

"Loud please, louder" called Scott; but more whispering, a tidy quiet in a real lesson; the young faces blanched in distraction. An atmosphere Scott could easily identify when they breathed deeper and heads settled onto arms or shoulders; as hearts and minds were taken away by Noyes, just as he wished.

"A bit louder" he called, made no difference to the quiet rendition of readers; but confirmed Scott's presence and marginal control over real learning, real school, real material -- not at all correct or fashionable. They sighed and yawned as he brought them out from the spell and gently hearkened them to home, leaving Scott with a tired dusty room. Loud cleaning staff came next yelling over the top of a vacuum cleaner, to force him towards the staff-mess-room; where more teachers left over from the rush away, faced dirty-sink cups and lumpy chairs. To finally force Scott home for a full evening of teacher items; food-papers-cocoa-nap-walk; like it was a whole day at home.

On Friday the kids left twenty minutes early and ten minutes more the staff-do began; with complimentary wine and 'kiss-o-gram' surprise for the Deputy leaving. She was a WPC with garters and he had to retrieve one without using hands. Anyway a fine time had by all, except his wife who went straight to their car with a bottle of plonk, the Deputy remaining with his head up a skirt. There was lots of roasting by then and chicken legs, bitters, custard and coleslaw. Five pounds per-head was gathered into a hat at half-time, relying on the honour system with no tickets. A pickled Head presided with his stand-by wife to produce a clever party-piece for the on-lookers and NQT's peppered the event like college bums at a union bash.

"Hils you're not drinking! No not-drinking; flirting okay and eat if you must; but no abstaining. Come on, we know you're a profligate like the rest of us -- face it".

"Okay Eamonn, you pest, you plonker! But I want to sit down".

"You already are sitting, to eat, drink and the rest. Is that your preferred position"? Eamonn was one step ahead of the alcohol and one step behind the victim.

"This yellowed trifle is my preferred option. Now stop the verbal junk, or pass it down the other way for a while. And bring over two glasses of red vino for us".

"I'll bring Mizz Raeburn over, to cheer you up".

"No, don't bother her or those on her flank; they

can be dangerous if the bait is taken away"!

The room was full now at five-pm, when alcohol had taken over the mood and transformed a dull coffee-room into a club room, with a new balance of libidos and egos. Papers and such still stacked the corners; but tables and flat surfaces served well for drinks, nibbles and buffet. The smokers unleashed their strongest reefers and occupied the wide sofas, or stood at drink corners with smoke signals drifting out of normal confines. Miss Raeburn was giggling, the Head gagging at her joke and NQT's conspiring -- just like last term's event. Everywhere in other schools, like a common communion across the country, they all taking the same sacraments together. Just then Scott noticed two older pupils at the garden window, with a camera. But it was too late for the kiss-o-gram lady upon a Deputy, too late with the indiscretions and too early for the next session of indiscretions after more wine had loosened a few belts.

"Judith do you like tennis, Wimbledon stuff? I have tickets for Sunday -- it's a great occasion..." Scott had risen from his stool left of centre and crossed over a big carpet area to draw alongside Ms Raeburn. He was being kind, an extra ticket, a unique opportunity; young teachers don't get a chance. Scott was tall and up-straight, to level his middle. He gestured like a happy man, overcoming his age with humour and guile; not concerned when he saw Eamonn approaching at left, in fact welcoming another player.

"Excuse me Mizz Raeburn, is this man bothering you"?

"What can you mean", she giggled?

"He can be a terrible pest; all our department think so. Quite the ladies man we hear, since he left his own department last term. Anyway we don't want him anymore and you don't either".

"What department is that", she ventured?

"The bargain basement department; Eamonn is stockeeper".

"Put the claws away ole man" demanded Eamonn.

"Put your mixed metaphors away old stick"!

But the prized object of this tussle lost interest in the fray. She suddenly heard her NQT friends calling out, saw them signaling at the door --

"Sorry I'm off; we're meeting in the pub across the street. Thanks Scott, see you Sunday".

She went off with a quick hop-skip-an-jump to the doorway; twisting through to the outer corridor on two crossed footsteps, like a theatrical exit.

"Sunday what? Never you for the chapel old chum".

"Tennis, actually, Wimbledon".

"Now you've done it; gone too far this time. No wonder your career is on a slippery slope. Right here in the staff-room too".

"I'm not fussed; a 'career' is your idea not mine. I just want to be a teacher and Jack-th-lad after work -- always got more action than you anyway".

"What d'you mean"?

"More girls have crushes on me than you ever had Eamonn; all my Year-Ten in fact".

"San-fairy-an; codswallop"!

"Yuh see where an education got us; just a load of fancy abuse and sour dreams of a romantic ego".

"So glad I'm an apologist, or revisionist sometimes -- you big spiv"!

"I used to be an existentialist, an individualist, you said so. Still I got the biscuit; a ticket for the main game in town and a chance at Miss Oomph".

"Better finish your trifle before I help you out; before it gets away from you and slips into your empty lap"!

They all had plastics to drink from, to cut or fork something organic and two sizes of paper plates, one for the hand, the other on the lap. Scott was now perched on a radiator facing centre; with Eamonn less secure against a chair-back, with a large cup-drink and no plates. It was six o'clock and there was talk of decamping to the local cafe-bar; lots of cigarette smoke to see now and unfinished eats/drinks on every flat surface. The Head was starting to move, gathering his wife and making fond farewells. Two Deputies were left quietened over a warm tea-pot, sharing the last peanuts; the Maths head at a table space with register-an-pen to claim his work-aholic status.

By seven o'clock it was the same blocking on the stage-scene -- because the party had gone on too long; like a mock-drama, where the spoken lines were beginning to repeat. Scott was still lingering up-stage and left; Eamonn withering at his side playing both friend and foe, colleague and adversary, teacher and parent…

"One more week" Eamonn said, "before study release", as they got out of earshot at the school gates; "then Year-Eleven will leave us in peace".

"You dare me to show in casuals on Monday", said Scott as he tugged off his tie and loosened up for a walk to the bus.

"I don't have to dare you -- you big ponse"!

The sun saved its best shot for teachers plodding home; always reliable like this, always the last straw to the mounting fatigue of a week.

But before the last week, before the last round of classroom antics, there was Sunday; tennis and

Wimbledon. Scott got to church at morning, early for once and renewed his singing voice, took the communion sacrament and fiddled over his dibs. He also took the post-service coffee in high confidence in his clean tucker. Rector Evans button-holed Scott for a new charity project and the widow Carey cheered-up at his elbow -- all very satisfactory for him so early in the day.

At one o'clock prompt he was spruced-up again at Wimbledon station main exit -- waiting and parading.

"Hils, hi, you look great". Miss Raeburn stepped infront of him.

"Hello" he returned nicely, averting a direct gaze at her.

"I love your sun-jacket, why don't you wear it for school, the kids will be impressed".

"No, not for school" he grimaced.

"So stuffy and inhibited, that's what we like about you; our gang depends upon it".

"Right you are. But you look amazing, Judith, how do you do it! Got your sun-screen and a hat"?

"And you got my message this morning? We have to ride the bus, then a short walk, okay".

"Yes, on my ansaphone thanks", he confirmed a call left while he was in church, about first going to someone's house in Colliers Wood and round to the stadium later. Scott thought the message left same time as the sermon -- he would be pondering a clever piece from the Welsh priest.

"Let's go, Virginia Wade is at centre court today".

"Virginia -- not today; that's years ago"!

"No, great commentary from today's woman; she still infront you know".

He was concealing his disappointment about the tickets; now this political polemic rebuff. True the weather was 'iffy'; but he had the silks out, a tie and kerchief in his breast pocket; with straw trilby and bottle of Pims in paper-wrap under his arm. In short, he needed a venue, to be seen.

"It's going to rain, silly, come on"!

Forty minutes later they were walking down 'nondescript avenue' in a mediocre suburb and Scott was supporting some fizzy chat from Ms Raeburn with his own sanguine observations.

"A tennis party Hils, no worries, you fit right in".

They stopped at a family house, at the front gate; where Judith said they could be outside if it cleared-up, in a garden setting with lawn furniture under the trees. But Scott lurched as he saw the doorway and a name over the letter box.

"You been here before? He said it had a garden for

our strawberries, cream and the whole bit".

'He' was the proprietor of this semi-onth-hill; a corner lot with cherry trees at the side and trellises on the wall. Ms Raeburn rang the bell.

"Scott, glad you came" soon as the door opened, "you can have front seat at the 'tele', to hear the dulcet tones of Miss Wade; she's calling the shots you know".

"She's too old, Eamonn".

"Not too old to talk about it and remember, yeah"?!

"I take your point, ole boy. But I'm a bit overdressed for your place, don't you think? I might not stay too long".

Of course his colleagues were happy, carefree and heaven knows what drives a seasoned professional to score points in mixed doubles, when mens' singles drew the most attention. It seems he needed to re-read 'The Feminine Mystique' or some Simone DeBeaviour. Scott doffed his hat somewhere and tried a position at the elbow of sunny Ms Raeburn for the next game, for the rest of the set.

DOWN and OUT

Of course the countryside is very alluring for an inner city teacher; specially since winter was coming and if another colleague was involved with the planning. Scott Robinson knew all about country life from before, when just out of school and knew how a break away from Kensington was the best kind of treatment for a sore head.

He was on the telephone one evening, to the other teacher --

"Nine-am or nine-thirty"?

"Yes, an early start; because it's dark at seven".

"Listen Scott, call me from Victoria; after you get your ticket, okay"!

"How's your school? What's your new place like"?

"Let's talk about it tomorrow, alright".

"See you then -- bye".

Scott cut the TV-film short and had an early Saturday night. He found a travel bag to pack his picnic and sweater/jeans/flask. John was meeting him infront of the station at other end of the line, with his budget banger, to get toast and coffee at his cottage. Then they would be off, like only teachers can on Sunday morning, late summer; like early bird watchers. John was the complete teacher cut out from a college stencil and Scott the professional loose cannon; a real matching pair. But there were no mistakes and lots of caffeine-rush from the kitchen, to the car and B-roads to the Weald.

"How's the beer I made, ole stick", Scott inquired after a few miles upon their way.

"Terrific! I was going to say, it's more than alcoholic, more like narcotic. Definitely an evening beverage, a witches brew. I got the empties ready for you".

"I got another two bottles and wine, my best red of the summer. We don't do reds much in England, because not enough sun. The vines we see today are going into white wines, Riesling from Germany, the northern regions".

"Well, how can you make Burgundy"? They were both talking sideways; because John had to look forward, infront and Scott could look out his left-side window at changing pastoral views.

"Boots"!

"What's that"?

"It's Boots -- grape juice! I got a 'dry red' for you and it's a French grape. Don't say I'm cheating because I started from tinned juice and recipes. I intend to progress and prosper".

"Sounds like you really are taking the bait; sublimating, I suppose".

"We know I'm divorced, but I still go into the clubs/pubs and get on the phone to some likely targets, you know. How about you"?

Their noisy roadster raced up the Downs and ran a twisting course through villages, farms and animals; like it was a fair-ground ride through a tunnel of blurred scenes, like a carousel ride. The October light was like July at the windscreen, producing burnished colours again; like another Bank holiday or a holiday tour. They chatted a lot and sparked each other like valves out of phase, out of school. They were both relieved to step out twice, for eats and car supplies; then continued the jokes about school and London kids.

"By-th-way, how's your little girl; seen her yet"?

"Now you've done it, why d'you ask; you corker"?

"We need to unload; go ahead, get it off your chest

if you want".

"I still write, rarely phone and go to court again next month".

Scott delivered over some city news to John, whilst grasping the essence of Kent weald orchards and fields, like he never could at home in Nottinghill. Essentially there was a contract: his London piece in exchange for pastoral idylls, some city energy from him, for John's scenic grand tour. All relationships were such and humanity teachers, college types, made good contracts; full and fair; they also exchange humour.

The road was climbing and narrowing, till the roadside hedges switched against the car windows and five-bar gates became more imposing as the hill tops were reached. 'Biddenden Vineyards -- 500 yards ahead', assured them of good judgment and instinctive directions. Teachers are good travelers, good companions and good apologists. Scott was relieved to see vines on the slopes behind the wine shop because he had dreamed of such; rows and rows of ripe fruit, hanging imponderously upon stalks across wire trellises. Stretches of grass underlay the straining stems and green markers instructed the visitors to follow the pathway. It was a perfect afternoon because he thought the place to be the same, the air was right, the time, the pieces of his wishes. So by half-way round he declared to his companion, that he too was going to have a vineyard; he would be returning, because he was a country lad before teaching. It all seemed to fit together that afternoon; so he pressed on with his declaration, to the disquiet of John who was now a little shy and unexplainably guilty with his part. By the time they tried refreshment at the picnic tables, Scott was completely nauseous and eventually brought it all-up onto waste land near the gates. They said it was a nervous breakdown. He began with a short stay in the wards at Paddington hospital, then was released on medication after nine days. No escaping the classic case history; teachers at the end of their tether, overwrought and undermined. John visited the first week and took some reading to him, but he had pressing duties to attend, class prep he said and headed off. No one else came to the ward, though he was glad of it because no visitors would believe such an obvious sham; as he organized his year for work again, took the Times Ed supplement from the hospital shop and dreamed of going to a good school. By the time he was due to leave the hospital, he was friendly to anyone with spare moments or spare baggage; he had adopted the routine of treatments and was a model patient.

At home it was dark and dingy, obviously been empty for awhile; with more quiet, more sleep; but a better TV and walks out for milk and bread. The phone rang Friday night, with an up-beat voice on the other end --

"Scott, can you still dance"?

"What about it Charles, who needs to know"?

"How about Saturday night? I know you were ill; but time to get out".

"I don't know".

However, next evening they met up and squared off for the bus. Scott had a fresh haircut and Charles a good aftershave; otherwise they looked like two teachers at an interview, presentable but nothing more. Before they launched onto the dance area they were at the downstairs bar to drink and think it over. Then upstairs they focused onto the nice circle of young Asian ladies in dancing kit with lots of black hair and ivory smiles. Two or three were children catching more attention with frills-an-ribbons and a baby nodding to a rhythm of drums over the mother's shoulder.

Charles and Scott went among the male section with lots of beer bellies, rubbed shoulders with blue suits and wet glasses; as members moved for positions before the target ladies. Scott mouthed into Charles' ear at intervals and Charles preferred to return facial expressions like only London Irish can, above the force of loud dance music. All very basic: two genders, drink, drum beats, late night moods and zygotes. First the warm-up, with the tender gender moving towards sounds together; happy to start off with each other. The next group to warm-up were first filling-up with amber brew, then squaring up with a likely lady. Scott and Chas needed to split-up a pair and did, not once but twice. Scott was pretending to be young, pretending to be single, happy and free. Maybe Charles was doing this too. The silent men near him were not pretending like this because they did not dance, or engage a lady; they kept a place at the bar, except for purpose excursions to the water-closet, till very end of session. They scratched their gray bits and enjoyed a lonely smoke like it was a tobacco advert. There were some very good profiles holding their own against a backdrop of moving colours, stupid joviality, loud happiness. Charles whispered across loudly --

"We taking these two home Scott"?

"What"!

"You know, back to your place for coffee eh"?

It seems one lady had just learned to dance and this her first time, as she leaned on his elbow when they made a good turn or back-step. The other was a sexy creature who retreated as fast as men approached, teasing; a great prize in a contest, but nothing to take home.

"No, not this time" indicated Scott to Charles, "let's leave the honour to our belly brigade or the two squaddies over there".

"Yeah, alright then".

"Don't worry, they will get taken care of soon enough".

"But I gave our address out, sorry and my phone number".

"Well, that's the last card to play in our game". Their evening had reached a turning point. "You want to go"?

"I think so".

Next day Scott doubled his medication for the morning and indulged in washing and tea over TV for a wet Sunday; remembering his illness and how his head did not always keep up with his leg-work. How he needed sit still to rub his face/head and think of getting well, good thoughts with no action. He spent time with Kay's dolls and toy kit in the corner, dusting/tidying them on the shelves. She would have them on the floor, spread out, making new noises for about an hour; a set of model vehicles, attractive miniatures for anyone who can enjoy cars cut down to size with fresh colours and no oily dirt. Eleven dolls had been left behind; a Japanese figure in Kimono, teddy bears, a frog and baby-dolls -- she had more taken away with her, many more. A lot of attention for the first child; basic family psyche, a college 100-course. But from 'Health and Family 100', it was now the 'sex war' between the male race and the female race, where health courses were obsolete. Feminism had hardened, broadened and intruded into mainstream families, not just college eccentrics; now middle house-wives were also militants and children exposed between.

By lunch he sat near the window with tea and bakery pieces to leave the toys for a while, to guess what his wife would do on a lovely October day; if it would be anything like what he does on such a day. Like Sunday two years ago, when three went out to the park again to draw lots of envy as they proceeded, after a morning of angry dispute. Kay was still happy in the centre and pulled them along to the gates and beyond to the emerald groves of Palace Gardens. One of many Sundays, out in the car, on a train, out to relatives or to church. He could sit and pick out scenes to dream of, like going into a picture scrap book. Like the day at Kew Gardens where he found the Sequoia, two California redwoods in the tree section and got a lot of nagging when he chased up to them to exude silly passion and falsetto notes at big deaf timbers. Kay was near three to be shown-off in a two-tone sun bonnet and socks with trim, enjoying a ride in her chair. Scott was in shorts and open shirt looking like a tennis pro from the rankings; the mother a woman in jeans, blue jeans and lots of hair over her face. Lots of signs then, signs of distance and anger. Next page from the scrap book was a Valentine's dance; the mother was at the food in the community kitchen. Kay in a scarlet frock with white lace, kept going for the floor centre to dance with her first man, her favourite, the one who tickled and carried her. Her own father of course; who felt he needed her more than was healthy, loved her more than was right, wanted her more than she wanted him -- a sunburst of excitement with forbearance upon the older partner.

It was Halloween last week; now Guy Fawkes night, when he was to go out and see a bonfire in Ladbroke Gardens, with mulled wine, a hot-dog and fireworks. When he walked round there and returned, he could hear rockets bursting in the sky above; but only see a few of them between brick silhouettes of Victorian houses. To underline how restricted his view was, how closed-in his home. He was buried in the city far from Kent and sunny rows of vines, far from elysian fields; buried in a small flat on a dusty street. Not unlike his ward in the hospital last month: a bed/bed-table, books/book-stand, tea/tea-tray. But even a small place can be found out --

"Scott how are you"? The telephone had intruded into the afternoon.

"Back in school tomorrow, part-time".

"Are you coming down before Christmas? I need more brew".

"Not sure, I don't want to repeat my malaise. Maybe Kent had something to do with it, the vines or the ripe air"! But the response was still adversarial --

"It suits me well enough".

"Because you can't dance"!

"What, neither can you, give me a break".

"Charles and I attended a club event at Swiss Cottage last month".

"Is he one of the gang now"?

"Yeah, he took your place".

John added more tags to an ordinary Sunday, riding over the rude snags. Scott promised to call again then cut it short. Time for some walk treatment; he added a coat layer and scarf, to catch the last light at Kensington Gardens. He jumped the lanes of Bayswater Road to defy mortal injury once again and accelerated through the heavy gates along with dog-walkers, child-minders and skaters. Straight away a breeze picked up; he sighed into the wind and hurried to catch dusk closing round the water at the pond. Black boughs and wet tarmac should be a dismal exercise, but not today because there was still more oxygen in here; more greening, more sky. Two ladies from church stopped and spoke to him about some God nonsense and waved hard as he moved away. Scott also spoke to a skating gal; he asked about the-going for skates when she landed on his bench in her bare cut-offs and emblem T-shirt, like it was still August. All very satisfactory last hour of day. No summer tourists now cos' it's winter coming, no squirrels because winter coming; no boats because dark coming, no kites no balls, no chairs no sun because it was November. Scott saw the 'big bird' going right over the palace towards West Kensington; the Concord bird and he shouted out, tugged an elbow of a fellow park prankster. Together they saw a big silver dart score the dull sky one more time that week; one more hat-full of New York travelers who were looking down upon his park, his path, upon his sore head. By the time he re-entered the street he was excited for tea again at home, excited about a TV evening and more eats. This park really was a 'moveable feast' as Hemingway would say. Not a Paris feast like he wrote about, but a London feast moving from summer to winter and back again; always somewhere to eat to see, always someone to talk to, something to love, work and art and risk. Ernest left a comfortable America to starve in Paris, but he endured and benefited. Scott left his comforts to struggle in London; another great European camp sixty years on and realized the task, the benefits for an American down-an-out in London or Paris. Scott had done the reading course at college and was a graduate fired up for the distance. Lots of preliminaries like Henry James in England; Eliot, Pound and Joyce in the same direction from Dublin. What a trail, what casualties, what stories/dreams and what ruin/decay. But they did not have breakdowns; true they drank, later Hemingway drank too much; but no breakdowns like his.

Instead of going home Scott headed to Queensway, a dynamic shopping street adjacent to the park; he padded down one side to the end and back again. It was the 'Kasbah' of London; not a village place, no writers/artists; but noise and light every day every night like it was burning, burning up at both ends. Every shade of skin, every kind of race buying and selling, earning/spending, playing and working. It was nothing like the London Scott expected, or known to James or Eliot. This street was London in the new post-war Europe, post-modern England, post industrial culture.

Next day was a half-day at school as beginning of re-hab and re-employment. Scott went in for morning break: coffee/chat then quiet in a library corner till lunch. Eamonn was now department head, a new area,

126

community curriculum; eating more lunch now and loads of custard, as Scott sat opposite in the formica canteen. He was lashing the ketchup round like it was a murder, getting some onto his fingers. Scott had to watch him sucking his hand clean infront of a small gang of Year-8's, who were gorging warm chips like a famine was coming.

"Fancy nipping out for a pint" he said?

"What, a quick one you mean"?

"No, not a 'nooner' – some liquid cheer".

"What's in it for me" pleaded Scott?

"Your 'favoured nation' status; a hands-off memorandum". But there was an edge to their slick chat, because Scott had breached his new contract with early illness absence and autumn was now a terminal contract.

"Well how's your French, or History even"?

"You know about my French. But I like History". Scott re-aligned his future with some clumsy fibs.

"Yes I know you, but not your favoured states; sorry you have to go for it, ole pal".

All this was very ominous, when Eamonn usually preferred sex or sport for lunch topics; Scott was disinclined with both topics, missing out on in-service training these last years. But sex and sport went together for Eamonn, as healthy diversions and good alliteration. The name-ofthe-game for Scott had changed to survival. He needed to be sleeker, meaner and get new spots.

The kids were clattering in the room like it was a prison meal, because hardware was either damage-proof metal or disposable. But it was important play for them, like play mating, play fighting and play manners. Eamonn was good; he hit upon two scalawags messing up the slosh bucket and stopped an argument between mouthfuls of burger and fruit crumble. He could play two games at the same time: his kids game in the lunch room and a wicked staff game with his colleague. Scott was still a sick teacher-patient; not up to a full charge yet, not ready for any encounter.

"I know you're not bonkers, just the same, get a doctor's note for the accounts office and" --

"And say it was exertion, stress, chronic domestics"!

They were ambling across the yard again and Scott could feel a nip in the November noon, a promise of worse things to come. But Eamonn let his jacket open and showed a striped club tie to good effect, for his new slot in the management. Scott was keeping step but feeling the chill and gripping his case very hard as they re-entered the main building.

After dinner at home Scott pulled out a sleeveless

woolen in dark blue and laid it on the breakfast chair. He cut short a TV item and went into bed with a journal and whiskey from Canada in hot lemon mixer; thinking of an early start with his half-day at morning, then afternoons till Friday. Of course Eamonn knew something because he was on the inside track this year, by luck and pluck; but Scott needed more hints by week's end. The flat was dark at seven-am with a west-facing window; so he made warm porridge, crisp toast and got to the tube by twenty minutes-to-eight.

Eamonn was starting to brew tea in the common room and enjoying an early chore, as part of his new department role.

"Just talking about you Scott"!

"You mean milk and sugar, thanks".

"Yes of course you do. No; listen, can you switch today? You can have Eleven-C and I'll take your Year-Nine's. Alright"?

"Okay by me".

"Next week you will have Year-Ten for a while, because they have no assessment yet, it should be a safe bet for you".

A real buzz was picking up by eight-thirty-am, as NQT's made up the volume and two deputies brandished paper lists to pin on notice boards. Fifteen more minutes it was over the top for everyone, up and out to the fray; each teacher heading off to the kids unarmed and defenseless, like lowly traffic wardens on the beat.

7-P were good at morning registration, subdued and kind to Scott, kind to a teacher not quite bonkers yet. They went to places easily and Jim at front helped with the names and home notices.

"Right Seven-P! Please, listen! Yes, listen for once and you two at the back"!

"Sorry Sir, it's swimming today, we have to leave".

"Leaving early, I know... but this is your last warning for parent notes and homework; on my desk by lunch time.

Right, off you go"!

He was in clear voice, loud and projecting; but not angry just persistent, teacher persistent. They flowed out the door like fluid from a jar, like water at a sluice; while he glanced a note from the Head in the register, for him today.

All through the lesson with Year-8 he kept getting it out of his pocket. But no guessing what it was. He mentioned it to Eamonn at break when he seemed a bit flush; though he gave nothing else away, pushing round the hot-water cistern to make his coffee ahead of Scott again.

Next lesson it was Shakespeare and 'Merchant of

Venice' with Year-11. Two responsive girls at the back took his mind from the villainy in the text, the malice and danger ahead. Even four-hundred years ago was no different from the London of Eliot and Pound, or this day at Hammersmith in a Victorian style school of mixed immigrants. Scott took up some reading and went ahead to scenes after the court hearing, to get a hint from the Bard: Joyce said "cunning and exile" and Will said, "cutlers poetry upon a knife"!

Later the Head started off with: "sit down Scott you look stressed. Been at your Shakespeare again. 'Kill the lawyers' is what I remember and 'beware the Ides of March". Lots of smoke like this from the Head; a good academic screen, when teacher types get together and have a parting of ways. Mr.Slipper was well away with the 'thank God it's Friday' doctrine, which today sounded more like some of 'Murphy's Law'; ending with 'don't call us we'll call you; the cheque's in the post'. And 'it hurts me more than'... Scott did not even get to say 'bye' or 'have a nice weekend', because the Head was already up at a cabinet; heaving the drawers open as he called out, "leave the door when you go, please, I have to see Miss Raeburn next".

On his way out Scott did indeed leave the door open and the front gates unlocked; to head off for home full of expectancy, full of myrrh -- but empty on solids, empty on substance.

SCOTT on PARADE

'Location, location, location' Scott kept hearing on the High Street, mostly about property. It was also true that a good location might find something new in people, might benefit them a lot; whereas another situation may overwhelm and show a person in bad light.

Scott Robinson was known to his pals as Hils, short for Hilliard, his middle name from a maternal grandfather in Minnesota. Anyway, he was far away from Saint Paul now, far from the great American corn belt. He had been transplanted into the home-grown sections of Kensington; able to take full benefit of the Royal Borough as best Humanities teacher, a good bon vivant replicant, with some left-over collegiate charm. If he could not follow his own career sojourn, or yet make sense of it, he definitely had a good opinion of west-by-west London; how this high district afforded him better entrees and catholic tastes.

Scott was living above Kensington Park and working in a school at Sloane Square. So he could walk back in the evenings; up Sloane Street to Knightsbridge, into Hyde Park and diagonally across to Kensington. In Spring he forgot about the tube train at end of day, to make for home under his own speed and set off with the aim of getting into a healthy pace. The best section for him was on the south-side footpath along the Serpentine Lake; going westward swinging his familiar school bag, vaporizing a lot of cares and concerns of the day.

Reaching the Round Pond he sat on a bench for a while and picked up bits of conversation nearby; like it was another staff-room and the grown-ups letting loose their hopes and fears, their wit and malice. Three Japanese girls came past, chatting freely and nodding a lot. They wore black coats with coloured running shoes, to set a new student style; active but still cold to the wind. A group of Arabs came next, for a full contrast; covered in black burkhas and pushing their children in strollers. Finally, a real London gent arrived, with heavy shoes and trilby hat; he walked with a brisk flourish and easily sped through everyone. It was amazing how much began to happen, or began to be noticed, when Scott paused to stop like this; like you notice everything better after stepping off a children's round-about, getting out-of-step can focus perception. Kensington Park was never a sleepy enclosure, but a busy thoroughfare; because it was the major pleasure garden for loads of people before reaching their Nottinghill housing estates.

During this year the park had really taken hold of him, cast a magical spell, because Scott always had such a difficult time exiting his park; after evening strolls he would hang around the exit gate like it was his last visit, his final exile to the suburbs. He came to realize it was the 'heart' of West London for him, always fresh and cool being on a hill covered with trees. Maybe it reminded him of other losses he had before, jobs he lost, or people and faces of years ago lost again in the fading light; because the park was also a sweet melancholy for him. Finally the gate was pad-locked by a keeper and Scott went away thinking he at least put the place safely to bed again, for another day.

The sun was not yet warm that week, that afternoon, so Scott picked up to continue his stride, trying to make an exercise of it; swinging and stretching for the final distance up the broadwalk to the northwest gate.

At home he got the kettle on and jacket off quickly,

like he did it before and rushed up a nibble and drink; usually tea with raspberry jam at his couch seat to see 'Grange Hill', the TV drama about school. It really was 'school' and he believed it to be written by teachers for teachers. He noted the plots were never resolved, never sorted out; they were always eclipsed by another conflict, a new crisis. But the dialogue seemed so fitting, that it was cathartic for him, at early evening. Scott was duly attentive, fiddling with his school tie and checking pens in his shirt pocket; because it was beguiling he told his colleagues in Sloane Square. But obviously it was not a London school, more like up-country in the Home Counties.

He then took a nap in readiness for an evening out, at his church, for a fund-raising 'bazaar' event. He was to sell door tickets, then attend to second-hand books in the corner stall. First off he looked for a good book 'find' before anyone came over and picked out "Spy Catcher". He already got through twenty pages before a church warden arrived and greeted him keenly: "Any sales yet, Scott"?

"How-do Miss James".

"We did very well last year, you know".

"D'you mind, I'm taking this volume for myself", he explained.

"I thought it banned by Misses Thatcher".

"How amazing it lands here" Scott exhorted!

"Anyway, he's dead now; Peter Wright I mean".

"Well, then it's okay – here's my payment in the tin" and he let a few coins fall loudly from his hand.

Nothing very arduous for a first division teacher, but big pay-offs in the tallies by Sunday. The busy book-keeper was a lady from the choir, downstairs at the cash table and the grayest elders were at a tea-table pouring beverages and presenting home-made bakery. The attending vicar was front-man for the church, suitably roving through stalls and people alike, with fresh white collar and ruddy complexion. He stepped round the hall like it was a country fair, with 'Miss Marples' at his elbow. All very pleasing for everyone to see him being glib, in earnest and happy, at the same time; like one of those 'Ian Carmichael' movies. Scott got the magic touch from him at his elbow and a generous grin, enough to keep going at his task --

"Good show, Scott. Nothing like this in America, eh"?

"Nothing like this anywhere".

Scott even went to harassing young ladies passing by, catching their eye and pushing paperbacks into their hands. And the same cast of characters appeared at Sunday morning service, with gleeful calls of success, fiscal success; posted up at the main door. Scott was always amazed at final figures from his meager efforts. But seems nothing could deter the event, not even dotty ladies at the bric-a-brac tables or bumbling gents at their service. Of course all this was good diversion from school. This was the whole idea for Scott; a big departure from grinding days of school duty, where staff were left in the classroom to fail alone and God had already gone absent.

It was now ten years of teaching this year and he beginning to get used to the persona, finding his place in the firmament of things. But nothing as planned, nothing like he wanted out of school. In fact he did not want to be a teacher, he told his grandfather once upon inquiry and thought instead of farming work or traveling to Canada; something more adventurous and wholesome. He kept recalling this same conversation, about his vocation, at every lull in his career.

Yet there seemed to be real connections between the church and teaching. No avoiding this so long as Heads kept talking about school 'spirit' to the assembly gatherings at mornings, with all kinds of charity days included into the year calendar. In fact lots of schools were still governed by the church, in name and form, with florid priests and frenetic nuns running amok in the corridors. This became a happy association for Scott, a long-standing accommodation, which put his difficult duty infront of a bigger background. This broader attitude to school care also appeared to sit well with the children, because they never rebelled against class prayers or services in the hall, like they rebelled normally.

Attendance started for Scott the moment he exited his front door, clutching a leather bag and checking his pockets for necessary items. It did not end till he finally swung round to his street, at the last corner. Mrs. Jennens, from the church gang, saw him from her window in the mornings and told how she checked the wall clock because she was surprised with his early rising. Scott was often very tardy for her Saturday clean team, so they sometimes crossed paths, when he was going there and she coming back. It became quite dramatic, because Mrs. Jennens went to 'Rada' before marriage and said she still liked the theatre: "My dear boy, what the --"

"So sorry; was out drinking"...

"But everyone has gone home now", as she pulled up straight alongside of him.

"Friday night, you know…

I have to meet my Irish friends, more teacher types". By this time she was always calmed and duly sympathetic, because she was also worldly and feminine.

"Alright, see you afterwards dear; come round for coffee. But don't be late". When the weekend was over she made sure of Scott's Monday-am, to check his haste down the street, on-th-double to the corner again; because it was an amazing turn-around from Saturday.

One early morning at school, in good time for a nice 'start-up' beverage, Scott was slow to leave the staffroom and caught out by a very eager Deputy. A sudden cloud of icy cool descended over Scott as the Deputy began to lean on him with mean/exacting demands and a small group of NQT's nearby went very quiet. There was a distinct threat in the air, so that Scott went motionless, as the Deputy seemed to bristle and burn at the same time. The NQT's were listening hard and when the Deputy finally departed, the group gasped openly out loud. Then one said, "can you get to all that by break, ole chap"?

"I hardly think so", said another. Scott, still standing, returned in a pivotal moment – "listen, at my age, you don't **have** to do anything"! This was accepted by more sighs and grins, which helped break the ice away and Scott could be at ease again before exiting to lessons. But he dodged the Deputy for the remaining day and re-made an alliance with his own department Head, before conceding a win. Not so easy to win out at that school, because four Deputies roamed the campus, along with Year Heads, House Heads and the like; they chased up everyone with daily demands, sudden appearances and other sorts of nuisance.

By October Scott was riding the tube again, to obviate an unpleasant journey, to arrive home dry and warm. By Advent he was ready to ride both ways to school, at am and pm. But there were benefits for such, entailed for a resourceful teacher at his post. On the way home, the train was best for some writing, when frustration and opportunity came together for an hour; when he wrote poetry on the back of notepaper, because he was a humanities man and had to try his hand. Scott was spurned to action if he sat beneath some 'Poems on the Underground'.

A change of trains was required at Earls Court; where the renown Mr. Piper was on the station platform, at duty, moving the boys on and keeping the girls away. He paraded up and down the platforms in full voice, for thirty minutes, in full view of boys; then again at morning. Occasionally, Scott said a few words, to cheer him on --

"Any extra pay for this"?

"A ticket for lunch and tea; at school that is".

"Excellent, by Jove".

"You want my duty then; you can have it you

know"?

"No, nothing like that".

Mr. Piper was fully absorbed with his singular duty; he was properly loyal to the cause and Scott deferred to that. Pretty good too, the way no one else in the station recognized him on task, only the boys scurrying away with his shouts. Long after Scott moved schools, moved on, he would look out for the lone Piper at the Warwick Road end of Earls Court and would sometimes see him unchanged and unfinished.

After Christmas Scott took another rebuke from the admin, a final dispute and had to accept re-location to the outskirts of London. True, he could still occupy the journey to advantage, writing or dreaming and such; he would parade his persona in foreign territory with special teacher's pride, a sort of gallant secondment. Of course he still lived in Kensington, resided in a shadowy corner of Nottinghill; where he enjoyed rubbing shoulders with the 'top-draw' coalitions you could find west of the centre. But every Monday morning he had a long journey east then north, to a new school post, a new London patch. Scott knew that location was everything and districts in the East were in strong contrast to Kensington. It was not fair to him after all the time he had before, because the kids were going to be very demanding; colleagues inclined to be burnt out and the vistas of terraced housing from the train, disheartening for a teacher well past forty-something. In fact, without some skill and some luck, the young intake at school could be dangerous; they were the diverse progeny from farthest parts known. Selima was from North Africa, only a few years before and her name came up for Scott the first day, first break.

"Try humour with her".

"That's not enough; how about some flirting"?

"What d'you say" -- Scott rarely retained a 'teachers pet'!

"Yeah, can you turn-it-on for her"!

"She needs to be distracted, with lots of attention. Or she will blow-up, for a big problem, like she usually does. Bless her cotton socks".

"Okay, I see her next period".

"Gud luck t'you".

Scott found his classroom at the very last minute and right there was Selima in row two at the side, near to the door; a power position for her.

"Right class, page fourteen please. History on Mondays – is that right"?

"No Sir, that's Wednesday", she calls out.

"Today it is Maths", from another body.

"No Sir, it's football. Ha-ha", from a boy.

"Check the timetable, over there Mr. Robinson" --

from a friend this time.

"Okay, thankyou".

It was ten more minutes like this, a poor start to a new school for Scott and a new area of London to conquer. The kids were mostly African/Latin/Asian and Irish – with a few English kids between the cracks – a melting pot of new kids on the block. Scott was the Western interloper, the easy foreign target. He had to travel on the Central Line, each morning; through Liverpool Street to a district in the North, almost out the city. It was about an hour riding on two tube lines, but enough to wake him and enough to rub his face into shape in a quiet moment. Going to school was good prep. Scott often shaved at the station, using a reflection in the bill-boards to get his small electric razor going; because his face would not take the shaver till an hour after waking. Then he was ripping-up papers on the train, bold enough to ignore lots of bumph he got and shining scuffed shoes at his seat.

Dress was important too. Scott had learned how to look like a teacher, specially for the kids -- jacket-an-tie but no suit, formal shirt but not white, dress shoes not black; red and blue pens at his breast pocket and flag tie loose an' free. Altogether, probably more like a racing tout, or sportsman at the club. The message was flair but clean, tidy but loose, smart but inexpensive.

This was only fair, in London, when chasing after kids for school uniform. Scott had begun with a closet of sweaters in American High Schools, nylon wear and nondescript pants; more like a follower of golf, rather than an educator.

The last walk from the station to school was a re-entry to deprived areas of rental housing and mean streets, a fractured community; unhappy people full of want and ignorance. As he walked he caused little attention because it was a brief exposure to the locals. But Scott was different, because he did not belong; he could never belong and knew he stood out, dressed like a county gent with an obvious touch of college. His pride was enough to see him walk tall and look straight at passers-by, sometimes greeting or nodding to them. He never paused to what they might think, because he was a practical man with his time and his worries.

By third period, Selima just wasn't biting; she didn't take to his board figures, his questions on money problems. She was turning in her place, fiddling with her stuff and floundering in the cool winds of cerebral effort. This situation was an unpleasant malady for her and difficult task for a new teacher on the block.

By three o'clock came another break, another fifteen minutes in the staffroom, with more warm tea and friendly fire from associates. Scott heard Selima was from Morocco, ten years ago, with a big family.

"How is she"?

"Okay so far, but restless".

"Next session she'll be tired, so be careful. We know what she's like and the Head knows her parents. Nothing like the 'Von Trapp family'; more like Nancy and Bill in "Oliver Twist"!

"Well, here we go again. Thanks". Scott sped off up the corridor, as if this would also speed up his time and shorten the period.

"Right class -- let's do some answers on the board".

"No Sir, you do the answers".

"Who can show us number one"?

"Nobody can".

"Alright, then; you can mark your own work today, swap books I mean. We trust you".

"Makes no difference"!

It was going well, Scott steaming down to end of day and not an incident in sight. Till ten minutes past four, trouble spilled out next to Selima, with a boy shouting out; he jumped up and lashed at her. The boy was West Indian and had been offended by some rude Arab words from Selima's direction. Scott ran up to separate the two hostiles, but too late to stop Selima hitting the boy and connecting on his nose. Scott went

145

into some quick action, for damage control, with gentle platitudes and lots of body language to send the heat away. It worked, because he was bigger than primary kids and not tired yet like his young charges. They sat down, cooled and re-occupied with books and pens again. But nothing for him to report on paper, nothing to spoil his success that first week at the blackboard jungle; maybe just a few rye comments to the Deputy Head. Ten minutes more and they would disperse like damp squids on the street, run off in every different direction, if no parent arrived at the gates for them.

The school was within forgotten parts of London; a left-over area of industrial housing, generic pubs and Asian stores. It was a large brick institution with desolate corridors and padlocks at every entrance. Inside, the staff were very young and blanched; looking like they spent too much time at their college union bar. But they were also very green to the protocol of professional relations. Possibly they failed to notice how the common room area was so unpleasant, off-putting. A dirty sink was filled with items from last week, unclaimed oddments on the counter-tops; with chairs round the room lumpy and old. At one end was a smoking area, small and dingy, lit by one small skylight. A few patrons were well ensconced in the corners, puffing away in earnest; lots of bleary eyes and busy ashtrays everywhere. Near to the kitchen section two or three young men sat around 'Miss Ooomph' every day, like suitors at court, like alley cats on the wall. She had dark hair long enough to fiddle with and cheap air of 'top-cat', enough to draw out some appeal. When Scott accidentally sat next to her on one occasion, he got cool airs of embarrassment and furtive looks from the ready suitors. To resist saying anything regrettable and to disallow an assault on his dignity, Scott suddenly thought of something daring; enough to confound his worst mess-mates and rushed out in the direction of admin offices --

He got along side a front desk, to a startled assistant and asked her -- "Is the Head in"?

"Just a moment, Mister Urrrrhhh…"

Because Scott was bored and brazen, he stepped ahead without waiting, into a back study. Without prompting, he immediately argued about needing a good Irish lady to work the staffroom; how at his last school there were two such ladies with hot-milk coffee and bakery bits. Why all this improved school spirit, even down to the lower kids; how he saw this again and again in good schools. The Head was crouched over his desk, he looked up but never flinched or spoke, this was definitely something new for him. Before he could gather himself to think of responding, Scott was withdrawing with more last words. Retreating with a nice coup, he turned smartly on his heel to get away. Not surprising the Head appeared to snub him that week, seemed to be seeking opportunities to do this, rather than try a blunt summons to account; likely it was the prudent option for him. Anyway, it was the Deputy who handled Scott on daily duties, to allow him escape and justify his actions.

Teaching like this, for Scott, was like playing a vaudeville review; he always found himself up-front on-stage without props, without a script and infront of a flagging audience. This was not a desk job, or office work, it was more a performance effort. So that Scott believed he actually grew a half-inch taller; after continually pulling himself up in front of the class and lifting his chest to exert authority on a rabble at variance with his code. It was all strength and guile for Scott, to fight his way through each day; with the kids then the admin, the parents, colleagues and inspectors. Yet it was still London; but Scott dearly remembered the other half, his Kensington town. Like he knew two cities in one -- his very own 'tale of two cities'. We know of course that Charles Dickens learned about London too, better than anyone, how malady and misfortune made a continued calamity for author and teacher alike.

A Hearty Polemic

There was nothing better to spread upon thick slices of crusty bread. Raspberry jam was a special delight, the way it was always there in the kitchen as prominent icon for him; all that was good and interesting about Britain. It was the teachers' choice, the Yankee's idea of high manners and Anglo civility. The jar stood at one end of the shelf, for easy access and the label at front pictured red berries with seeds on a white background; a quintessential ingredient of home for Scott. Usually he enjoyed this preserve alone, with black tea and TV. The afternoon series of 'Grange Hill' was a suitable school soap-opera for a teacher decompressing at home, lounging on his sofa by the open window. By the time Scott got past his second mouthful, all was right with the world, it was Voltaire's best of possible worlds. It was a daily act of 'Zen', as healing and tonic, after the ravages of repeated wage earning labours.

Scott was home a few short hours and stirred from quiet rest on the sofa, with his shoes off and his hands/ arms across his eyes/face. He was not asleep but silent and still, drawing upon reserves of energy; letting his breath sound gently, coming to life again in a mere thirty minutes. Then the telephone rang out --

"Scott, how goes it ole man"?

"Not bad, Charles; just having my cocoa is all".

"Your what! Does that mean you have a lady over there"?

"Nothing of the kind; it's cocoa time at the 'home front' and getting cold, it doesn't stay hot very long".

"Thought I'd drop round to see you, maybe go out for a jar – what d'you think"?

"Sorry, afraid not old pal. This is Tuesday, a school night, thought I told you; can only go out Friday evening or Saturday. I am free Sunday too, but not after tea-time; then it's preparation for Monday".

"Marking you mean, papers and lessons; yes"?

"No. Apart from all that; really need get into my 'deep therapy' session; thought to explain before". Scott spoke a little more then hung up the phone. He still had to go on a short run for air before turning into bed. The one call was alright, but no more; he had a regime to follow and only halfway through. All this developed since he arrived in London and into schools full-time. Because next morning he had to be ready for anything, any eventuality. He could arrive at school a little sad, a little happy, in a good mood or a bad mood; but he could not arrive tired, unwell or unready. He must get to school in good time with fully charged batteries, all his fluids topped up; refreshed and awake, upbeat and up-to-speed. There were absolutely no exceptions to this preparation, no excuses and no allowances. Otherwise, the kids would walk all over him; get out of control, create dangerous scenarios and drive him out of the classroom. No one explained this to Scott when he first left college; but he heard his colleagues talking and each day found kids pushing/pulling to the limits of his strength. So at evening he took his 'nap', ate sensible food and enjoyed a little 'basket weaving' – a whole mix of rest and recreation. He knew other teachers did the same and accepted it as part of good professional discipline. They all looked forward to the 'school hols'; because not till then were they free to break out, kick over the traces and enjoy 'town and country' pursuits like other young unmarried professionals.

As it happens the very next morning was a major trial, a severe test of his new found prevention therapy. His class was in the annex, a cluster of new rooms which were largely temporary; built of pre-fabricated sections with a clear space under the uplifted floors. Because this area was constructed apart from the main building, trouble followed more often; the kids felt it was off bounds, out of range from normal concerns.

"Ouch", came from back of the room; then again. Scott looked up from his desk at the front and tried to see who it was. "Ouch", again! He stood up and traced the cry to a girl sitting in paired seats with another girl. They were Spanish and looking remarkably alike.

"Anything wrong, Gabrielle"?

"No Sir". But she squealed once more, like before.

"What is wrong"?! This time Scott was not to be put off. Fortunately, the rest of the class were happily occupied and not over-reacting to the sudden cries.

"Something is sticking in my leg". Scott bent over to show interest, when it became apparent the other girl was also involved, the way they faced each other to giggle and squirm. Scott's instincts told him it was serious and must be dealt with immediately, he sensed danger.

"Stand up girls"! When they rose from their seats he quickly stood infront of them to make his intent clear. But the girls were evasive and coy; they knew how difficult it was for a man teacher to confront a girl at school about anything. He was on shaky ground, yet determined to show some authority and resolve.

"I said, Gabrielle, what is it" and he glared at each in turn, daring them to resist.

"Maria keeps pricking me, Sir; it's a knife". The whole class gasped and turned to look round. Maria looked sheepish; she looked guilty and ready to acquiesce.

"Can I see it please"? And Scott saw a big hunting knife, with six-inch blade and stringed hand grip. It was a scary weapon. He went quiet and put his hand out – "you better give it to me"! But Maria held onto it, claiming it was for protection, because she felt threatened. He asked her again, with no success. Clearly, there was now an unsatisfactory 'stand-off' between them, needing to be resolved quickly and safely.

"John, go to the office and ask them to send someone here immediately". The boy rushed out the door to leave Scott as before, standing by the girls with little he could do. Tensions had risen as the class were not keen on the idea of a knife like this; but they could not be relied upon to support their teacher. They would enjoy seeing Mr.Robinson in an awkward situation and at a loss for words, to see him in trouble. Scott well knew he was in difficulty, becoming heated and red faced, waiting for a senior staff member to show.

The boy soon came back alone with only a message;

that their teacher must take the knife and send Maria to the office. This failure only made things worse; so Scott had to come up with some of his own initiatives, fast. The girl stood impassive to the message and clung onto the knife; though she never looked like that sort of kid, she was not aggressive or any trouble before. Most likely other kids in the room would be sympathetic to her, she would have friends among them. Scott had to tread carefully in order not to alienate the rest of his class. Gabrielle had taken her seat again, she sat down, now her part to play was over.

"Alright Maria, keep your knife, hold onto it; but go to the office and explain why you feel threatened".

After a little more persuading and some negotiating she left the room with her friend. Scott hoped they would indeed go straight to the office and not think to go on a wander of the school. That would be very bad news for Scott, when he finally reported his account to senior staff. It was going to be unlikely for Scott to look good at the end of all this.

Suddenly the Year-Head burst into the room a little breathless; she was a youngish woman been at the school many years, a well known face and usually on good terms with everyone; not really a 'heavy' admin type.

"What is wrong Nine-B; I heard it was urgent?

Can someone tell me, please"!?

"They have already gone, Miss"!

"Who have"?

"Maria and Gabrielle; said they were going to the school office". Scott retreated to the side of his desk and went silent, to watch how this scene might unfold. He tried to appear uncommitted, neutral and knew he had few cards to play; except for candor and brevity, when he faced the music at end of day.

"They're not there; I just came from the office. Do they still have the –"

"Yes Miss"!

"Alright; I might know where to find them. But if they come back, Mister Robinson, you can confiscate it and see me later. Thankyou". She went off in a hurry and the class were more at ease sensing the conflict was past; they were getting noisy and excited, laughing and calling out to each other.

Scott did not see the Year-Head till afternoon, when they bumped into each other in the staffroom. He was never called to account formally and only heard vague remarks, concerns, from the lady. This worried him, because observations and conclusions would be made without him, near certainly not to his advantage. Miss Swanson offered to complete the dreaded 'Incident' form for Scott and ran off joking about it. But it was still on his mind the next few days, especially when he saw the same group twice more that week. But Scott expected a quiet few lessons ahead, without any more incidents; because 'lightning seldom strikes the same place twice' he thought. It turned out like this; the peace and quiet after the storm.

This incident was dramatic and alarming as Scott ever knew. There were no arguments, no disputes, claiming otherwise; nothing to divert attention from the violence following teenagers in the city; staying close to them at home and into school, as part of their city upbringing. The other kind of trouble was not so direct, not overt; more like a general malaise that seeped through cracks in the school establishment; like toxins in a stream, sand in the fuel, water in the oil. In this way a darker attitude emerged, moving towards an easy opportunity for more mischief.

"Scott, come and see me at end of day; please". Mr.Palmer ducked his profile round the door when it opened and quickly retreated safely to one side when the kids poured out of the room on way to the canteen --

"I can't talk now; it's my video club today, this lunchtime".

"Yes, I know".

About fifteen pupils came into Scott's English

classroom, mostly boys, to see a video film. There was always a video player and screen already set up in his room, to facilitate easy use.

"It's 'Robo Cop', Sir. We saw half last week; let's rewind it a bit".

"Good idea Rodney, we need a bit of continuance".

"A reminder, you mean, talk English"!

"Okay, let's roll the celluloid; now take your places please -- action"!

"Very funny, Sir; but you're not a Hollywood type. Just a boring teacher".

"No he's not! Mister Robinson is really nice and my mum says the same. Not like you Murray; you're a real pillock and that's the polite word"!

"Alright class – I mean group; forgot this is not a lesson. Quiet please"!

The video-tape flickered a few moments, then began with a robot called Murphy walking the mean streets of America; fiddling with his weapon and talking to his female partner, a young brunette who looked more like a model salesgirl than a city cop.

"If not finished today, you can come back later. We need to start something new next week"!

Scott heard about the movie, but never saw it before. He enjoyed the crisp action and the tongue-in-cheek dialogue. It was good to see America again in full colour at school and British kids reacted to scenes in unexpected ways. They saw the story with very different eyes and with a lot more humour.

The opening drama was very brutal, when patrolman Murphy encounters the bad guys in an abandoned area, he is trapped and overpowered. The gang set upon the cop viciously and inflict squeamish injuries; when his partner is lost in another section of the building. But it gets your attention, thought Scott; gets the audience hooked on the action, the violence; to create a lot of sympathy for the ordinary person as decent cop and good family man.

"A bit louder, Sir, the next bit is really good"!

"Yeah, when he gets back on the street in his new gear – great"! Obviously the two boys saw it before.

"No, later; when he gets miffed and wants revenge"! Scott finally realized they all saw it before, to become a sort of catch-up for Scott; a narrative on modern teen culture at end of the century, where futuristic ideas were posted for all to contemplate.

"Five minutes to the bell; let's leave it for now. Who does the tape belong to"?

"How about tonight, Sir, you promised"?

"Sorry, almost forgot; I have to see a parent".

"But Sir, you said tonight, after school; we all heard you"!

"Maybe tomorrow; if Rodney wants to leave it with me. Now off you go, next lesson in two minutes. Take everything with you, no time for homeroom visits"!

By late afternoon Scott was tired with that special tiredness from school stuff. He was a bit light headed and flushed, like his blood pressure went up all day; thirsting for a cup of tea, when he should have a cool citrus drink and cup of yogurt. He managed to get his afternoon groups onto quiet reading/writing activities, to avoid a lot of demanding discussions into soul-searching problems of the world. But still the sore eyes and sore joints, for Scot; when he got to the staffroom sanctuary to remember his meeting with the Deputy Head. Not a parent, like he said to the kids. He lied sometimes, if he thought to get away with it, because it obviated trouble for him. Scott dashed into the toilets and cooled his head with handfuls of cold water to his face and hair. He brushed off his shirt collar and went out along the corridor with the mug of tea and his bag.

The door was ajar and Mr.Palmer sat at a big ugly desk leaning into a bakerlite telephone receiver, looking towards the doorway and new entrants appearing.

"Come in Scott" he called out and waved at the chair opposite -- "sorry, I have to go dear; there's a teacher here I must speak to. Bye"!

"Who was that, Sir, your wife"?

"Yes, I forgot you met her at the end of term bash. Yeah, these women, I can't even hide from her at school. Anyway, Scott, thanks for coming".

"I needed an excuse, to avoid more of my video club today".

"That's what I wanted to talk about".

"The what"?

"Your video club. We have some complaints, I need to relay".

"So long as my lessons are good; who would worry about it"?

"Yes Scott, we appreciate it's a voluntary activity. In fact the Head was applauding just that, when he assigned me this task".

"I thought my inspection comments were good this year? Who cares about movies and videos; except for a 'Religious Oversight committee' or the 'Women's Institute'!

"Quite so, ole stick. Listen, let me explain".

Scott finally went very quiet and sat very still; to take a good punch, to face a plain insult and not flinch or react.

"Two or three parents phoned the office about the videos you show. Apparently they think your choice of content is not suitable material for teenagers. And

Mrs.Potts doesn't like her son staying late after school, to see entertainment, like he was serving a detention".

"Can I respond"?

"No, let me finish. Two of the parents also spoke to the Head; about unacceptable levels of violence, sexuality and bad language. One of the mothers – can't say who – is coming into school tomorrow".

"Anymore to hear"?

"Well, yes; but speak, please do".

"The videos are not my choice; I never saw them before, except for a western movie".

"Which one was that"?

"They brought them into school, not me and brought them from home! So what's all the fuss"?

"Don't get irate Scott; I have to ask. Who brought in 'Howard the Duck'? Reading the 'Playboy' rag and trysting with his girl at the end! I heard".

"Hilarious, really".

"Well, it does seem like a double-standard. I can see it would be confusing for you".

"Annoying, would be more accurate"!

"Leave it with me for a few days, okay".

"I can disband the club if you like. No real loss to me, if you understand".

"Let's not get hasty; we can say it is suspended for a while. I will leave you to make the excuses. Right, I must be off; my wife is waiting for me".

Scott finally traipsed home, to get a bus at front of the school; a bit more weary than usual, another big disappointment for him. Too much hypocrisy for one day, too much deceit and too little support. He was beginning to enjoy his club and thought the kids were too; not being a classroom subject he thought to be free of restrictions, grades or 'big brother'! But politics with a small 'p' still lurked around every corner, hid in the closets and was alive-an-well.

Scott was in a Roman Catholic Church school and enjoyed the cosy atmosphere offered in the staffroom; a gentle approach to the curriculum and better behaved children. He was carried away with these comforts, garnished from lots more manners and consideration shown by everyone. He began to think he made it into a sanctuary, safe haven with a big family; began to relax and be himself, lower his guard with the staff and in the classroom. But this was a mistake; after ten years in the profession he should have known to be watchful and careful, not to confuse relaxed appearances with strict attitudes. The Head might wear coloured shirts and ladies might wear pants; but kids were still the same, capricious and bossy.

Scott was teaching RE to Year-8 and the class were half boys and half girls – a nice group and happy with their new subject teacher; no hint of misunderstanding or dislike. That morning Scott had been reviewing a section about the church in earlier times, Europe in the Middle Ages. Lots of kids hailed from Italy, Spain and other Catholic nations. The lesson unit entailed information and discussion on monasteries, nunneries and the clergy. Of course they all went to church on Sunday, as demanded at the admissions session; they knew about monks and nuns. Three of the staff were teaching sisters and different priests came into school for Friday Mass or on festival days.

There was about fifteen minutes to the end of lesson and lunch was the next event. They were getting restless and hungry; so that attention to exercises and text books was beginning to flounder, lose some appeal from a good start to the period. Scott must change the pace and the mood, before they rushed off --

"You can put your pens down and close your books; we will continue next lesson. I want to ask, I mean discuss, about the monasteries and monastic life".

Many of the kids did as suggested and sat with arms folded, up straight and curious.

"Let me ask the boys first. Right; how many of you thought to be a priest when you grow up, considered the priesthood as a vocation after leaving school? Anyone"? About four or five hands went up in lazy relaxed fashion.

"I don't mean you decided or even talked about it; but think it worth a chance"? No more hands were raised and the boys seemed to regard it as a fair question, something that might have been mentioned at home in any proper church-type of family. They were not threatened or particularly worried about it; just a lot of blank faces looking back at Scott.

But the girls in the group, who were sitting apart from the boys to one side of the room, were reacting differently. They were getting tense and beginning to glare hard at Scott at the front. He turned in their direction, cleared his throat and began to speak. The tension was building when they seemed to guess what he was going to say; arms tightened across heaving chests, mouths drawn firmly and Scott could see all this. But he felt compelled to continue with this line of thought, with his inquiry; he did not want to be diverted or made to look weak --

"And the girls…" Their temper was now clearly visible and he should have declined to press the discussion any further. But oh no, not Scott the seasoned teacher; the old pro pressed ahead.

"Girls; how many of you --"? Those at the front, nearest to Scott, were taking it very personally; not like rational intelligent thirteen year olds. They even lost their sense of humour.

"How many of you considered becoming nuns; taking church vows and joining a religious order"?

There were absolutely no responses, no neutral positions and no sympathetic listeners; just a solid wall of anger and impatience. None of them spoke, muttered or glanced away; they were all staring ahead at their target of stupidity, disgust and disfavour. Scott had made a terrible mistake and fallen into a pit-fall of his own making. Open, honest liberal discussion held no sway for Year-8 girls; they were not impressed, not ready to entertain such outlandish notions. The boys took the idea of priests, lightly and without concern, but the girls could not distance themselves from this idea the same way. He should have known better, as any trusted colleague could surely confirm. So Scott did not relate this faux pas to anyone, he let it drop; to forget he said any such thing, hoping it would fade away in time.

The girls in his class did not let go so easily. They were offended and surprised in a way that unsettled their young egos; someone was clearly to blame and must be held to account. Their strongest weapon – to shun the respective teacher, refuse verbal contact, ignore him and make him feel their plight – was made to reciprocate their distress. It was almost two weeks before the girls started to break their silence with the teacher, an action they construed as just and fair.

"Scott, come and see me at end of day, please". Mr.Palmer was in the same queue for tea at afternoon break, in the rear --

"What again; we have to stop meeting like this; staff will talk".

"About the video club".

"But how would they know"? Scott noted it was now 'the' video club; just a week ago it was 'your' video club. A shift in noun declensions might mean something, might be a clue for Scott concerning school clubs and parent influence. He wanted a resolution to the complaints and he was curious. He also knew an eagerness to confront issues in school was not always best tactics – stalling, being obtuse, ducking-an-dodging was better regarded; given more respect and often diminished the issue to smaller proportions – this was less risky.

"Sorry, not tonight, I can't – maybe tomorrow".

"Alright, soon as you can Scott, let me know".

At home Scott went to the tape player and inserted Glen Campbell, then Kenny Rogers – as antidote to the day's upheavals, pacifier and soother – better than a dummy in the baby's mouth. Glen was singing out plaintive and melancholy like a siren; the effect was pabulum and tonic for a lonesome teacher returning to his bunk-house. He needed sweet sounds and easy lyrics before setting down to eat. After he started teaching he was all 'country and western' music, more and more; the only albums he could benefit from in the evening. He had other vocalists, who were also slow and harmonious, yet often he heard the same tape over and over; knowing by then it was no longer music he was listening to, it was his own special remedy for raw nerves and disillusionment.

At college Scott relished the classics and got out his Beethoven stuff when he hit the typewriter, to enjoy the complexities of a great master. He benefited from all the subtleties and nuances at variance with bursting passions of a Germanic soul; as a student he was open to difficult composition and serious themes. At school his needs had greatly changed, they simplified so much it seemed like regression; but this was unfair to Scott and unfair to the realm of music.

High Stakes Winner

In training college education was bits of paper, lesson plans, learning theories, famous books and at the end a certificate. But the kids never asked to see this certificate and they never cared about ed-training. They did care about their teacher, even if they might get angry with him, or behave badly. They were also curious, wanted to know more about Mr.Robinson; because after parents he was the important person in their lives, first real friend/ foe outside the family. Scott dismissed all his college bumph, very quickly, when he realized he must learn to think and speak on his feet. He must be a worthy adversary, strong advocate of the good; when faced with laziness, deceit, hostility and ignorance from pupils/

parents/ the admin. No – timetables, curriculum, registers and grades – were the minutia. The major concerns were, first and last, his relationship with each pupil; the class together or the whole year group, quite a handful, tiring and exhilarating.

The first thing he must do is find a way to learn the kids names, all of them, not just ones in the front row. It was the association of seat positions which started him off. Then he was on the way to facilitating scores of names, first and last and how to spell them. By four-pm, on Friday evening, the nomenclature would fall away and relieve him of their burden. But by Monday morning, the great list of handles re-appeared again.

With the staff, his colleagues, it was a very different exercise. Scott noticed how at this school teachers never used first names, not even in the staffroom. This was not the important one to remember, specially infront of the kids, when there was a large staff and many names.

He was in Chelsea, at another secondary school for boys and girls. It was History for the rest of the afternoon and Scott teaching a unit on 'Roman Britain', with an important introduction to begin --

"Quiet please, for a moment, till I get through this"! But girls at back of the room were still noisy – two in particular.

"Lesley, please, can you talk later" – still did not work, as she and her neighbour started laughing too, on top of their animated talk.

"Alright Lesley, go outside please, wait for me there"! Suddenly the fun was over; but Lesley got out of her seat to find the door. She became quiet, dignified and went out.

"How long for, Sir", her friend called out?

"I really don't know" and Scott began his intro at last. He drew on the black-board with chalk colours, made a short presentation from the text and turned to a preliminary exercise for the class. He forgot about the girl outside and was glad to get the lesson going again --

"Mister Robinson, Lesley is crying out there". The boy was correct, seen through the side window; she was staying very close to the doorway and looking in, appearing down-cast with glistening eyes.

When the class were settling to their task, Scott paced up the room between rows of desks, heading to the exit. Without any fuss he went out and stood directly infront of Lesley, before saying anything. He could see she was duly crest-fallen and tears running down her cheeks. But Scott had to justify his action, chastise and explain for her -- "I did ask, several times, to be quiet; you know I have to start…" but more tears came. She had only been out of the room about ten minutes, yet obviously devastating for her; probably something new, because she was usually a good student. No need for Scott to say anymore – "come in now, please". She went quickly to her place, pulled out a tissue and leaned over to confer with her friend. Scott thought it to be the end and strolled normally back to his desk. Everyone was now involved with the exercise, happily absorbed in questions from the text and answers into their own books. Scott busied himself with looking ahead in his notes, checking his board work and glancing round at faces in the room. All seemed to be going well. But Lesley's friend unexpectedly rose out of her seat, heading purposefully towards Scott seated at front of the room. She was clutching a visible piece of school paper and got to the waste basket adjacent to his desk. Scott looked up, not knowing what to expect and saw her angry, very serious.

"This is your Christmas card, Mister Robinson" as she began ripping-up the paper, violently, shoving the pieces forcefully at the basket! When finished, she simply turned smartly round and marched back to her seat. No one else took any notice, except for Scott, the intended party. Firm notice was duly served upon him; he was distinctly out of favour. He checked the calendar in his school planner and noted: Tuesday, the 9th of the month. He went to check again; yes, it was only November! It was almost amusing; if not for the unwanted antics of twelve-year-olds in school and Scott the provisional 'straw man'. But maybe some folk prepare early; young pubescent girls might do that, the way they could be so fastidious with paper and pen, always tidy and prompt. After a suitable lapse of time Scott dared to look towards Lesley, but saw no change; she was bent over her work, her friend had regained composure and resumed her work too.

Lesley and her cohort were usually good with Scott; they liked to tease him and added lots of 'fizz' to a lesson, all to the good. But it was two weeks till they resumed normal play again. He was perturbed how they were in the wrong, yet wanting to set the trouble at his feet. It was another glimpse of marked disparity, for him, between boys and girls in the class.

Though there can be romance in school too; not always a battle of the sexes. Another girl, in a different school, was soft over Mister Robinson; while she was in Year-7 and he their form tutor and History teacher. Sonia was very shy in a girls church school and Scott a temporary teacher in a working district; he still young, slim and tall. Sonia took to Scott first lesson they had and the other girls quickly knew this, to call out confirmation to the surprised teacher – "Sonia likes you, Mister Robinson"!

"More than that, real love, looks like" someone else shouted out.

But Scott was a seasoned teacher by then and took it all in his stride. He already knew about girls in school and the way a teacher-man had to walk on 'egg shells' in the classroom. He dared not mention it to anyone, not to colleagues or friends; it could easily reflect badly upon him, better to let the girls monitor the situation. Sonia's classmates would know if anything was wrong and could direct Scott safely away from pitfalls and gaffs. Otherwise Scott had a full day; with other kids in that school not relating so favourably towards him. There was little slack time for him that term, with an extra class to teach and a new department head stirring-up more demands. The week was just flying by, Monday blurred into Friday, so that Scott had forgotten about his Year-7 class --

"Mister Robinson, Sonia is crying, you have to visit us. We haven't seen you this week"!

"Okay, at lunch break; I'll be on duty in the playground, see you all then".

After a quick bite of food at noon Scott hurried out to the school yard, without even stopping for his jacket; it was Spring in North Kensington, a warm breeze ruffled his shirt and tie like it was holiday time.

Year-7 were in the far corner, playing a very gentle catch game. He simply went forward and joined in the circle, while the ball continued to be tossed across the centre, because the game was not very competitive. They simply stood and threw an old tennis ball to each other, passed it round the circle. But if you fumbled to miss and drop it, then you were 'out'.

"Come on girls, a bit faster, this goes on too long" Scott looked to tease them.

"See, how he throws it to his girl-friend. Sonia, watch out"!

The girls could be a bit of fun, inspite of Scott's awkward demise, his professional risk taking. But Sonia never approached him out of context, nor spoke to him directly. Except for her friends, he would not know anything of her sentiments; she was always well behaved and lacking confidence to be the contrary. Scott was disinclined to see her school work, to examine it, in such case it was disappointing; her hand-writing was good but the sentences short and often incorrect. He could easily sense she was not academic material and would be far happier when finished with schooling. Meanwhile, their lesson with Scott was first thing after prayers, when he enjoyed beginning a new day with them --

"Please stand-up everybody. Thankyou.

Now; good morning Seven-P" he called out!

"Good-morning, Mister-Robin-son" they returned slowly, with a lot of plaintive chords and a little dissonance.

"Good heavens, Seven-P, I can't hear it. Wake-up please, it's already nine o'clock.

Good morning, Seven-P" he cried out!

"Guurrrd morn-ning, Mister-Robin-son" they returned a little louder and a lot slower.

"Again please"!

"GURD MORN-NING, MISTER ROBINSON" -- seemed like a rousing rebellion was finally happening!

"Thankyou, now sit down, please" was the way class began on Monday morning; the weekend made his girls rusty with their skills and lazy in responses. But underneath, there was good heart between them, enough affection and respect for the week to come. Sonia was in the back row, silently imploring good cheer and understanding; because she wanted to be happy and so easily could be the opposite if things went wrong in their lessons together. The other girls knew this too and wanted to be kind and protect her.

Children have to be happy at school, to enjoy the lessons and learn something. Girls too must be happy and not so easy for them, like boys in the park at their football. Of course Scott looked his best at school, he attracted attention; because he learned that smart apparel and good hygiene were essential for image and authority. After school it was an entirely different matter; though he might be seeing a student again, this time privately at home, in the evening.

"Yes, it's the tutor – don't look much like a teacher tonight, we know, but I am"! Scott was bundled-up for winter, like a vagrant, unshaven and undistinguished. Finally, the door opened into a typical council flat, just off the Edgware Road. The boy was about twelve, in the kitchen, waiting. His half-sister was in there too, round-an-round with a doll and bright chatter. The boy was more serious, more anxious about seeing his tutor, this first time. Though only a few years older than the girl, he already understood how this meeting was important. Scott worked easily with the boy, for several weeks; drilling core subjects for an entrance exam to a private school, down in Sussex. He was trying for a scholarship, because his mother had no money; she was an office cleaner and his father gone, moved to America years before. His mother had a new man visiting now, every evening a tall West Indian; but by lesson's end he too went off somewhere unspoken. The mother was from Morocco, dark and exotic, tired and fretful; she was still young, but anxious and heavy laden. Life in a government flat was beginning to wear upon her, though she was a good mother, to find an unsung teacher-hero like Scott. He glanced round the rooms occasionally to see nothing of any import, very down-market; all the usual home fixtures. They had been assigned to the kitchen table, a yellow formica top upon a metal frame. Scott took out his papers-an-stuff and proceeded with best efforts; working with an unknown boy from the precincts who was uncertain and quiet -- as potential winner in the education stakes game. He was thinking of the new school waiting for him in elysian fields, summer cricket in house blazers, happy dormitories with matron, classes for classics and well mannered masters. All this and more for the unsuspecting boy next to him at his elbow; maybe only months away, before beginning the next term.

The big exam came-an-went quickly, but weeks before any results were known. First to know was the mother, of course, by letter-post; it was surprising and formal, nothing like any notice the mother had before. A day later, she phoned Scott to pass-on the good news -- "Great stuff", he kept saying, "I want to come over and see him, kitted-out in the uniform"!

"Oh no, that's months away! Sorry, not tonight, we're heading out the door in a moment". Scott never did get to see his prize pupil again and wondered how quickly he would be forgotten. His special usefulness came to an end, without much ceremony or consideration; the boy became private family business again.

But Scott was not able to linger on the subject for long; he had another contact straight away; same age as the boy with circumstances very similar. He took another pupil to coach privately, this time up past the Harrow Road; a girl trying for another good boarding-school entrance, up-country in Buckinghamshire. Her mother was domiciled in a basic low-cost flat, alone with her child; no man was ever spoken of, as if there had been none. Except, the girl sometimes whispered about a father, out-of-range from the mother. Again, the mother was cleaning somewhere for a living and focusing all her aspirations upon her child; projecting her hopes and dreams onto a small girl, placed infront of Scott twice weekly for an hour or so. They occupied the kitchen to share toast and tea, where Scott could see some of his dictates stuck upon the fridge door; his 'study notes' were taped to the white front panel. 'TV is the enemy of h/w' it said, or 'Get to bed early and get out weekends', was another maxim Scott had written out for them. The mother was comfortably ensconced on a sofa before a small TV in the next room, fussing over herb tea and a newspaper; thinking she was out of sight. She was out of sight, but the girl knew about home comforts in the living room and how she must be denied this for weeks to come, till end of term. It was hard discipline for her; but Scott knew how to console, distract her and ply his tutoring trade in a seemingly adverse situation. But not so, some hardship for the girl in their scruffy kitchen went to favour Scott; she became more responsive towards her charge and more open to his new lesson material.

Twice a week, Scott bused up to Kilburn Road and found her flat number on the door panel. He pushed the button but did not hear any bell or buzzer; instead, the mother eventually appeared at the doorway, opening it wide for him, from inside the hallway.

"Hello Scott, how are you" she beamed out!

"Great thanks; sorry to be a little late", he always seemed to say.

"That's alright, go straight up, she's waiting for you". She went behind Scott, to step up the hallway stairs, following him with kindly words. The child was inside, already in the kitchen; standing up-straight opposite them, to show good manners and ready eagerness.

"Hello Stephanie, you look very keen tonight, well done"!

"Hi" she squeaked out in shy reply, starting to quiver a little at her place, nervous and uncertain again. But once they got down-to-it at the table together, her shyness started to recede; she began calling him 'Scott' and giggled over some intimacies they shared. Bits of homework lay scattered between them, her books were piled on empty chairs and school bags were left on the floor against the furniture. It became a working atmosphere for them, their own special space for a while. They worked well together, like a professional team at business; full efforts, frankness and good cheer over the school tasks ahead. Like the boy from Edgware Road, the girl did well. She left her mother and went to live in a new school, a few hours north of London; far enough away to prevent home visits till end of term. It was a dramatic change, a near trauma brought on by themselves, with Scott the paid accomplice. The mother was left alone to dream of her child in another bed, eating strange food, making new friends. It was what they hoped and planned, for all those months; but the new found reality was a little frightening for both of them.

The next pupil, for Scott, was not so fortunate; evident almost from the beginning. There was a portentous sense of doom from the very first phone-calls.

"Is that Mister Robinson", the voice was impatient and tense?

"Yes, it is".

"My boy is sitting the exam just after Easter. Can you help us"? Scott already knew the facts of their urgent situation from a previous call.

"What's your address? I better come tonight", he decided.

He set off walking the darkened streets, after a hurried dinner, to arrive at a modern basement flat by Westbourne Park Road; in time for an evening session.

The mother was young, she was tall and slim, a bit glamorous. So that if Scott heard she had been a model or something, he would not be surprised. But she was also frenetic and unhappy. Her son was about twelve, solid build, dark and a bit surly. Scott often found it difficult to teach him; when his hands and elbows flew about, threatening a hit to the head. The boy was very unsettled and a bit angry; Scott merely a likely adult within range, an easy target to vent frustration and vexation. Several times, Scott had to stop and speak firmly. But learning proceeded, because he saw the lad two or three times a week. The mother said her father was sponsoring the lessons; the boy's father was unavailable and out of contact for years. In fact, when this subject came up, it appeared to cause the mother distress and panic. Nothing came from Scott, though he would normally ask about parents, to learn if home-life helped. It occurred to Scott the father may have been in serious trouble, the way her boy became reticent and sulky.

But the boy also had strong ability and desired to attend a boarding school. He may have wanted to leave home to get lost in a new world of playing fields, cadet games, a small town and no girls, no females. It might be the right time for a boy to leave his fretting mother, for awhile.

The exam came closer, only a week away and the pupil was well prepped, with a good chance to succeed; but the mother had made plans to scupper their efforts --

"We're going on holiday but coming back the day before", she said.

"No, go after the exam; far better" Scott pleaded!

"Sorry, we have no more chances this year"!

"Where you going"?

"The Camargue, in France; staying at a friend's house", she explained.

"You must take his school books and help him every day; or he will get rusty, go off the boil" – argued Scott, thinking it should work.

"Maybe we can; we have a lot to carry".

The mother insisted they both needed a break and the boy did badly in the exam, as Scott had feared. She phoned him after Easter and was not embarrassed in any way, with the bad news she offered. She accepted it as another disappointment they must learn and get used to. Scott could easily see the sour influence of the mother upon their fates. He visualized the boy at his desk again getting angry with fractions, disliking his homework assignments; hating the whole idea of school as happy opportunity and fair chance to succeed.

No matter what success Scott had, with students, the failures also clung to him. He did his best for the boy, but still felt badly and there was no consolation. Scott was a little more thoughtful, somber, in church on Sunday; when he had many more questions unfolding before him. After final hymns and prayers, there was a coffee service open to everyone, but he still very quieted. Another teacher approached him head-on, regarding his mood; a college tutor, pressing a printed mint card onto his chest--

"Here Scott, take this. I rarely attend".

"Okay, what is it"?

"The Royal Society – lecture series. Next week, on the future of novels. Take my invitation. Tell me what you think, next Sunday, if you like"!

"Wow, I never been before – thankyou"!

Sure enough, the next Tuesday, Scott headed off after a full portion of raspberry jam on toast at home.

He did not change his clothes, only took off his tie and added a coat layer, because it was still April in the city. He took a straight bus-ride along the top of Hyde Park in the direction of Marble Arch and found the premises behind Bayswater Road, at an old Victorian house with plaque infront. It read: 'The Royal Society of Literature', engraved in brass beside the door; nothing else, meant to be quietly understated. He went in cheerfully and flourished his entry-ticket; handed his coat over to a doorman and began to circulate the chairs set out in the main room. He was attempting to savour the mood and work out the mechanics for this evening. There was a surprising good turn-out on such a miserable night, a wide cross-section of literati types.

At the front was a head table with three chairs on a raised platform, facing back to the audience. It was a familiar scene, a pedantic form of event found at any kind of forum. There would be a chairperson, minutes-taker and guest speaker. Scott knew the scenario well, knew the drill from years back; it was predictable and a bit confining.

After a warm drink served-up in white china cups with tea-biscuits, the event was called to order and Scott sat near the middle to one side; a good position he worked out at college. The lady guest was quite young but already a teaching fellow at London University and reading a 'paper' on British novels. She was young but also stiff and formal, with no humour, no pauses and no change of pace. If a listener missed a line or two, they would be lost for the evening; because there was no going back, no chapter summaries, no repetitions. The lady set a brisk pace with her polemic and held onto it. 'Take no prisoners' – Scott mused, as he glanced round a room full of heads bent over to one side or the other. People were obviously trying to catch-on and pretend to be conversant. He could also tell, from the room suddenly becoming warm and stuffy, that people were already tired from a full day at work.

After standard courtesies in conclusion, the chairperson invited everyone to mingle and chat. Scott jumped at the idea and headed straight for the honoured guest ahead. She had stepped off the platform and stood at the front of everybody; hoping to see someone distinguished appear, but not so. Scott was suddenly inclined to mischief; he quickly became a little familiar and probing at the same time. The lady enjoyed a spirited encounter at first; but soon began squirming when his curiosity became a little ambiguous, his intentions unclear. She looked about to see a friendly face, or someone nearby to verify Scott as legitimate guest, literary devotee, or honest gent – but he stood alone and suspect.

"Who are you; what are you doing here" she finally blurted out? But the lady continued to feel under threat, when Scott merely flinched and continued with his one-sided observance. She had to escape, had to move and finally stepped sideways to turn a shoulder towards him. By then the chairman had spied Scott in opposition and got between him and the lady. He also took opportunity to try a bit of chivalry --

"Good evening, Mister Erhhh – I don't think we know you! Our speaker tonight was excellent, don't you agree"?

Scott managed an oblique response and lost interest in the proceedings; he went to get his coat. The show was over, his part at an end. A lowly teacher came-up against the frosty academic elite; but it was their choice of materials and their 'turf', so had to be a no-win situation for him. Scott was reminded how this also reflected upon his daily duties. How at school he was not expected to win or shine out; how he was meant to be servile under the administration, co-exist with his colleagues and to suffer under the next generation.

Scott At Large

Scott Robinson resided in West London; it was nearby the famed 'Nottinghill Gate' area, attracting visitors world-wide. But his was a very modest abode; because teachers are not well paid, in fact everyone said the same. So they must think of another kind of income to supplement them; but this must in some way compliment their professional skills, it has to fit in with their life-style. Taking a lodger can be one option --

"Mista Robinson, this is Yoo-ehh", came a voice over the intercom.

"Come in" and Scott buzzed the door open, to see a Chinese girl about twenty-two years, thin and pretty.

"Thankyou" she gasped, stepping in from the street.

Scott felt scruffy, but managed a happy intro and cup of tea for the lady. He was renting a room and wanted her straight away. She was beaming all over, but struggling with English, enough to produce a lot of gurgling tones meant to be polite and friendly.

"Yes, I know", she kept saying.

"I'll take you upstairs" said Scott, going ahead with extra keys. It was bright and warm that part of day, to show the room at its best; desk against the window, small TV on dresser, a bed and cushion chair made by himself last year.

"Pictures, very good" she said, glancing round at five small pastoral scenes hanging under the picture rail. They were from Portobello market and period water-colours from Edwardian England. Scott also lingered upon their pastel images, heaved and sighed next to the girl, then went quiet with her; opening up a space between them as both invitation and distance.

Next morning he went up with early coffee for her, pulled back the curtain and spoke: "school today, okay, eight o'clock now"! After five minutes he left the drink and went down to his kitchen for porridge and toast. Before going out he opened the bathroom window and left a note for Yoo-ehh. He was off to meet John in Kent, a day out with the car, as old teacher friends on the rampage --

"You can't have a lodger" said John, settling into the front seat.

"Oh yeah, why not"?

"But where will she sleep"?

"Upstairs of course".

"No, you can't share the bathroom, come on Scott"!

"Sorry, it's too late, she moved in last night".

"The police will be round, in fact I'll call them, or the church! I thought you went to church"?

"I do on Sundays; but that was Friday and today is still Saturday."

"Well, what's the use of me talking"?

"That's right, just drive this bone-shaker will you"!

"Alright. By-th-way; Ray should meet-up with us at the 'Bishops Head', for a lunch-time drink".

"His 'round' remember… and I need an appetizer first, then a constitutional plod up the hill afterwards, okay good".

"I know Ray likes to chat and eat; not work to pay your mortgage"!

"How so"?!

This was very much like another time, when he was running the open roads, with the same bad company. Going south that time to the hamlets of Sussex, to scoff their ales and view the women; flaxen-haired maidens, they were promised. Such an unguarded intake of fluids that day re-awakened youth in Scott and desire in his companions; maybe going to be the same today: "Sorry gents, I am always Ernest in town and Jack in the country; what else, with all those hidden hamlets, country gals and beastly bovines"! Nothing new about London gents heading out to fresh pastures, city boys trying their luck in the provinces. But this day started tame enough; beginning at Eynsford and the historical site advertised --

"I'll get the tickets", as John went forward to the kiosk. "Three adults please", he insisted!

"And I will find some guides for us" as Ray gathered up a few coloured pamphlets, then handed over a crumpled 'fiver'.

"Now I'll lead the way, gentlemen; this way if you will allow me, thankyou".

"Leave out the 'wind-up' Scott. This is not our staff-room and you're the one on the carpet all the time – you plonker"!

"Yeah, blood on the carpet, every damn day"!

It was not a tuneful trio, not a harmonious ensemble, moving round the Roman ruins that day; but they enjoyed pushing each other's buttons like this. The kiosk lady seemed nervous at the confusing way the men interacted. She could see they were friends the way they looked the same: overweight, over-confident and over-th-hill. They also looked worse-th-wear from lunch time drinking; like those 'Three men in a Boat', or 'Mr.Polly' and his mates. But nothing like this in London; a whole ancient villa laid out under a canopy; with frescoes, statues and household artifacts rescued by archaeological graduates. It was all there: function rooms, baths, mosaic tiles, garden walls and courtyards. Scott was trying to imagine himself being there, what it would be like then. A subjective exercise for him; which meant he was glaring at the scenes intently like he really had 'negative capability' he talked of. John read all the info texts out loud, as if teaching it; there were lots of written pieces with each show item, to validate the broken urns and rusty ornaments. Ray was twisting open his flask of coffee to taste; a departure of comfort unknown even to the best Roman consorts in their lavish villas. Lots of other visitors went round the lay-out like it was a leisure park, or an amusement pier – relaxed and carefree. Not like Scott et al, who had to be very thorough over it, as prize teachers made-over into students.

"Nothing like this for miles around; not in Kent anyway", John exclaimed!

"Come on, what about Pegwell Bay and the Viking ship display over there"?

"I mean an ancient ruin. The Vikings were only punks, really, bums of the North Sea; a bit like Scott's Year-Ten, last term. Ha-ha"!

"Yeah, the Romans were better; they gave us central heating, sport and homo-sexuality"!

"What about their wine and their literature; I often enjoy some Ovid", claimed Ray.

"I prefer beer and skittles, or our school plays".

"That's enough! Let's get moving, we're off to Whitstable", urged John.

"Where, what, today"?

"No, not today – now"!

Back in the small import sedan another flask was opened and passed around, during a journey sufficient to put enough distance/time between an ancient site and a seaside habitat. Whitstable was very different. The windy promenade overlooked a cold edge of the North Sea, its choppy waves breaking loudly onto a stony shoreline; the streets were low cost housing with salty air and seagulls calling. Next street back from the front featured oyster bars, fish shops, crab stalls and drinking houses. The town was small enough to catch sea views and a hinterland from the High Street, without confusion, without getting lost. Not surprising, John insisted on a blue-an-white café, a sort of generic outlet in such holiday places. It was ordinary and familiar like old slippers and offered a table at the window. John led with toast and poached eggs, while Ray wanted sardines on his toast and Scott paid for the tea-pot after he perused the menu wall writing.

"It was a great day; we have to do this again, yeah".

"We're not finished yet"!

"This is good grub; puts lead back in the ole pencil".

"Can we forget about school, please, you promised us"!

"Do the honours, pass the pot round, before it gets cold".

"You can be 'mum' for us" --

Scott was lashing away at baked beans, while counting the cafe patrons and thinking about them. John was right by the window but ignoring the view opportunity. Ray was looking over the heads in a dream, then down at his place to mop the plate with bread to sip the tea like a tonic chaser. It was all familiar and harmless; but comfortable and satisfying, like home away from home, like knowledge and enjoyment were one. Memories of another visit last year, came floating by, because they were pleasant and a good omen of time well spent --

"It was August".

"Charles was here; remember he went out

swimming"?

"Me too"– and Scott had a full memory of that day, coming into view over his café scene; it was a flash-back to a serene moment in the warm sea a few yards out from the shore. He went out beyond what was safe, swimming a great stroke he got from college days. The water was murky green and he could not see into it when opening his eyes on the down-stroke; which could be dangerous, because he did not see the bottom and would not notice obstacles. His chest heaved well and pleased he could still get arms over high, again and again, as he pressed on away from the beach. Out there the water rolled and swelled over a large expanse, so he had to feel small and vulnerable; but also feel free, free of the town and even free of himself for a while. When he sculled upright he looked back to the town-frontage to see people and cars carried on as ever, as dots and marks along lines of residence. The place took on a dismal hue and flat aspect, nothing special or dignified like Brighton was heralded to be. This town looked different from out in the sea, like he felt different away from London and his home -- But not this visit, not like this today; the view from the café was not yet high summer.

Their journey home was more subdued as each passenger went quiet then thoughtful. Three heads turned at the windows and stared out to a darkening melancholy of evening. Shadows reached down from uplands to cover the fields, the dwellings and the road they traveled upon. A lingering denouement for three lively plonkers heading back to their city nests, like rooks to the belfry, like crows to the tree tops. The road into Kent was crowded and welcoming, now the road back was empty and bare; like a lonely place no one visits, like a dangerous place people avoided. 'Cats-eyes' at the road centre ran ahead relentlessly and the car's engine whined or groaned in a way unnoticed during day-time. Finally Scott was deposited at a terminus, to catch a short train ride home; he said last comments, zipped-up his coat for the late walk and prepared to end his day. Back to home he found no one in the living room, no lights and no voices; which meant Yoo-ehh was upstairs for the night. He could catch a little late TV before lights out, instead of putting his gear away. It was good to go out of the city for a day, but always sad returning to a silent flat and a cold bed.

A week later he was not so sad, he was a bit nervous and a little scared --

"Last bets please" he heard, "place your bets everyone!

And… no more bets now".

Scott fingered his chips in a side pocket, then

glanced round the gaming room like a gambler would. But he was a teacher and down-on-his-luck; fishing around in a Mayfair locale on a weekday afternoon; trying to gain another income from a college approach to Lady Luck and the house reputation. The club menu was a four-star event, followed by tea-an-biscuits. He got out some bills/papers and pen, to square off his lunch with good intent; beginning to think of gaming and the difficult part of his afternoon; sitting down at a large green-felt table with fifty pounds of chips to make it a hundred pounds or more. He was scared to lose, but knew that was no good; he had to decide on some numbers and play. He always sat on a stool furthest away from the wheel, to give him more space more time between spins; checked the red and black numbers against his card, to find a winning sequence. It was not luck for him, but intuitive reckoning and daring. Not to make it sound easy; right infront of him thousands of pounds were disappearing into the table gullet, as coloured chips were quickly swept away by the house lady at every game. Men and women, mostly men, were studiously unmoved when their money vanished at a steady pace all afternoon. But one hour later he had eighty-five pounds and when the croupier turned his way and glanced hard at his meager efforts, he thought to leave the table action. The cashier laid out the money like a hand of cards, on green felt again. Scott said something a little funny yet terse to the young man, and got a quick reply.

He stood behind a young lady at the cash desk, who had played the card games. Scott tried to see the amount of winnings and followed her to the side area lounge for more tea, while she hid her money and got out cigarettes and tissues. She caught his eye and played the mystery a little further, whispering to the waiter and fiddling with her hair-strands. Now he was a gambler/ladies man, as he squirmed in his seat thinking of something to say, to break the hard ice. By then she was whispering again and talking to the man on a bar stool about her system, her lucky days of the month. No intros yet for Scott as gambler-at-large, new ladies man and furtive winner behind his tea-cup.

The house ladies employed to work were mostly mutton dressed-as-lamb, in velvet gown uniforms with deep neck-lines and some jewelry. But none attractive for Scott, even as middle-age plonker. It was just after lunch, but they all wore evening wear; because there were no windows in the salon rooms. There were window recesses round the main room, which had been filled in, but with plaster not glass. Parisian style lighting decked the spaces with light and shade as required. The men employed were in dinner outfits, all

clean-shaven and straight. Clearly he was in school/
college long enough years to taint his views regarding
sex appeal and formality. But it was irrelevant, because
they would not notice him; unless they saw he did not
fit in, a sort of reverse attention. But then again, he was
a counter-puncher; they lead first and he responds, a
middle-weight teacher persona.

Outside the sun was still waiting for him and the
city tempo had moved to late afternoon when people
were leaving work to head for buses and trains. Scott
got safely across to Green Park and sat on a vacant
bench, to check his pockets and move the money to
his wallet. Two winnings from two sessions felt good
for him that Friday; to make up for no school, no kids,
no salary for the term. He was a gambling man this
year, but still wearing his school kit; sports jacket and
tie, slacks and kickers, a red marking pen in his breast
pocket. It was a healthy walk through more park to
Kensington Gardens for the ends of late afternoon.
No more 'lady luck' for this week. But children were
yet at the playground and on a warm day Scott liked to
hear children at play. He sat on the sand-pit wall, to be
amongst happy people and remembered his own child
at such play; years ago when he was an active father, if
failing husband in a failing marriage. He could only
think of the good things then; the importance of a

child's attention, a clear time in the long afternoon and happiness safe from harm. Next to him was a Chelsea matron with loud tones after her charges and way too much food for two off-spring. On his left was a father at a sand-castle; a grand hard-work design for the warm day. Scott could have been at home with chores, or at school; this was better, a last time at a lost cause. Finally, an idea of food at home with the TV came over him, so he went; but after he got the kettle filled and heating, his telephone was ringing. It was a woman's voice again, an American woman this time --

"What you doing there Scott; London is a stupid place"!

"What d'you mean"?

"Who wants a Queen, real crazy idea. -- don't tell me you still have Lords an' Ladies" she said!

"Yeah they do. We have Dookes an' Duchesses with cucumber rolls, at tea stores in the arcade, every day of the week".

"When you coming back here? -- your father needs a visit, he's not well".

"But I got a new school; History and games in the afternoon.

Just a minute, wait, it's the door"! Yoo-ehh appears and points to the kitchen, then she giggles --

"...wasting your time you know, forget it and come-on home"! So it went, like last month and next month, till the summer when Mrs.Robinson gave up on her teacher son.

Scott collapsed on the sofa, giving some explanation to the girl at the sink and said he would try her noodles, like he never had any before. She found his utensils quickly to get the pots and pans steaming away and took strange jars of additives out the fridge to mix in. Scott allowed himself to recline for a while and enjoyed the domestic mood like it was his girl. He left his papers on the table and ignored the TV. It was just him, Yoo-ehh and the cooking sounds/smells. She never spoke either, like she was at home and happy, then remembered something --

"Mista Robinson... I mean, can I ask you?

-- I need an English name".

He looked at her directly: "what about Abigail"?

"It sounds like a flower colour --

what about Judith! You like"?

"-- sounds more like a laying hen on the nest", made them laugh out together.

"Hah yes, you think so; but my school needs a name and my job".

"Let's try Valery"?

"No I cannot, we have one in my class and she's my-friend".

"-- well I like Yoo-ehh, I really do".

"Ah yes, I know"!

Of course he did not take the teasing too far; no need, at such an intimate time. They continued a bit more like this untill the telephone rang again, when Scott prepared to leave for the evening. He went up and kissed her high cheek, like she wanted and made a comfortable exit to the noisy street. For a while longer Scott lingered upon the essence of a very young lady, alone in the kitchen messing about with his things; as he set off to Earls Court by way of dog-leg back alleys through Kensington. He went over the road to Brunswick Gardens to walk past large white terraces filled with chandeliers, oil paintings, pianos and spoilt children. This time of night lights were on but the curtains still open, inviting a hard inspection of up-market dwellings. He arrived at Duke's Lane to find the pathway behind, leading into a vintage street of old style cottages and flower gardens. Further on was the very heart of Kensington Borough, a small public rose garden next to Saint Mary Abbot's church. Old ladies were taking in the last gentle breaths of their evening and a young child went yelling from the trim lawns --

Yoo-ehh was now finished at the kitchen and savouring a rice dish in front of his TV; enjoying her clever life in a foreign city, her silly talk with a friendly landlord.

Scott continued over the main High Street and always tried to jog the rest of the way to Hogarth Road, where he enjoyed the desirable side of Earls Court. Two lanes off the main street converged at the 'Kings Head' east window and the houses nearby were Georgian and Regency dwellings. Some of the fronts contained appealing courtyards, which proffered both privacy and hospitality, when you pressed against their iron gates to survey. Ten minutes more took him to a rendezvous where the drinking began, when the full company of Scott's retinue faced each other, for releasing and exchanging the oddities of the week. There was beer, mild and bitter brews; there were assorted nibbles to eat; there was joking and laughing, talking and walking. For a full evening of rest and recreation in and around the popular district. The re-formed company were either pretending to be young and unsullied, or enjoying being seasoned salts on the full tide of evening life. For one night a week they had it both ways like this. There was to be a night-cap this time, at Ray's flat close-by. Charles began to brighten up at this last furlong and John was making an impressive assist with the entrées. So that Scott seemed to be the sole beneficiary of this happy activity; but then forgot himself and spoiled it, after he arranged sitting in a nice armchair to begin his Abraham Lincoln rendition. "Government of the People, by the People and for the People... now set them niggers free"!

"You're going to get us disbarred from school, carrying on like that. Behave yourself, will you"!

"Stop it Scott; you forgot your medication", came from Ray this time because it was his place.

"Free speech is free thought; a basic right of constitution in England after the 1688 revolution, for a healthy commonwealth -- yes? Cheers"!

"History was never your forte, ole chum".

"Listen then; what did the 'Bard' say about death and taxes..."?

"It was Emerson who said that".

"No, it was Franklin -- another American.

Sorry, but your poetic license has run out, ole man" John insisted!

"No **not** drinking Scott, okay"!

"How so"?

"Talk if you must, but drink up first", was enough to contain him for awhile; before Ray had to say -- "I must away to my bed, Scott".

"Me too".

"Then why don't you, off you go". Sent out alone he settled on walking again for a half-hour reflecting and some bladder relief in a Kensington alley, safely out of sight behind the church compound. He mulled over the Socratic discourse they had, to unravel the evening's verbiage and unravel a week of upheavals; to eventually arrive at his own front door suitably empty and tired. The Glasgow girl was still at business on the street corner and glared at Scott's passing; recognizing him as a non-starter, a hardened abstainer. In turn, he recognized her good track record of exposure to late winter evenings and fleetingly applauded her. For him too, it was another long day's journey to home again; every day he had much to do before he rests, with miles to cover and people to see, before he sleeps…

The next day Yoo-ehh finds Scott at first coffee and hands him a letter she found at the door. It is quality tinted paper and Scott sees a casino logo, so puts his cup to one side.

"Looks like an invitation card" he said, "a complimentary lunch"! He begins the new day at hand; now he is up-straight and moving again. "With two tickets; you have to come along, okay".

"Thankyou Mista Robinson. Ah yes, I will".

Yoo-ehh is learning about Scott and London -- one of them wants to be lucky, wants to win; the other needs good intros, new openings. She must also learn English, to speak and understand it, so stands near the door while he reads; she leans towards the letter and looks to the mouthing of his words. But suddenly finds herself thinking of another homeland faraway, where there is a real family for her with their own native language -- it is an identity check. Then she comes back, to think again about the Mayfair club dazzle she heard of and her new life with a silly landlord.

Private Lessons

Scott Robinson went to the telephone, on good impulse; to catch a likely colleague one evening and make timely arrangements for them. After teaching school for many years, weekends came to be precious and well defined interludes of escape. Sometimes a teacher can get far enough away at this time, yet still meet up with a colleague, because they understand each other best --

"Hampton Court for the day" -- an idea finally came to the other.

"Not sure..."

"Richmond then"?

"Why not Hampton Court and Richmond"? -- for yet another idea.

"How come"!

"They are so close together – let's do the palace in

the morning, then deer ranges by afternoon. Call again Friday, Stephen"!

Ten-am is early on Sunday to meet up with flasks, tucker and travel kit, for a tight car ride from Kensington. But by eleven-am they were on the parking cinders in front of the palace backs. The pathway detoured round the south-side to reach a big open patio, overseeing the water gardens stretching into a misty sunlight distance. The uneven foursome ventured further to the massed flower borders, enjoying carpet lawns and weekend people. It was a fitting area for family groups, as if ordained. The large Tudor backdrop screened off the drab residences of West Chiswick and afforded an imaginary period of modern gentility going out towards the Thames River thoroughfare; which beckoned a trip to heritage and intruded upon a geometric landscape. Everything worked for the best of all possible worlds, both the natural world and plant world, the river world and human world...

"What plans Scott, for summer"?

"Wine! Making gallons of it -- red/white/rose. Sweet and dry, strong and medium, clear and dark".

"How so"?

"On my own this summer; so it will be school chemistry all over again; my family are going overseas for the holiday".

It was also the best of all possible weathers, bright and warm; with a whacking array of floral colour, big lawn smells; lots of noisy people over every inch of grounds talking and exhorting as if everyone knew each other.

They laid out picnic items to share a space on the flat lawns in a spread pattern with other groups; everyone had a push-chair, children and too much to carry – so it seemed. Somehow, coffee tasted better outside from a thermos flask, squatting on the ground. Sandwiches were best this way too. This was to be a celebration event, because next week his family would leave and Scott would be at his own devices. At Richmond Park the sun was lowering across the grazing pastures, as the same group sought out the Queen's prized deer herds. Each herd gathered round a pair of male antlers and moved off like a flock of birds in the sky, like dumb sheep on a hill. The second try at contact Scott went flat upon the ground and began sneaking-up on them like a Red Indian scout. Stephen enjoyed laughing out loud; but the two females were unsure about the joke and more nervous than the animals, because of sheer numbers against them. The falling light made the parkland romantic and rueful, disconcerting to Scott a failing family man in a failing career. But Monday was just round the corner, school for another week, slogging it out in the blackboard jungle; a far cry from Berkshire Royal County theme parks --

Scott was eating lunch with the nemesis of his department, stretching out cafeteria courses over thirty minutes, with pungent exchanges of school chat info --

"On the carpet again, I hear, Scott"!

"Yeah. No one likes my humour".

"Why's that"?

"I mentioned the 'fat' word in our staff-room in front of the women. Big mistake".

"Yeah, I know -- how would life be without men? I heard".

"They all giggled a lot at first, the group with tupper-ware lunch salads, then they swooned; but I got no answer from them".

"And it was"?

"The answer was -- a world full of fat happy women! Never mention feminism in the staff-room either. Talk about sex or money, religion or death – but not the two 'f' words".

"But you already knew that! I can't decide if you're hopelessly naïve or a reckless mischief. Which one is it"?

"I give up. Don't desert me at trial, please Eamonn". Both of them took a breather for a moment, to savour the canteen fare and ruminate. One of them had less to chew over -- "I'm taking your groups next week, Scott, for a day".

"Well, I got nothing for you. Sorry".

"What d'you mean"?

"Just lessons and books and kids -- but no cream, okay".

"How's that"?

"Well, my best pupils are away at camp that week; so it will be real spade work for you. Alright? Get the details from me Friday-pm -- if you can catch me".

"On a course, are you"?

"Yeah, that's it – and by the end, wish I'd stayed at school. A long day-of-it ahead, with too many 'adults' and too many 'Ed experts' -- what a load of plonkers! Because the real experts are still in the classroom, doing it. Right".

"Yeah okay Scott -- but why d'you need to broadcast it! Why not play the game for once? Who knows, you just might get good at it".

"Just sport my pudding course, for once and I will shut-up put-up"! This was a customary lead-in for their prunes-an-custard, or such like.

The next week Scott was one of hundreds registered in the hall at the 'professional centre' in North London. Some big-wig at the podium was casting out his circuit humour to teachers who were mostly young, green and plump, like garden melons.

Each teacher attending held numerous sheets of paper to delineate the order of day – working format at coffee with Group A; lunch by twelve for group B; a discussion tea at four-pm for group C. He sat through three am-blocks, where one block was a discussion of conference topics already decided – a nice futile teacher-specialty. The pm-blocks were formulating issues/directives onto blue and pink sheets; to be correlated next day at a selection forum. And on it went – very much like the bingo session at Butlin's camp, a Scout Jamboree or one of those American conventions. Scott tried to enjoy his part and could never take these events seriously, after tracking previous events, when any effort he made was lost in the circus melee following. Oddly enough certain individuals did emerge as leaders or spokespersons, by end of session. Possibly they had a strong agenda set beforehand with like-minded comrades – everyone else was carried along like flotsam-an-jetsam at the seaside.

Not for him to worry. Scott was trying a lateral move, taking private students this term -- tutoring in their homes at evening or in the library; maybe at Scott's home on his round table under the wall pictures. Like the Japanese girl he had for three months; when she visited for English breakfast-tea and reading lessons. Scott sat on her left side so's he could draw his pen closer and actually see the lessons going into her ready head. This single teaching was very intimate and dwelt upon the intimacies of private life: love, pain, loneliness and happiness, family and work. All this, as she leaned over the table and fiddled with her fingers, devoted to the paper at hand for two hours every time. Yet Scott wanted to be kind and used his favourite writing material; he thought she might cherish this at home when returning to her 'Land of the Yellow Sun'. The lessons were to be projected through life-long years, maybe to her own children, rather like a ripple of water crosses the sea into the horizon.

But lessons could also be more demonstrative, much more dangerous; like a bomb blast – a sudden burst of energy behind him when two Arab men exploded with three West Indian street boys. The Arabs were noticeably well dressed, slacks and shirts from Harrods, shiny black pumps replete with small gold chain – but this did not hold them back from a full frontal assault at the West Indians across the café tables. All the cutlery and crockery shattered over the floor, whilst Scott and company went silent, only turning heads round to look-see. Scott was meeting with his post-graduate student on a top floor arcade, the bottom of

Queensway thoroughfare. He was trying to make a good mix of lessons and fees with entertainment – a necessary skill for adult students. He sat with two Arabs on that occasion: the student client and a London Arab gentleman of unclear standing. It was his idea to meet and talk, to enjoy a café in his part of London; but it was their money and their hospitality.

Ali, the student, lived above Marble Arch in the Saudi community, in a service flat off Edgware Road. It was seven-pm when Scott arrived, after Ali had eaten with his wife in front of their TV. Then everything put to one side and a laptop computer came out with papers and notes. An hour later the lady served tea and dates; somehow she knew Scott was ready. His wife was from Algeria and showed off her spoken French to him, while they forgot the papers awhile. Her eyes danced like gypsies when she spoke, her speech full of laughter, after she had been alone in the bedroom waiting. Scott could see Arab women must be beautiful or lively and set to wait upon men at any time. They had been married just that afternoon, in the Mosque at Regents Park, with few witnesses and simple prayers; then home again to a thesis on plant germination. This occupied the two men till ten-pm or later, four nights a week; to show their friendship and age across the bounds of race-an-creed.

But race or creed can make a difference. One day a gruff voice on the telephone asked for Mister Robinson, Scott Robinson the teacher. I am a Russian writer, from Moscow, he said. Scott did not speak, did not answer, to allow a more clear request. The voice was formal and a bit angry; but Scott needed students and needed teaching hours to log-on for more professional credit. Georgio met-up with him early evenings to talk books and academics in Britain. He was tall and guttural as he told Scott about the Soviet Army as conscript, life in Moscow and his wife a Russian style model. They were staying at a no-frills Bayswater 'benefits' hotel, within sight of Hyde Park railings on the North side; where they took to walking off their anger and frustrations about literary prospects in London, as ex-pats. How the Oxbridge crowd were the gangsters on top, how the 'old boy' domain covered scholarship/media/publishing – to always include them out. They walked like this, from the water fountains along the dividing road and back to the railings, each time they met. He said there was no seating in his room, so they started from the lounge lobby, then returned to the bench cushions; trying to ignore the lounge TV blaring away, so they could talk that last bit more. It was three weeks before Scott saw the model lady, after wondering if she really existed. She did exist and it was a disappointment in the making, when Scott could see how she had moody cat's eyes to appear lean and cunning. Olga was young and slim but not pretty; she enjoyed smoking too much and dressed to impress. There was a boot lace round her neck with a rifle cartridge hanging from it and one evening she wore a military waist-belt upon a cotton dress. Not to fool anybody; because she was actually tougher underneath.

But George did not have any money; so there was no gain for Scott, except an outlet for dubious frustrations and vexatious energy. Soon after this his luck changed, because his next contact was very different; it was exciting and promising after a surprise phone call one stale morning. Scott was pressed to see the new client that same day, only a few hours later. She called Scott's mobile phone when he entered Kensington Gardens --

"Please look for me near the Elfin Oak"!

"I'll be there in five minutes", he returned.

"By the playground, wearing a tan rain-coat, okay". It was like a chase; a bit of cat-an-mouse play.

"I can see you now. Welcome to Kiddies Korner"! Scott shouted across the pathway and hurried to the waiting figure.

She was tall and her hands cold to clasp when Scott took hold as a greeting. He offered some lame apologies, warm gestures and happy intros --

"I like this park place; it's a good idea", she said.

Much later Scott realized they were being watched, by her chauffeur bodyguard, when they sat at a picnic table and scrambled over her books; poetry technique and lit-crit texts. He must have been positioned on the other side of the central driveway, but close enough for him to re-act. Scott had been sticking his neck out when he greeted her so enthusiastically and warmly – such was his opening gambit with foreign students, young lady students. Later, he came to know she was closely related to the King of Saudi Arabia and that her father had been Ambassador in New York. But she was still a pleasure to deal with and set a diligent attitude to the demands of her course, her instructors. Scott was so pleased with her as to fumble and stumble over the texts/notes and her explanations – repeating his queries and her answers at the wood table; but she was confident with strangers and hard work. In a short while they began walking away from the open table, to find a warmer space in the Orangery café, because it was April and not warm enough to sit outside. Scott ordered something modest from the buffet display, to validate their comfortable occupation of an inside place at the window. They continued with their books after she took a mobile phone from the coat pocket and laid it beside her plate. The lady seemed at ease with her lesson and the cafe services, to also include Scott.

But by six o'clock she made another call: "wait, ten minutes by the gate – alright that's fine".

It seems he was only yards away, the whole time. Scott could finally see her guardian as British, looking well trained and capable; a bit younger than Scott, enough to be fitter and stronger. Before they went off together, Scott tried making another arrangement: "how about next Tuesday"?

"I will call you. Thankyou. Bye".

The next moment Scott was alone with a dizzy head after the whirlwind session; the best kind of adventure for middle-age teachers -- a foreign lady of good family, with royal connections and poetry. She was his student princess for the term; Scott had finally landed a prize pupil. He went straight round to Ray, at his job, to retell of his lesson encounter and Ray took his opportunity to play with the response --

"Watch it mate! You might end up in Riyadh, before long, with more royal maidens to teach".

"Yuh really think so"!?

"Why not! I can see your place reserved on the desert caravan train; relocating you to their summer camp, to get ready for course work under the tent awnings. But first you have to become a 'eunuch', you know"!

"How so"?

"Well, can't have you distracted and then the pedigrees to consider. You heard how Arabs are great horse breeders; they know all about husbandry. At end of contract, you'll qualify as late entrant for the Gelding Stakes"!

"What's that"!?

"When you seeing her next, let me know; I want to meet her".

Ray was executive doorman at a swank block of flats in Hammersmith and enjoyed entertaining business from extra sessions at his work station. Scott sat in the blind side of the doorway chamber, taking tea and pound cake, in exchange for his story – like another knight's tale from the sacred grove, another quest to the secret heart of the city.

Not surprising, the next lessons were equally worth telling, equally successful and exciting. The lady did not pall with instruction or with exposure to his quisitive probings and Scott was certain her bodyguard was always close; like the unseen hand of Allah, like a God-father's agent. Of course she never hinted at anything, did not give anything away. She was well versed to prudence, discretion and tact; like any girl who was a princess from pre-pubescence. It was nothing new for her. For Scott it was very new, very compelling and good story telling for his Friday-nite teacher friends.

By September school was in full stride and Eamonn rubbing on his weak side, the kids tickling his funny bone. He was not ready for a full timetable and return of his family, making it a congested term till Christmas; a time of trial all over again. But first there was a country weekend to enjoy; the farmer was an old friend from early years before college. It was an hour on the train from Kings Cross, then a land-vehicle ride to one thousand acres of empty fields, empty lanes, empty woods – well, empty of school children. The first evening was a breath-taking expanse of peace and air, a ringing excitement of old acquaintances re-made; the village pub a well-spring of merriment and amber tonics. Saturday he flexed his strength with a hay scythe, when he chopped at the nettles in a pony paddock and alongside the grass verges. He had escaped the city a few days, escaped the modern world and his own small enclosure -- to follow the farmer on basic chores, a brief church attendance and happy exchanges over meal times. Caring for animals and fields was more healthy than caring for people, more consuming and less waste. The farmer was browned and calm like a holiday person, his wife constantly on the move round their house. The return on Sunday evening was worrying, to consider if Scott recharged his batteries; or had he merely made a short futile escape from Londinium Fort. Monday came round again too soon. Eamonn was ahead of Scott at each break, kids were loud and stupid and the farm outing quickly became a dim memory for him.

The next Sunday were more private lessons, better lessons, more work and less trouble. He got to West Acton early evening for a short walk to Princess Gardens, to his Arab family pupils from Libya. Right in the heart of detached suburbia was a quintessential brick home at end of a leafy cul-de-sac. The elder sisters were returning from a walk, in full covering garments and hijab; they greeted Scott at the gate and went ahead to open the door. He was shown into their front room to view the showcases and family memorabilia from the sofa furniture. The son came down first and had an hour's English lesson, followed by a handsome tea-break, delivered on a silvered tray by another child. It was best china and Arab sweet cakes, while Scott rubbed his face and stretched his legs. The lesson was hard work, though the boy-student was exemplary and mindful; but it still gave him a long thirst and need to laugh out at his own jokes. Next hour, the sisters came for exam work; because the family worked well together they benefited from pairing to answer Scott in turns with comfort and assurance. Their father was actually younger than Scott, but very firm and loud on how he saw his role as fierce guardian. At the same time Scott noticed a display on the cabinet, an Arab-style gift-set in plastic viewing box, a silvered dagger weapon on blue felt cloth. It seemed to be a prominent item.

The lesson was two hours, but there was always extra time and last chat/review with the father, before going back down the street. He was happy, but tired with a full bladder. Getting home again, Scott simply collapsed with a mix of TV and hot whiskey. He had earned a modest fee and spent good time with up-coming Londoners from a very important group: the children of immigrants with two cultures, two languages and a future somewhere in between.

Next month was no easier, with the weather turning down and nights closing in, the future prospect was Christmas. This was exciting stuff for kids, but not for Scott or other staff; with exam prep on top of Christmas prep, it was a strained combination. Once again Eamonn was teamed with Scott in 'forward planning' work, curriculum through the term; he was also teamed against Scott with grade results across Year Nine and Ten. Which meant they sat together too much at lunch time and even phoned each other by Wednesday evening. By Friday Scott was desperate and down. But after his fill of dinner left-overs, a lucky chance brought Charles to his doorstep; accounted by the subject as missing a bus and passing his road end, then an unthinking impulse. Charles was an ESL teacher, which was less gain but less strain; a smart choice within a mammoth profession. Before he could sit down, Scott called out an imperative to him --

"Listen, I need a drink, Chas...

I mean tonight. The first round is mine, okay".

"Where to"?

"The 'Rat an Parrot', in the back lounge, at left side".

"Why not"!

"Because school is killing me; don't you see" said Scott, as he got his coat-an-hat and turned Charles back to the door.

"Yeah my students are great; lots of young ladies from the East, with spices an' silk. No complaints. But I never taught school kids".

"Don't think about it; government service makes duffers of us all"! Before long they were fitted together into a corner snuggery, onto a second round of elixir ales and their talk becoming more fluid less anxious.

"Move over to the cream, with me; kids are too smelly". Scott was beginning to get real sympathy.

"Tell me more. I had twenty years in school, you know; it's hard to leave".

"Never-inth-world" -- Charles was punctuating his responses with the aid of his drink, lifting the glass up to offset Scott's frustrated outpouring. But there was comfort from the crowd too; a ground swell of weekend promises for other patrons also dissolving their weekday concerns with friendly frothy liquids.

"Glad you came by, Charles".

"Sheer impulse, an itch I couldn't scratch, to be sure.

I'm also Irish and need a drinking pal".

"Good on yuh".

"What's on tomorrow, Scott? Let's cross over to the South Bank; visit the Globe Theatre and get two *groundling* tickets! How say you, knave"?

"Well I say thus: we might be lucky and find 'All's well that Ends well'; I mean the play of course. But we could settle for 'Midsummer Night's Dream' instead, couldn't we? I don't really know what's showing this weekend – except for 'us two fools about town'"!

"Sounds like more irony from the Bard, eh what? But you should know the 'lit-crit', squire"!

"No irony; more like a bad omen for us, I'd say! Anyway I must teach first; a young Persian gal; then I'm yours for the rest of our day -- you scurvy rascal"!

Scott slept without dreaming that night to arise happy enough for 'breakfast-ina-tin' at morning and got to his pupil before noon. She was a shy girl, much like a Victorian child would be; a polite waif keenly wanting to please the adults. Scott arrived in casual gear, but still very imposing, conscious to be considerate and gentle with his young charge. They went to an upper room of a grand terrace house off Marble Arch, where Farzan stood silent and still, untill Scott invited her to sit. Not till then did she exhale and ease onto a splendid sedan. The room was gently lit from an old-style sash window and there was elegance in the furnishings, the décor; while they spent vital time together on her English books for homework instructions. She had large soft eyes and quiet laugh, as they ploughed through the exercises and reviews. A very pleasant task for Scott, as burnt-out teacher gallant. A wonderful scene of adult and child at a most worthy activity; satisfying for Scott in a way he could not have with an adult; because the very future was sitting/working before him and it was open and accommodating. The world was beginning to be a good place for him again, from the time they had together.

SCOTT at PLAY

S cott Robinson was brought up to believe he should enjoy working; that he would find a profession and make it fun sometimes, not just for himself but also for others. And even more so at school, because this might be an 'end game'; a terminal posting for him and kids could not 'vote with their feet' anymore than Scott could avoid monthly bills. Kids needed school as much as they wanted to be free of it; equally Scott struggled with his own career paradigm each and every day.

It was first lesson of the day, first day of term and a Monday. Two boys about fourteen years old, were hitting out and shouting at each other. This would mean a sound beating at Scott's school; this would easily mean some rough handling and more punishment later, from any teacher Scott had as a boy. Sometimes the strong contrast, between behaviour in school then with behaviour now, was overwhelming; it seemed to mock Scott and his whole generation. He could recall how long it took to be a teacher, standing now before them, all the years at college and working periods between; it clearly seemed a mockery. Scott had been a weak student as well as a good student, an average student and exceptional sometimes. But he was never given to fits of rage against his classmates, or needing to blaspheme every week. He had been treated harshly as a pupil and to have the next generation abuse him all over again, was a disturbing consideration, a ghastly observation. It had been a long journey to arrive in front of London 'hellions'; maybe a terrible mistake; but maybe not the end, only an unpleasant period before rewarding times to come. It was one of the two, Scott thought, as the lesson came to a close; then made sure he was smartly out the room a clear first, set to enjoy his coffee and break in a complete way.

The staffroom was a special sort of club where all kinds of chat, gossip and plain info was swapped around; while tea and biscuits, coffee and buns, were sipped and slurped in a short interval. Making it a brief theatre of the absurd, a pantomime set for adults; like prime numbers in a set together, only recognizable to those on notice –

Two seasoned Irish ladies brought in hot milk and warm rolls at break, so that Scott always dreamed of free time just before break, to facilitate a quick start in the line --

"Gur'd morning to you, Mister Robinson" said the first one.

"Can I have two buns, with cheese; thankyou? Just the one coffee. And how much is that" Scott declared openly?

"The same as yesterday, my luv"!

"Sorry, never remember anything. I have brain damage from the kids, you know".

"That's alright my dear; see you tomorrow".

Scott turned to find a ready pal and circled a few tight clutches, till he spied an open place at the elbow of the French assistant; "Bonjour, bonjour" he hailed. She turned and blushed at such simple efforts, but could not come up with a good response; she wished he had not appeared, it was too awkward for her. This was a ready scene for Scott, going into his favoured play of coy alumni mixed-in with school patter. So much teasing, that Miss Guillot was confused and amused, then dizzy at her place when Scott made another smart exit at the sound of the next bell. He heaved his way up the corridor with his lesson stuff, after this small display; it set him up ready for the next session of

227

children hell bent on infamy and damage.

Later that evening his phone rang after the TV news; it was the familiar voice of a colleague from days of yore. "Scott, you ole bean, I switched jobs this year"!

"You did what"?

"Am a solicitor now; way out in some great farming country. Not a teacher anymore, I'm afraid, sorry". He was very up-beat and a bit triumphant.

"No, sounds a good idea. So where are you" Scott had to counter?

"Up in the Cotswolds, a lovely town called Cirencester".

"Up where"?

"Well, Ciren means round in Latin and cester is a fort -- the Round Fort, get it! It was an ancient Roman site, now a small town. Can you come up and visit; you just might enjoy"?

"Yeah, of course I can, definitely ole stick".

A week later Scott was on the train from Paddington Station, going west past Berkshire; finishing with a short ride on a branch-line from Oxford, in old pre-war carriages that featured big cushion seats facing each other. At this end of the journey he chanced to sit opposite three young men who stood out from other passengers, because they were well dressed but comfortable with it, happy and talkative to each other. Clearly they had been outdoors a lot, having a ruddy colour and bright look; not really office types. They were young enough to be students, but were not introverted or inhibited. Scott was intrigued; yet they took no mind of him glancing across at them, hinting at a marked departure from metropolitan connections.

No surprise, the town was very different from London, beginning with the honey coloured sandstone everywhere; stone walls and buildings bright and clean in the sun, with much less traffic and much less noise. The busy pace along the main streets, was brisk and upright, but it was also gentle and safe.

Justin was to meet Scott at 'The Black Horse' free house in the town center, for a liquid lunch, then off for the day. The two friends sat over pints of Farmers ale and refreshed memories of their time in a church aided school down in Fulham. Justin was an underdog in the Classics department, Scott in the Humanities. They always sat together at lunch in the hall canteen, where they groaned about the same old sausages or the lumpy meat pies put before them. It was a noisy group of boys, so they cut this time short to go walking by the North End Road for an orange or a couple of pears off the market stalls. The Sixth-Form prefect, on duty at the back gate, took some teasing from Scott each time;

but he was glad to see the two friends set upon their rounds.

But there was no need for them to escape and hide today, so they spoke out easily --

"Just couldn't stand it any longer".

"Why not"?

"Masonby, the old scroat, terrible department head. That's it ole man".

"What'd'you mean"?

"I mean, when you have unions hijacking the profession, when inspectors are making the job into civil service routines and top heavy with trendy politics…"

"Steady on chum, you will get us arrested" squirmed Scott!

"…when all the teachers are pushing and shoving to suck on the same 'tax tit'… yuck! You know the parents don't care either way!

Now I have my own shingle on the High Street and answer to individual clients; with no assistant or office protocol to crimp my style".

"I got a contract at another church school; not too close to home and far enough away for a nice train ride" said Scott calmly.

"Come on finish up and let's go"!

Two young pretenders took to the open streets, setting a fit pace towards the west entrance of town for a look-see at the Roman ruins; next going onto the cattle market arena for a view of Cotswold rural types. They finally began a long sojourn into Bathurst Park, which stretched longways for miles; an old hunting estate for the Earl and private heritage for his family.

The old pals happily followed a main riding avenue to the west. This ride went out for twelve miles to the next model village; through well established beech and oak, across working pastures holding prize cattle and sheep. Footpaths criss-crossed open ground by way of a folly, or a small summer-house. The riding they walked over was for horses to gallop out in full stride, with rough holed sod under foot, with enough distance and space to get a few horses pacing against each other; good recreation for a by-gone age.

"What's over there" Scott pointed round, when catching his breath?

"Our Royal Agricultural College, no less, squire".

"A great looking place".

"But too many 'hoorah Henrys' and a lot of horsey gals".

"It's amazing"!

"Not like your campus in America, eh Hils"?

Scott strained to see yellow-stone masonry piled up high as residences, a tower and long frontage. He stood still, to check the scale and the impact it had upon him.

"We are going-up to have tea tomorrow".

"How's that"?

"My new client is a 'husbandry' teacher of sorts. Stock farming, I think; crossing different breeds of cattle or something like that".

"It sounds terrific"!

Scott was obviously entranced by such a lovely pile of collegiate in a rural landscape; a bit like an Oxbridge college, but built too far out of town to matter. He was reminded of his Oxford, his town college; only thirty miles away and also a small town. But nothing else the same; Oxford had lots of ladies, several river streams to follow and foreign students everywhere.

A little later, upon their jaunt, Scott wanted to ask Justin about women. Maybe there was romance, some love or sex. Was this the reason for his satisfaction in a small town without walls, a small job with no contacts, a small home without prospects? Scott had masses of gals at his very doorstep in Nottinghill, there were school jobs galore and glitterati everywhere in Kensington. Even when all this passes him by, every day, it was still close enough to bring hope to a middle-age leftover teacher. Nottinghill made people come alive; even dullards and the inadequate were faced against each other and made to tramp the same routes as high fliers. They are dragged out of hiding and made to catch-up. Scott remembered how a neighbour said to him, at his front door respite, how she was not leaving the area: "because people mind their own business here"! Someone else said: "lots of bad things happen in London, good things too; you try nudging one above the other". It was Town versus Country, all over again; so that he must re-read Oscar Wilde's popular play.

Before the sit-down tea, next day at college; the First XI were fielding their best side, at cricket, for a benefit match. Visitors were expected to make a showing and take an interest, even it be reserved and contemplative.

The playing field was beyond the East Wing, nicely bordered by chestnut trees and a canopy of big beeches, so that supporters were well shaded in their lawn-chairs. The team pavilion was at front-left, with lots of men hanging about in fresh white garb. Scott strolled the boundary line, with Justin, round to a small seating stand and studied the scoreboard behind them. The college was ahead after four overs, two hits for six and lots of extras from wide bowling. Ladies were in attendance too, with respondent spouses, enjoying a sporting afternoon that required summer stuff and cool tresses. Younger ladies leaned against the front of vehicles parked in the shade, with jeans and boyfriends; not recognizing much play, or noticing the pair of intrepid supporters infront of them --

"Who are we against today", Scott had to ask?

"Our local police force, pretty hefty fellows, but slow on the field".

"Not good at bowling either, I see".

"But this is their rugger squad, doubling up for summer events".

"Very gallant, to be sure" Scott sounded out.

It was quiet and slow, almost motionless; but punctuated by a crack of bat on ball, a sudden flurry of activity and some shouting; then returning to first positions for the next over. Nothing quite like it in sport, a bit studious and reflective for a field game; yet eventually absorbing, if the weather plays along and the spectators are not ignorant of the form and context. The whole afternoon presented a lot of esoteric stuff; an exclusive slant in the game, rarefied airs of sovereignty and a gentrified version of competition. Scott was easily taken back to his own youth in America, when balls and bats were above all else for a while, more important than parents or school grades – not much different there – when boys are free and happy, successful and healthy, fit and friendly.

The tea at college was an affair to remember, because it was a simple and engaging event. He sat together with Justin on a bench seat, across from four farm students groomed as country squires, with Oxford jacket a'top county shirt and club tie. They were in high humour and very comfortable with the familiar; altogether a shiny confidence he found both appealing and annoying. He could not decide, if it was envy or repulsion resulting from their brassy confidence. Meanwhile, they devoured most of the edibles on the table and slurped all the tea; winning against the furtive nibbling of Scott and his one successful grasp at the teapot. Clearly, a social gap was apparent; maybe a generation gap or even a psychological one. On Scott's side he was holding up a mirror to see himself in segments and wobbling; obviously not at ease with his own performance that day.

The refectory room had a high vaulted roof and large portraits of elder fellows upon the walls which no one looked at. There was heraldry and arms over the doorway, a head table for college admin and oak paneling on the surrounds. It was medieval and lofty, old and cozy, it was privilege and conceit.

"I say, you were very quiet in there, ole boy"!

"Quite so, ole chap; out of my depth with the Socratic dialogue, you know" --

"How so"?

"-- with the Cartesian axioms they were expounding".

"Hey Scott, this is a farm college, what d'you expect"!

"I expected your pal, to engage us with vertical integration in the feed industry; so where is he"?

"Maybe out chasing milk maids for us".

"Instead, we had the histrionics of Aggie Freshmen and a crowded tea-party more like another game – too many men without women, I'd say. Bahhhh"!

But Justin was set to cheer them, so authorized to haul his pal back to the sports field again, which they had to themselves by now. "Come on Hils, show me what you're made of"! It was a call to rally the disaffected.

"Okay Jus-tin, let's have your worst"!

Down at the practise nets, Scott took off his jacket and proceeded to swing his arms about to stretch. He held onto the heavy red ball for a while to remember something and turned the seam in his fingers, before running down to action.

"A good length, topping, ole fella"!

Justin was at the wicket end with a new three-spring 'Slazenger' bat, which showed fresh red marks on the face of the blade. He was swinging it across his shoulders and ahead, till the ball came, when he paused at the crease for a moment.

"Good straight bat, a clean center hit"!

It was the incomparable sound of leather on willow wood, which they knew from years before and what they each wanted to hear.

Scott completed four overs before switching with Justin. He was always a pace bowler, with a bit of an in-swing, if the pitch was good. He was trying for the space between the bat and Justin's reflexes, right for the middle stump. One ball out of six was too wide or too short; the rest of the bowling was well pitched-up before the stumps, to confound Justin and his choice of strokes.

Bating was not so good. Scott had the nerve to face-up and take the ball; but he too often wanted to hit off the back foot, which required a lot of practise to use a deft stroke of style without effort. But when it really worked the satisfaction was full; it was so complete that even the bowler was happy to see the ball bounce merrily away.

Finally the sun was cooling and shadows spread over the grassy field, far as the nets, to dim the play and make it end soon. It was reluctant and poignant for them, at the same time, when they retired indoors to gather up and leave.

Before Scott returned home, they had lunch together at 'The Black Horse' again; half pints of ale and a pre-cooked pork pie. The pub was more like a private lounge space, like a middle sitting room and the other customers were obliging and genteel; nothing like a noisy London club, nothing like a Kensington style tavern.

"When you coming up again"?

"No, it's **up** to London and **down** to the country" insisted Scott.

"Okay, touché".

"Better start reading some 'Tatler' or 'Country Life'; Ju-stin my boy".

"Oh dear, what a ponce you are. I almost forgot"!

"My train goes in a half-hour. You can see me to the station". Scott continued with lots of fibs about enjoying the sleepy weekend and wishing to leave Kensington, to fend off a sloppy good-bye. But they managed a firm handshake and some big waving at the end. Teacher types always get together again.

The train ride back to London was restful for Scott, because it was forced confinement and too dark to read. Of course he was glad to reach Paddington; how a good weekend away was meant to end. He was also glad to get back to work; just not ready to tend a countryside hearth even though it be lovely and clean, quiet and modest. A holiday place is quite different from re-location, he discerned and must not be confused.

Though he had to leave Londinium one day, he

knew that; but how and where. This concerned Scott that evening, because it would be like leaving your parents, but you must go. For an hour or so he listed events since he first arrived in the city, credited them by calendar years. Without a ready comparison it seemed to be a good account and years well spent. Certainly better than remaining at his previous post in America; any kind of move was better than stagnation and festering over lost chances.

Next week at school, there was a new coffee lady; she looking like an Italian woman with young kids, from the dark areas under her eyes and scratches upon her arms.

"You want coffee, Sir" she pleaded?

"Of course I do, is the Pope not Catholic" sounded-off Scott!

"Is who"?

"The Pope my dear" urged Scott.

"Mama Mia"!

"Thankyou so much and two cream buns if I may".

"Hurry up Scott", came from behind "and don't take all the goodies"!

"Next please, who's next"? She was nervous, but clever enough with getting rid of Scott, by latching onto another pundit in the line. It was not fair of him to tease the kitchen help like that, everyone could see it was unfair; so he went off to seek-out his playmates --

"What's up Scott; Year Nine is it"? Someone was sensing his soreness.

"How d'you know"?

"Same for all of us – ole bean!

Here take this seat, now surplus to requirement, like you in the department".

Geoffrey was an old fellow of the school and an unlikely 'bon vivant' of the staff common room. He was always 'up' and looking to roast someone. He was tall, so his range was long and his large grin gave way to a lot of verbiage. But Geoff was also 'bonafide' with the Head, so dangerous too if really crossed. He knew this made his baiting and banter more wicked, gave it more edge; enough to make Scott reconsider sitting --

"Listen Geoff, I must away to Year Ten, top set; the cream of Humanities".

"What say you"?

"History today: Fascism and the 'White Race' complex. Lots of dubious politics and doubtful dialectic".

"Right up your alley, ole chap".

"Right up your arse, you rat"!

"Come on Scott, where's your college repartee; you sound like a pedestrian proletarian this week – oh come on, cheer up man"!

Scott had enough of this to make a fire under his belly, enough to get him moving, but not enough to stick in his gullet. What the common room was intended for, not a place to sleep or hide away, but to refresh and re-direct.

Lunch was a non-event for Scott at his new school; there was too much serious eating and protracted dialogue from sedentary staff, which sent him dashing to the nearest exit after a few essential mouthfuls of sustenance. Scott needed air and kids again; he went out for a free-for-all on the west side grounds, where bits of cricket and soccer were spread across an old London green field. In fine weather Scott readily responded and forgot himself, diving into impromptu games, gate crashing if you like --

"Can I bowl, just one over, please"?

"Not again, Sir, oh no"!

"Pass the ball, will you". Groaning protests from victim kids were closely followed by some sterling in-swingers from a happy 'has-been', who delighted in the occasion and the upset he caused.

"Okay, that's it Sir, you had six balls".

"Thanks a-lot boys"!

But he proceeded across to the next group and repeated his exercise happily, again and again, till the school bell rang out loud for everyone. It was a glorious short interlude of magic gamesplay come to an end. Scott ambled towards the classrooms in no particular hurry; baggy pants flapping at his knees, gusts of air spilling round his sore head, his old college tie waving about like a torn flag.

School breaks like this were important; each has to be different, yet each equally important to measure the rhythm of the day. Breaks were also important for the intake of fluids and solids, food and drink at welcome intervals. This could be difficult when kids ate and drank at these same times and at same outlets. But some kids held up signposts for Scott, to assist him, when they pointed the way or shouted out hints; usually thirteen year old girls, the newly caring age.

"How are the chips today, ladies"?

"That's on Wednesday; only Wednesdays and Fridays", she said.

"Well, excuse me then".

"That's alright, Sir; today it's a kind of pasta".

"Teachers always sit over there, Mister Robinson, at the High table" said her friend. "So they can watch us. Ha-ha-ha", they went giggling together.
"Thankyou, very helpful".

Scott learned to enjoy various levels of tonics and pacifiers, learned to snatch bits of fresh air and how to make a breaking stride throughout the day long.

In addition, all the bumping off other teachers and the kids, set to keep him spinning; kept his internal gyroscopes going well, to produce the best balance for a very hazardous occupation.

A Season Travel Pass

Scott Robinson was from the mid-west in America and never lived in a big city before; to get around back home he rode the bus and later drove a car at college. But in London he never had an automobile and had to adjust to mass transit, like the New Yorkers on their 'subway'.

Twice a day, five times a week, Scott went up-an-down the escalator from the street level into the underground travel system; to join with thousands of others also going to work or home, going to visit or shop, or who knows where. It was the city underneath a city, where people met and talked; where they sat and watched each other, read and studied, relaxed and slept. There was excitement too: back to work on Monday, or sitting next to the rich and famous, journeying to romance, danger and darkness – a full experience in any life.

One episode stood out a long time, it was beguiling and dramatic, so he retold the story over and over to any ready listener. About ten-thirty on a Saturday evening, Scott was traveling home in the tube train; the carriage was empty and quiet, after a full evening out visiting another teacher friend. The doors opened at Oxford Circus and two young ladies entered infront of him, but each went to the far end of the carriage and took a seat alone at opposite ends. It was so deliberate as to seem rude to Scott, offensive, the way it suggested disdain and possible threat from him. He looked both ways to make sure of the situation and took hurt at the cutting slight made clear to him. Was it 'feminism' again, or just rude people – he could not decide.

He still could not decide two stops later at Marble Arch, when the doors opened again and this time about ten drunken people entered. They were young, flushed and excited from their night out, loud and profane – probably one of their first drinking bouts. It was so distracting that Scott forgot about his first problem with the ladies and squirmed in his seat at the onslaught, not knowing where to look. But suddenly he did look, to see the two ladies again; this time right next to him. They had moved from the end seats without notice, to sit either side of a very surprised middle-aged teacher man hastening homeward bound. It was amazing: how one of them leaned a little towards him as if they were together; the other sat very straight with legs crossed over tightly. But Scott was enjoying the poignancy of the situation, re-thinking through the dynamics and inwardly mocking his detractors proved clearly wrong that night. It was the apex of his evening moved over to the end position and he enjoyed knowing how the ladies had been forced to turn over their cards, to show meager value; whereas Scott did not have to give anything away. But not finished yet; because Scott had to get off at Nottinghill, had to leave them defenseless on this night train; desert his post if you like. He leaned over both ways and said to each: "Sorry, next stop is mine; I'm getting off". Nothing came back from them, no words of return, as he suddenly jumped up and stepped to the doors. He grabbed the shiny support bars, waiting for the doors to click open and did not look back or round to the merry pranksters. He got off like it was a normal journey with no probs, like a regular afternoon jaunt from school or somewhere.

The next day, up on the street, was also rather annoying – when a noisy black cab came over to the kerb. "Taxi, taxi, over here", someone hailed right beside Scott. "Where yuh going luv" came back, as a woman leapt into the rear seats. It roared off in a cloud of fumes and made Scott shrink away from the road. He was repulsed by this raw ugliness; it was for him the most reprehensible aspect of the city and he always shuddered every time cabbies sped close to him. But they were everywhere and everyone seemed to use them – except Scott, who resolved not-to when first arriving in London. With certain activities he was a hardened abstainer: like nite-clubs and taxis, no taxis; he also steered away from call-girl stuff.

Scott never used the bus services much either, but he did enjoy coach journeys from school. Next week was the annual trip up the Thames with Year-7; a half-day event for younger kids. Runnymede was a nice distance for a school trip, for a good afternoon away from their Chelsea brick house school. About forty minutes of riding the coach, after getting off the Windsor road, they arrived at a car park and pulled over to the river bank; then kids and staff all piled out like it was summer hols starting.

It was an open meadow along the Thames River and two entrance sites provided visitor-info, maps, guides and such – obviously aimed more at American tourists. Scott thumbed through the brochures and walked over to the JFK memorial first off. It was a long stone structure, with a plaque from the US Bar Association; rambling-on about first tenets of liberty transposed to the Americas, then returning this icon after the death of a young president. His kids would never be interested in this kind of serious item, as it sat in a lonely corner of the field, waiting for friends and countrymen.

Scott retained a copy of the famed charter at home; to often glance at sections regarding "noisy fish-wives on the river bank" or censuring "money lending to minors". The language was blunt and short, not what he expected. References to 'Magna Carta' were in all the public info; but not so easy to track on the site, because it was simply a grassy lea, with one road through following the river and two small gate-lodges at either end. It was a modest site, but sufficient to mark out the ground, to provide service and welcome for countless history buffs. There was also the opportunity for return, for someone like Scott, to stand on the place and re-cast himself in 1215. To think how it was, what was said and done, as big story of the day. Not so much dates and facts, but real people at an important event; different kinds of people doing different things, such as boys tending horses and men dressed in tunics with swords. There must have been women with food, hangers-on and baggage, priests and officials in long tiring arguments; not forgetting a restless king bored and vexed. Maybe it was raining a bit, or cold enough for gloves and woolens –

"Sir, can we get a drink"?

"A what"?

"A drink Scott, want some tea ole chap", came from behind this time. "You kids can get something later, be off now -- cut along will you"!

"What's that"?

" -- cut along kids".

"We don't say that now – we say get lost, okay". It was a terrible return to 1990-AD, a sudden rush of immediate concerns, a sudden crash back to earth. But to attend such trivia, such tedium -- after considering the Magna Carta issues marking the destiny of men-at-arms on a cold river stretch; a nowhere green pasture halfway between London and Oxford. Which begged the question, why here, why meet on this patch of ordinary wet river land!

"Sir, where's the toilet"?

"Not now boys, cut-along will you"!

"What"?

It was no good, no use trying anymore; Scott had to concede a loss. He had to attend his charges albeit mundane and pedestrian; had to leave his college musings and try re-connecting with his dream later at school with the guide booklets.

Miss Hazlehurst was the French mistress, not

without inference and sitting beside Scott the following morning at break --

"How was it"?

"What, oh yesterday, not bad".

"Ten years here and I never get away like that".

"Not even trips to Paris"?

"No, we stopped all that, after Year-10 disgraced the school; seeking French letters and French kisses as trophies"!

"I see, Madame…"

"No you don't; it's much harder for women. They take no notice of me", turning her nose towards Scott.

"No, you'd be surprised how they look-up to you; yes really" said Scott, knowing how she usually warranted uncommon attention.

"They call me, Hazelnuts"!

"We all get tagged".

"I heard you are, Old Hils" and this seemed to restore the balance, restore her composure.

"Well that's my name – Hilliard".

"But how would they know"?

"Lord only knows"! It was time to focus on last sips of coffee, without talking, before getting off to classes.

Miss Hazlehurst was good at 'break' chat. Because it was short, you had to get your point across; slurp the coffee and swap info, ply some new humour and hints -- all in fifteen minutes. It was an acquired skill, all teachers undertook and she was at it for more than ten years. He looked round her eyes as they shone and squinted, if he could see the years in her face, but he could not. She was beautiful and fresh like a college girl, with a lot of vitality under covers; her skin looking like she spent the whole night in a bath of creamed milk. So Scott glanced at her hands, another area of age evidence; but apart from pen-ink and chalk-dust, he could not see any tell-tale marks of the years she counted. He had to conclude, that she was obviously in league with the devil, or had a favoured alliance with Venus. The lady did not appear in afternoon break, so Scott sat quietly with his tea and day-dreams. He considered walking home that night, but sudden rain sent him down to the tube trains again.

Going to work was made easier on the tube because everyone was doing the same and the vibes were good. Scott would hold the upper rail and swing at his place in a full carriage, next to all kinds, mostly the young and smart going to the office with fresh newspapers and neat apparel. There was style too -- dark shades of colour over mint new shirts and soap fragrances, quiet chat and happy giggles. When the train stopped, everyone going out slipped easily past others like snakes in the grass and landed squarely on running feet; to speed-off to the exits like fishlets in a river stream, like birds in a flock --

Coming home one day, from school, Scott was on the platform in Victoria and waiting for the Circle-line. He was standing behind a tall man and it was 'rush hour'; but he noticed how the man wore a wide-brimmed hat and stood very still, obviously not part of the rush home. Scott noted upon the signal board, how a Circle-line train was due after three more District trains; so he could turn again to the man infront, for another look – surprising too. He wore a light cotton suit with large pleats across the shoulders and silly string tie – it was western movie garb – and the cowboy boots confirmed Scott's notion of American visitor. But he had no camera and no cases, just a shoulder bag and a steady pose as if looking with disdain at the place. It was Jack Elam -- Scott could now see his bushy eyebrows and the squinty-eyed profile; very much an 'ugly duckling' of the movies. No one else noticed, or saw how Scott was on track with a Hollywood icon from 'film noir'; through all kinds of B-movies, right up till when Sergio Leone transformed him into movie character legend. Two trains arrived and departed, but Jack stood firm among the commuter hostiles, to look strong and well. He turned his head a little, but not enough to catch Scott hiding in plain sight.

Jack was very quiet for a show-biz person, somehow not expecting recognition or attention – showing the strong silent side of American life – that ordinary day beneath the big city streets.

But Mr. Elam was a visitor, obviously to leave town in a short time, heading off stateside towards his home on the range. Scott's work mates were very different and not going anywhere; yet one of them still appealing. 'Miss', was always an intriguing notion for kids and 'Hazlehurst' is real old Yorkshire nomenclature. She was tall but not too tall, enough to be seen above the kids; was proud but not too proud, enough to be with kids. She had a penetrating gaze and alert posture, so stood out each and every time she appeared with the kids or in staffroom gatherings.

Scott was with Year-10 for a trip to the Globe theatre on the South Bank. Miss Hazlehurst decided upon a tube journey to the embankment, then to cross a bridge over the river at Royal Festival Hall. She insisted it was only a short walk along the famed bankside, to see 'Macbeth' at 2-pm.

"Why you Constance"?

"It's Connie, please. The Head of Year is away and I'm the deputy. But I like live theatre and saw lots of Beckett in Paris you know".

"Who's that"?

"Samuel Beckett, the Irish ex-pat, you should know".

Scott was to follow-on at end of the group and Miss Hazlehurst at front. He pretended it was boring for him and pretended he never went this way before – but not so -- not to let the kids in-on his true passions. He loved the Globe more than anything else and walking across the footbridge was a perfect entry into the South Bank scene; like it was in the Tudor Period with the bear-baiting, flop houses, stalls and taverns – the very first 'red lite' district in London.

Fifty Year-10 students straggled across to the south-side walk and gathered together for five minutes to catch-up and redirect. Scott was hovering round the outer edge and eyeing key individuals, most likely suspects to deviate and delay the process. Then they all off again, in two lines, to arrive at a ticket-gate for the playhouse. He could see groups from other schools in different uniforms with their teacher escorts, bunched together at the same gate and pressing ahead towards the starting time.

Scott's group were going to be 'groundlings' at left side of the stage and the weather was safely holding out for clear sky and no rain. While the kids talked and shuffled about, Scott surveyed the venue from end-to-end to savour the Tudor theatre; recreated in all its wonder in all its charm, for people such as himself, Connie and colleagues. Not really for West London school kids, who hankered after bags of crisps or sweet drinks; to think an outing like this as good escape from a predictable afternoon timetable. No, this afternoon was really time-out for Scott and his like; when he actually benefited from being a teacher, at long last. He was gloating with the idea of getting paid to see the 'bard' in action at this premier venue – his chums in America would be green with envy, he'd make sure they were.

Miss Hazlehurst sideled over to him at the interval and said a few saucy words, to confirm her real interest for the afternoon; to stir-up Scott and get him going on some direction she could follow. She was playing a teacher game, along with other games of fun, not least the basic gender game at the theatre. For Scott's part, he did not have to pretend how 'the play was the thing'; it really was and let the kids guess he cared less to be with them that day, than they with him. He knew they needed him more than he needed them; because this was his territory, 'artsy-fartsy' London and him 'Jack-th-lad' about town; not really a teacher lackey to sallow fifteen year-olds --

"Sir, where's the toilet"?

"Not now Gregory, not now laddie".

"I sent him over to you, Mister Robinson. I'm dealing with the girls today, okay, alright". Miss Hazlehurst was the cat with the cream again, as she broke into his quiet mood.

"I'm trying to follow this production, you know", Scott enjoying an honest irony for once; "and you're spoiling it for everyone", he added for good cover.

"Alright Sir, I'll find it later, cheers". Miss Hazlehurst was hovering within reach, as back-up for another teacher and also as child advocate. She decided to get between a teacher, declared drama devotee and a child in trouble. She sent the boy away on a diverting errand and came back to Scott with a surprise: "a drink Scott, want some tea ole chap"; exactly what he wanted to hear, even if it be only a promise. "Wait and I will be back; but watch my lot over there". She waltzed off to the right, into the mêlée and was gone a long ten minutes out of sight; to find a concession outlet only she knew of, adding more scores for her today.

"Well, what d'you think"?

"What's that"?

"All the jazz stuff – come on, Scott, you must hate it"!

"Well, I dunno".

"Macbeth in sun-shades and singing witches... even more freaky than I remember at college"! She was holding onto a paper cup with both hands, at her lips and talking over it.

"Only the RSC could pull this off; it seems to work. I like the asides to audience; it seems to be real" -- had to be a full answer from him.

"Notice it was the kids responding"?

"Not our kids, I hope"!

But the last Acts were long and hard, continuing with the modern music themes; which only added confusion and anxiety for Scott. He preferred 'Hamlet' or 'Romeo and Juliet'; something of ideals and humanity bursting with youth. This play was too dark for a Yankee like Scott; certainly darker than Eugene O'Neil or Tennessee Williams.

The theatre shop was full of fodder for tourists. But Scott spied some good prints, full-size pictures of Shakespeare and Kit Marlow; alongside a prospect view across the Thames, featuring Southwark in the foreground. The theatre images were marked with names, streets and alleys sketched in roughly, clunky sailing ships were painted on the river. He bought two coloured guide-books and the three prints, all towards salvaging a spent afternoon.

After the performance their classes were let loose in the courtyard for thirty minutes to extend the visit and assist the learning, while Scott perused the café outbuildings looking for himself among the happy punters. He saw lists of patrons upon the wall, headed-up by Mr. Sam Wanamaker himself. His profile was etched into a metal engraving above the name – another Yankee had made it across the pond to discover his final habitat, a fatal quest in the making.

When they gathered outside, to return, Scott managed to glance across to the Rose Theatre site; where he knew a plaque and basement ruins lay beneath a new office block. It was a very unsatisfactory outcome for another Tudor theatre on the South Bank. He continued to look over in that direction as they marched off back to the bridge again. It was a tinge of sadness for him at end of his outing, because no one else was bothered about The Rose, not even Miss Hazlehurst.

On Saturday and Sunday Scott tried to keep above ground out of the tubes, to walk. Surprising it was sometimes quicker to walk to Earls Court than ride a train; there was no waiting at the stations; the air above was wide and open, the streets worn and friendly. He would strike out to find a new route hidden amid back lanes and stride across historic cobble-stones, or slink along narrow alleys; to arrive at a familiar place like he found it for the very first time.

But walking and discovering the sights of town was

only for weekends – on working days it was back to the underground, because time saving was important. One such day Scott was happily tired, but unprepared for the kind of trouble passengers can find sometimes. He was dressed, for school that is, with nice pressed trousers and jacket; sporting an old college tie, traveling home on the tube again. The carriage was full with mostly working people, going home at end of day and Scott had a middle seat opposite some good reading of bill-boards: "Poems from the Underground". He was scanning through lines of John Clare, enjoying a sighted position infront of an old favourite. A young black man across from him was not so enlightened, not distracted with pastoral lyrics; he was eyeing Scott's school bag and the brief case next to him. He had two friends, very much alike; extending the same unwanted attention and venturing to finger a lock, when it looked like theft was the intent. The atmosphere suddenly became tense as tired travelers sensed awkwardness and some hostility. Scott moved his own bag between his feet, squeezed hard and leaned forward a little. Murmurings were sounded out, when an old black man started singing out loudly; an obvious response to the strained atmosphere. It was worrying when Scott could see the travelers were tired and vulnerable going home, Scott too – and it appeared to have the face of racial trouble.

What Scott relied upon in the city was quick judgment, right or wrong and even quicker action to obviate trouble. This was a danger zone, clear to all and everyone had their strategy, their own defense in the underground jungle. Scott's plan was simple and well practised; he left the carriage at next stop, then walked ahead and re-entered the same train to find another seat. He was lucky with finding a comfortable place between two Arab women laden with big shopping carriers. He leaned back and let his feet bump upon the floor as the train raced-up to speed into the next tunnel. Infront of him was more reading on the bill-boards, but no poems this time.

Travelling the underground could also include some amazing exercise – the way Scott would take the outside track on the escalators and proceed to run-up the moving stairs alongside his astonished fellows. Because he could never ride the moving steps or even walk on them; this felt like slacking, like he was losing the race to live; if ever he admitted to himself that he was tired or forlorn. 'Rush, rush, rush' -- was not a bad agenda, if it was shyly disguised. The trains and the stations were not just functional; sometimes they were a store of likely surprises for people, for those already acquainted --

"Hils wait", came from the staircase one evening.

"Hazelnuts…"!

"Oh, stop it will you"! But he kept on walking ahead.

"…what you doing here? I thought you went to Surrey"? By then she had caught up and two consenting adults got into step along the platform and found a space at the end to wait.

"I'm going to my sister's; she's having a baby".

"Good, we can prepare lessons together".

"Huh; since when did you do French"!

"That's right, double-Dutch is more my forte" -- they continued with this till the train came and found two empty seats together. But a little tiredness was showing on her face now, a trace of unhappiness behind her strong repartee. Scott gushed about timetable changes, his kids; filled her-in about where he actually lived, because she was struggling with the route plan stuck above them. He thought it unfair to tease about babies or family, or Surrey even; though he did most of the gabbing, while she faced other people in the carriage, taking his info from the side.

"Sorry, next stop is mine; I have to get off and leave you, desert you". She drew her mouth firm and wrinkled her nose in objection. But it was the end game today, after closing comments; time for her to withdraw and rest, time to be a sister and aunt for someone else.

"Alright then; goodnight, Mister Robinson"!

"And bonsiour Madame". When Scott regained the platform he looked back to wave and saw her already impassive and silent to the surroundings. She was facing the opposite window, without looking, when her train rushed into the tunnel as if never to re-emerge. But Miss Hazlehurst was like a beacon for him; a small torch of clear light inside their opaque profession, journeying with Scott or without him, through the remains of an old Roman city.

Scott at the barricades

Scott H. Robinson realized he had been a teacher more than a decade and was glad to hold onto a profession in his middle years, after lots of upheaval earlier. He first went to work on farms, then construction projects in the north, gas stations and a cannery; constantly on the move to new work, new places and new people. But, equally, he was unsure if he could stay in education till retirement. Was there something else he wanted to do; could there be anything left for him after long years in school? Did teaching define a life-cycle, which firmly set out prospects and guide-lines; though little understood during the time passing? He had some vague notions inside him, but was not sure if these were real options or just fanciful whims –

Scott was beginning to think all this through again, one long sunny afternoon, but still not getting answers. He was out up the Thames River, among all sorts of others, when his attention was distracted. Someone was waving, an arm held high and the hand moving; it was meant to be strong and clear. Scott moved closer to recognize a colleague from his last school, in Fulham; a language teacher terminated in July same as Scott. The man was standing amidst a busy café near the entrance to Richmond Park. It was late summer when Scott paraded his family out for another day. He wanted one more Sunday out of the city and Richmond was an easy drive from Nottinghill.

"Hello Mister Robinson" came from the friendly figure; who immediately gestured at Scott's summer shorts and threw out both arms in mock alarm.

"Greetings to you" – Scott gushed out as the two men squared-up to shake hands.

"This is my family…

And this is Mister Roget, our French teacher from last year". Scott made a half-turn to introduce the principal parties and enjoyed what seemed to be a happy event for everyone. The sun was cooling enough to signal evening coming next, so Scott declared it to be a way-stop. Everyone found cafe chairs to occupy, then the men went off to a concession stand for refreshments. Scott et al were ready to stop and sit; a child needed to drink and eat frequently. Round picnic tables were spaced along the terrace, which overlooked a good Chiswick vista; lots of green-growing portioned over desirable residences. People gathered in groups obviously concluding a day out somewhere, at recreation or something. One or two individualists remained standing and surveyed the afternoon panorama, at the same time attracting the last warmth of late sun; their foreheads glistened and shone from an abundance of light and air. Scott could see who had been out all day.

"Looks like there really is 'life' after school" exclaimed Scott; "I was hoping so"!

"What ever do you mean" asked Mr.Roget?

"Well, you're not going back there, are you? Neither am I and you know how it is"! -- seemed Scott had primed his questions well.

"No, I don't".

"Terminating your contract means you drop-off the edge of our planet; you are banished from Eden into the infernal grove, forever". He insisted boldly.

"Yes, there is a certain amount of shame and pity, when you leave. But it's not like a death sentence, is it"? Mr.Roget wished to be reasonable.

"Of course it is, you are meant to crawl off

somewhere and die horribly, don't you know"! Hardly surprising, their good cheer was beginning to fade.

"But I feel very much alive on a day like this --" served to cool down Scott's rhetoric.

The two colleagues rarely spoke last year, because in different departments, no need for them to trade any banter. Yet Scott saw Mr.Roget every day, at the coffee urn and smoking in the corner. He was tall and affable, merging into his department identity, same as everyone else. But last school get-together in the hall, his name was on the 'thankyou/goodbye' list, same as Scott. A deputy-Head read out the notice after opening prayers, before the Head's general remarks.

This was a lovely day, as Mr.Roget said, though meeting-up like this sent Scott into a cloud of doubts and anxieties about his job. Still, he had to be fair and recall another encounter in a very different neighbourhood, with a very different kind of person --

Scott had a lot to do on weekends; he needed to unwind from the week past, prepare for the new week ahead and enjoy himself, cut loose for a few hours. Portobello Road took care of the shopping items, usually on Saturday. This time it was Friday, half-term; he hiked from the back of Nottinghill to the centre of Portobello by noon-time. Friday was market day; many more stalls set-out down the road, all the way from

Pembridge Road past Golborne Road at the north end, about two or three miles – like a long reptile snaking round the heart of North Kensington. He was striding out in civvies, aware it was a 'no-go' area for some of his colleagues; but a lot of bargain values to be had for the urban adventurer. Suddenly someone called out --

"Hi Mister Robinson"!

He spun round quickly because it was not school, and no one should know him on the far side of Westbourne Grove.

She smiled a happy face at him and said again, "hello"!

Scott recognized her, from years ago at a terrible school in Hammersmith. How could he forget such a tough assignment, when he clashed with gangs of boys in the classroom and hid away with a posse of tough girls at lunch-time. She was there too, an average pupil trying to enjoy her school days and avoid unnecessary trouble.

"What you doing here then", she asked standing straight and still in the street, near to a wooden stall piled high with apples and oranges?

"I like to check in Woolworths for batteries, then go over to Tescos for the groceries.

And how about you"?

"Well, I live round here". She was a tall West Indian

girl, medium build in a dark dress-suit, her shoes were glossy black with low heels.

"What you doing these days"? He decided it was alright to stay and converse for awhile.

"Me; working in a law office", seemed to fit with her dress code and the dark colours; "…about a year now".

"Good news; what d'you do"? Scott was thinking a typist or receptionist, something modest and stable; he remembered her a decent girl without any incidents.

"I'm a barrister".

"A what" – he blurted out!

She seemed to enjoy this response and smiled wider at the same time, relaxing like it was a load off her shoulders, like it was a necessary surprise in any encounter like this -- "Yes I know, from that school"!

"No one goes to college from there"!

"That's right; but I took evening classes…"

Scott was truly and happily glad, to stand infront of an old student and simply gush with enthusiasm. Why not – she had done her time on the playgrounds of West London terrain, then took life by the shiny horns and made something for herself. He was proud enough for both of them.

"You still teaching then Mister Robinson"? Her mild local accent was still apparent, a pleasant counterpoint to her new profession. He saw how others would also find her modest style a welcome contrast to old-style law offices.

"Oh yeah, can't quit now; too late, you know". Unlike the young woman he was dressed in street gear, jeans and non-descript jacket, unshaven and unkempt.

"Listen, I must go, before everything closes.

But great to see you –"

"That's okay Mister Robinson", as if he were dressed for that level of respect and herself in Saturday togs, when it was the other way round -- a bit of dramatic irony for him that day.

It was a chance encounter, but what every teacher needed; recognition, success and happiness for everybody concerned. He was swelling up with things to say, awkward emotions and clumsy gestures, but finally turned on his heel –

"Good luck to you, Gloria and well done"!

"Bye mister Robinson".

For a moment or so Scott forgot what brought him out that day, he was dizzy and dazed with shock and surprise – but okay with it. In fact, Scott had been set-up for the rest of the weekend, like he rose-up six-inches from the ground; not taller, but free of kerbs or holes in his path, free of trips and snags. Her happy words and that big unaffected smile followed him for hours, till finally he related the event to a colleague on the phone Sunday evening, he just included it into their silly exchange.

On Monday he was back to work and got as far as lunch-time, when he enjoyed a lively session in the staffroom. He looked across to a familiar voice --

"Listen dear, four-pm, see you then – no I won't forget – why would I – calm down dear, don't upset yourself…" He simply could not finish a sentence, finish any kind of thought; because the other end was tough and unremitting, for a good fifteen minutes.

Mr.Sweeny was on the telephone in the staffroom, making his daily courtesy call to home – a young wife who easily baited and roasted him, the way he squirmed at his place; twisting and turning like he was getting lashed with a whip, his face showing a deep red colour.

"Is that the wife again"?

"Fight back, John, come on"!

"No way, that was my mother-in-law, she's tough you know".

Three of his colleagues sat round one end of a long table – it was lunch-hour and time to ruminate just before afternoon lessons. Mr.Sweeny sat with them and finally let out a sigh when his own seat hit the chair seat. The colour in his cheeks started to lighten and a wry smile came upon his lips when someone pushed a mug of tea over his way.

"Now you can help with our cross-word"!

"Never the Express, try the Times, go for it"!

And time to the next bell was short, they each wanted to delay the moments left to get ready for the afternoon; it was an important last few minutes, rather like theatre nerves just before the curtain goes up. By then it would be too late for extra books, more pens, more notes and ideas; it would be time up. In fact one of the Deputies came into the room at this stage to start things moving – "Let's get to classes ladies and gentlemen, you too Mister Sweeny – let's go"! He was walking to the centre of the room, peering into nooks and crannies for maximum effect.

Over the weeks and months from September term, people start making friends or attachments, to other teachers and items of furniture in the staffroom. A regular clutch of four ladies occupied the far couches to make a square in the corner, good for gossip or sharing prep. Scott heard one of them say – "This is where ladies would recline, in days of old, with 'period' pains; they lay here and swooned from their vapours"!

"What can we do; we're not allowed 'periods' anymore"?

"Well my girl, I take the day off", her friend called out amid the giggles!

The head of History liked his own armchair and side-table; apparently he waited a whole year for it to become vacant. The younger staff moved around more, to-an-fro from the kitchenette and main door out to the corridors; or they grouped round the cloakroom where a big picture window let them spy out onto the playground all the way to the car-park. Miss White occupied a table by the kitchen area and ate from her plastic Tupperware, sensible foods like carrots and rice. She was not so young and needing to attend some work at the same time; she forked at her stuff in the dish with one hand and turned the pages of a text with the other – all carefully operated without fuss or favour. Her cardigan was expensive M-and-S wear, swung across her steady shoulders, like she might do relaxing at home. She did not listen-in to anyone else and rarely glanced up from her place; altogether a very solid account for the other staff and the kids.

She did not even pay attention to the school drama production coming up. But Miss White must have seen the big poster, tacked on back of the doorway, so that everyone could see it coming in or going out. 'Greek drama like you never saw before' the headline screamed out – 'Gods and heroes fight over Queens and maidens'! The drama teacher said he was competing directly with a bonanza edition of 'TV's Coronation

Street' that same weekend. So he was pulling out all the stops, to present a spectacle not to be forgotten, not to be missed.

Mr. Sweeny had a small part in the play; he was to be the ardent suitor of a feminine lead, costumed in toga with open sandals. His big scene came at middle of the drama, when he got down on his knees to directly proposition the lady. By this time the audience had settled in comfort, relaxed and unaware what might happen. The teacher-come-actor called out his lines, loud enough to be heard at back of the hall, where Scott sat next to some Year-Eleven girls. They were a savvy group, street wise, but not nearly as hard boiled as they thought.

"Mi lady, I must have you – love you – I desire you…" and more was delivered with considerable conviction, to any of his own class who might attend and sit in the furthest rows --

"He means it, yes he does, he really means it" -- exclaimed the girl nearest to Scott! It was an outburst from mounting teen tension; the girls were transfixed by the scene with their class teacher as persistent suitor, besotted pursuer, sex fiend. It had all been too much for them, when they finally gasped and choked, as if strangled with their own mired emotions. But one of them had responded aloud, loud enough to be heard on stage.

Scott knew Mr.Sweeny heard the outburst, he must have and felt his triumph as the scene continued. Eventually the actor had risen to his feet and given up on the lady. But still the girls shivered and stared after him when he exited at stage left. They had been well shaken that night, very unexpected, incurring a certain loss of face. Likely Mr.Sweeny had mastered the evening from start to finish, for the benefit of his authority in a tough school, to heighten his prestige with colleagues.

When Scott broached the subject next day, pressed him on it, Mr.Sweeny shrugged it off as if nothing happened – once again winning at the con and the bluff. But he did say, not in his stage voice, but resuming his West London demure –

"Yeah, they're alright those gals, a bit shy, that's all". And his colleagues rejoiced in his success, his surprise, his nerve.

Scott sat with Mr.Sweeny and his table cronies, almost every day. He liked to talk about teaching; how he came into the job, what worked, what kids noticed. Mr.Sweeny was serious like this and knew there was a lot to learn if he not to be overwhelmed by a steady intake of West London hellions -- you had to survive. He finally came up with: "when you find yourself making the same mistakes as everyone else – you know you're a teacher, you made it --

Come in early Mr.Robinson and share a pot of tea with us; okay".

Scott sometimes did manage to make an early start at morning and found the long table clean and tidy from the custodian's efforts; so he enjoyed some reflected order and calm before lessons. Teachers were quiet and either thinking of home comforts they left behind, or the next classes coming up. The table group consisted of Mr.Ellis at History, Mr.Patel in science and Mr.Winston with French. They were different ages, but all low-ranking classroom fodder; because Scott never mixed with management, senior, middle or lower heads. There was too much to lose if you said the wrong thing, even in jest in the staffroom. The atmosphere in the room was comfortable and informal; but also full of eyes-an-ears playing a game of oneupmanship, back-biting, back-stabbing politics. Careers and jobs could be lost, washed away with one careless comment.

Scott went by Portobello Road to walk home many times, it was curious enough for any interest, with a lively mix of racial groups doing low-cost business on the street each and every day. He should have met lots of pupils on the road, among the stalls, or inside the stores. There must have been hundreds of them living close to the market, but they never appeared, or he never saw them – except for one.

"Hello Sir" – a young man grinned at Scott and nodded his head. He was pulling a wheel barrow along the top end of Portobello Road and it looked like his real job, for quite awhile.

"Hi there" from Scott seemed appropriate, because he could not stop to chat, pulling a load of boxes and straining at the hill. Scott knew him from a local school and remembered him not too bright; but pleasant enough, happy to be recognized and greeted. From that day, Scott often saw him; sweeping the roadway where fruit-an-veg leftovers lay, or pulling carts and barrows at the market stalls. He was a bit shy to see Scott, his old teacher and looked a bit sheepish when they bumped into each other on the roadway. He wore working gear and woolen mittens with the fingers cut off – a professional touch for a young man at his new trade. Winter saw him still at his work, easy recognizable under warm head-gear and heavy coat.

Scott felt it necessary to resume his teacher role, on such occasions, even on weekends and out of uniform. He would never know what he managed to accomplish with the boy at school, what he learned or how he was influenced. But sometimes there was a reverse effect; if he continued to meet the young man on the street, 'the penny might drop'. Scott's mere appearance might confirm some ideas the boy had at school; to harden some vague opinions he needed, for life at work after school. Because a lot of Scott's work was in the dark; he could not know how his lessons, or his influence, might get across to kids infront of him. One day in late July they would disappear from school registers, to go into the adult world; garnered with the dictates of parents and teachers to help upon the way.

Scott also believed in structure, for himself, not only for the kids. He was at church on Sunday and on Saturday evening he went back into north Kensington for cod-an-chips, to occupy a table on his own each time. Scott went unnoticed, disregarded and in return he only expected to see more strangers. Untill another boy from school showed-up to cross paths with an off-duty teacher. He was quiet, impassive at school and seemed to be unchanged years later.

"Hello Paul" said Scott to a tall black boy who came into the fish shop. It was about six-pm -- cold and dark on the street, but warm and bright inside; with not unpleasant smells of fish and potatoes in cooking oil. It was a Chinese establishment, but they had taken over the shop as it was, the local 'chippie' at lower end of the road; honest rations for working folk.

Scott was half-way through his meal when he spied

the boy he knew from a church school. The memory was intact because Scott had over-reacted to a discipline incident. Paul had hit someone over the head and Scott had him out the room to chastise. But Scott overplayed his part and by the evening knew that other things were plaguing him, to cause his exaggerated responses at school. The next day Scott sought out the boy, to give a full apology and he felt better straight away. In fact, after this lesson, Scott learned to reduce his anger on such occasions and instead display his reactions in the form of frustration or disappointment; much easier for a boy to respond and remedy. Infront of him that evening he saw the boy had grown tall since school; but he made a half smile and nodded. He was still shy, like before and went off with his head slightly bowed.

Scott often trawled Portobello market to scout for discount items, needing to walk out from home and saw Paul again a year later. He had now grown very tall, broad and manly. Scott said hello gently, as it did not look like Paul was interested in continuing a school thing; it seemed a nuisance to him, but he was polite and kept moving. Leaving Scott secure with the idea that for Paul and many others, school was over and better things lay ahead, more important people and more important events. Scott recalled how he spoke to the boy at school and glad he made amends, seeing the lad mature into an imposing hulk of a young man. He had averted a possible problem and learned something for himself. He survived a minor crisis and the boy had moved on.

Scott kept hearing the word 'survival', in relation to school duties – 'you must survive first, then you can teach', or something like that. It was a basic tenet of schooling, which kept cropping up at regular intervals in staff-room chat. When Scott first heard these comments after college, he blanched at the negative slant; it could not be true, it was cynical and unprofessional talk. But this idea of survival kept coming up and Scott was forced to remember his very first year at teaching in America, when he attended a school camp for a week in early summer.

There were about a hundred kids and six teaching staff, out in old army barracks, up the mountain. One afternoon, a big field game was organized for the whole camp. The kids went off to hide, then three staff together with three class-seniors were to search and find them.

The game was to hide and not be found. Scott went off with other teachers and the children, onto a rocky bluff out of camp. There were lots of trees and thick brush to hide in, lots of good cover for beginners. He saw two boys go up trees, climb into the boughs and another teacher get behind a rock; but neither were good enough for him. When the shout went-up to begin, Scott went down to lodge near the water. The hunters were soon upon them, calling out names of those seen straight away. He had to do better and get closer to the water; so he went very flat and slipped down to the rocky ledge of the cold inlet, holding on with keen fingers. Scott was desperate and determined, because he must not be seen by the children, the teachers or anyone else. He didn't know why it became important, what had changed for him to be so anxious to win, never to be found in his narrow hiding place.

The watery edge lapped at his shoes and his pockets sagged into the wet as the minutes went by, when hearing the shouts of boys above. Lots of names were called out as boys were seen and found, to be sent-off back to camp. It was now early evening, still light from the summer sun when he held on and waited not to be found. The shouting died away; no more people hiding near him, waiting to be happily found-out. This was part of it; he was not happy, not happy to be found, he could not say this. Because he was keeping something back inside of him, something he wanted hidden, separate from the kids at school -- but did not know what it was.

When Scott finally stood up to leave his place and

go back to camp, no one noticed him return and no one worried about a teacher who took to hiding more seriously.

"What happened, did you get lost" someone asked?

Yes I did, that was it, he thought. "Yeah, anyone miss me" he said aloud?

"No", came right back to him directly.

Clearly the quandary was his alone. Yet it looked like he was learning something, a special lesson from school and for school – but what was it? Was it isolation or tenacity, was it maladjustment or pride; maybe it was loneliness and a profound sense of anger – but why! Scott knew at least one thing, that he was easily disappointed with people and sensitive to the trials of children. But would he ever reconcile this with himself, or with the bigger family he now had at school?

The Unexpected Teacher

Scott Robinson had been at teaching more than ten years, when he realized there would be no turning back, no other life awaiting him. It was now deep under his skin, like sawdust in the blood; the teacher persona had taken him over. It started innocent enough, when he thought to assist at schools over in California, to try his luck. But gradually the whole business re-directed his life; not through deliberate choice on his part, more by default than anything. He heard himself say – in summer hols – he would teach one more year, then leave to find something better. But he never did and after ten years he never said that anymore. The only thought remaining was, had teaching taken him over by force, or was his real persona sitting happily within the phenomena; was he victim or had education uncovered him. If he was in a church school, then the idea of vocation re-directed his thought to a more acceptable position. Otherwise the notion of fate and free choice, hovered round him like a dark cloud, when at his beer with teacher friends on Friday night. But weekends went past too soon; it was a fleeting respite for a troubled pundit of the classroom. Monday morning came round very quickly, to expect the unexpected, like he heard in training college --

'Silas Marner' was showing on the video and a class of boys, thirteen years old, watching the story over four days. Scott intruded a few times to help fill in the background and sat back of the room to watch-out for mischief. 'Silas' was a lonely character, making his way through George Eliot's old England – he had been terribly betrayed, then isolated at his trade with linen making. A small girl child had entered his life, to bring some happiness and hope; but surprises were still to come for him.

Scott too was alone in his flat at Nottinghill that year and embattled with school duties, at a demanding site down in Fulham. By the second day he related to Silas and his burden so much as to feel quite sad for him and sad for himself; by the third day weeping silently at his seat near to the door. He covered his face with one hand and squeezed away some tears with the other. At the same time a boy happened to turn round and yelled out -- "are you crying, Sir; are you alright"?

Scott could not answer; but he was not embarrassed or ashamed at his response to good literature. The video continued and the tears, till end of period. It was a boys school and they more keen on football at break than a teacher upset. They were always in a hurry and only worried about missing their time outside.

That same afternoon Scott was at games with the PE head and rode in the coach going to the playing fields; supervision duty for twenty minutes journey. After starting off someone yelled across to him: "Sir, were you crying in English? Russell said you were"! His companions looked round to see the action and Scott came straight back with: "Yeah, a big cry-baby, okay! Now turn round please and quieten down, thankyou"!

They were confused with an unexpected answer, but happy enough to say no more, except whisper to each other. Scott knew the boys were good and they allowed him to be himself, even if it be foolish and weak sometimes. It was fair weather and firm ground underfoot to enjoy a game of football; Scott went chasing after the ball and the boys, till well past three-thirty. All-in-all a good day at school, the quiet confines of the classroom before lunch, then out to run and shout with the games staff till home time. He never had it so good, because his marking load was cut in half and everyone was happy outside away from school buildings, away from the strict timetable. Back into school the next day, there was a power struggle still going on in the classroom and teachers left alone to their own devices. Scott was not out of the profession, or dead in his career, but he had been abandoned in a territory where kids could be mischievous all the way to life threatening. He felt like the sergeant on a lost patrol, cut off from the brigade and already regarded as missing-in-action.

But Scott was not the only hardship plea in the district; many more worthy people were distressed and unhappy with their lot. One of these standing at attendance, one clear evening, when Scott chanced in passing -- "are you okay, what's wrong" asked Scott? There was no reply from the man, stationary at his place, on the street above Kensington Park.

"Is there anything I can do"? Scott continued, to a man who was openly weeping on Friday evening, opposite the Queensway crosswalk. He was not young, but looking respectable in winter coat and scarf, with full hair and sideburns. Tears were running down both cheeks and he looked downcast; but his hands stayed in the pockets, he did not attempt to hide anything or wipe his face – shameless, positioned in an open space to be seen.

"I'll be okay son, it's alright" he finally said and Scott welcomed the response, to walk on. When he turned round he could see the man still on show; on public notice that the world could be a terrible place and even age no antidote to hurt feelings, disappointment or sadness. The man made no excuses and wanted to weep in public. This open show impressed Scott and would guide him when it was his turn to make sorrow and let go of hope and cheer.

But there was laughter too, fun in school, even if it be self-deprecating and laced with risk for Scott; grist-to-th-mill in everyday times of 'teacher man'. Take smoking, smoking in school, regarded as major infraction; searched out and firmly dealt with; as opportunity for more mock drama and unfair humour -- Someone at front of class, called out one day -- "Sir, Carrington is smoking"!

"What's that"?

"He always smokes in the toilets, Sir". Scott knew the boy, Carrington, was out of his seat to the loo; that he was a likely lad for early intake of cigarette pleasures.

"Are you sure"? When the boy looked back calm and serious Scott believed he might be correct, so had to react to maintain some kind of respect. He jumped up from his desk and rushed at the door to show strength and resolve, "Right, I'm going to find out"; then stepped out quickly to the toilets nearby and entered. It was another dreadful, smelly place. Scott never entered this one before, to see the only window vent high up was closed, water ran over the floor and the sinks were scarmy and cracked. Scott thought to at least try and open the window before leaving.

"Carrington, where are you"? There was one cubicle with the door closed, so Scott repeated, "what you doing"? But there was no answer; so on impulse he over-reacted with a big kick to the metal door, to burst it open.

Carrington was in there, but not smoking; instead on the seat at his ablutions. Oh dear, a bad mistake or a nice trick – maybe the boys knew he was not smoking and either way they laughed at the outcome. It had been a clever ploy from them and Scott was certain it was a conspiracy of boys in the corner. Maybe it was a few days in the making, before they trying it on a likely teacher target. They were turned dutifully to the books, but looking very satisfied with their big prank. Scott had to apologize to Carrington, who was honestly surprised and embarrassed. In fact he saw fit to apologize several times over the remaining week. A further problem for Scott was the name, 'Carrington'; the most feared Deputy Head in the school was of the same name. Could they be related, enough to take his error much further, all the way up to admin people? Scott had to wait and see what transpired, to see if he was held to account at a higher level. The boys in the corner really snookered him that day; he had to credit them with clever play for an extra shot! But nothing happened, nothing came from the senior staff; so Scott could forget about it by the next week and view the games-play from a different perspective. He would enjoy laughing at himself and admire his young charges, as part of bringing-on the next generation. To play and win or play and lose, it was all to the common good by the end of term...

When student teachers arrived for next term, Scott was again facing the idea of becoming a professional teacher. Not for himself, but to watch the struggles of others in the making; rather like seeing a young beast going to be fettered and trained. He gave a big sigh of relief when they left, because it reflected upon his own fate, which had already been sealed by then.

"Mister Dreebin"! Scott hailed to a student teacher and waved at him facing a tough looking boy in the playground. He came over to Scott and heard a general warning for NQT's – "That's Melvin Tombs and trouble; best leave him alone".

"I had to stop him bullying".

"Let the senior staff do it. He can be dangerous. Just pass his name along at end of break".

"I couldn't get his name".

"Well, I just might have saved you from a poke in the eye".

"Thanks Scott"; he blushed like a young man and chatted till the bell sounded, while Melvin ambled away like a quarry who lost his prey.

"Let's have lunch together – see you in the canteen at noon, okay". Scott wanted to mentor someone and Mr.Dreebin was a History grad from Cambridge, so would be good sport for a left-over teacher from the old school. They sat together on a big sofa in the staffroom, after eating, to sip tea from plastic cups and Scott heard how his friend was researching on weekends, as well as serving at school.

"How's that"?

"Lord Rothschild. I go to his library and find material on the Franco-Spanish war".

"I need air and space on Saturday/Sunday – not more dusty papers".

"Me too; my father got me into this. Next month we print the stuff, almost a hundred pages and publish privately for family members only".

"Summer's coming up – I feel sorry for you kid".

"So do I. But I might not stay in teaching and do more research. I don't know about kids, if I can stick with them for a lifetime".

"Yeah sure, never my plan either, it just happened. But it's not a lifetime; only till retirement – then I might take early retirement – see what I mean"!

"I'm only twenty-four; how about you"? Scott had to go back to the age game, start with numbers and projections for a career. Nothing really new for him from this student today, but he was intelligent and polite so Scott did not need repeat himself. He began in schools at thirty-something and before that at twenty-four was still working in a gas station over in the 'Golden State'. Nothing like these salad days of young Mr.Dreebin. All the student teachers he knew were just out of college and just after school. They never had a chance to kick-over the traces; so that Scott was always talking to an alternative generation, who would not believe his own story of mis-spent youth or young angst. But the kids liked Scott because he was not the status-quo, he was impulsive and crazy like they were and disliked the rules more than they did. In fact, Scott was becoming much like the kids; the dividing line between them very feint and broken in places, when a crisis loomed.

"Put that in the bin, or put away"! A thin black boy was drinking from a bottle, mid lesson, in a defiant manner. Scott had to react the right way; it was a challenge to his position as teacher and the class watched what would happen.

"You do it", the boy said after a quick gulp to finish! He held the bottle up for Scott to dispose of, like he was top-dog and Scott the servile lackey. Not a good play against a low ranking teacher, who was half Irish and half unknown origin, who noticed an open window back of the room. Scott often over-reacted in such a crisis, took an opportunity to up the 'ante' – so he ran up the aisle to grab the thing and threw it hard through the window, thinking it a plastic container. At rear of the school, beneath his room, were a lot of parked cars. A plastic drink bottle would simply bounce off the roofs, or clatter onto the paving and roll away. But the bottle was glass and they all heard the breaking noise, as it shattered beneath them. The girls at the back jumped up to see what happened and gasped at the shock drama. The boys were lazy and only turned round to hear the girls shout out about the cars beneath. But Scott still had another card to play; he simply carried on as if nothing happened, as if he did nothing wrong. Another fright for the class, when they realized their teacher-model had malfunctioned and was very human, hostile and dangerous. Not till they all left the room, at lesson's end, did Scott glance out the window to see the damage – but saw nothing. The boy who drank from the bottle had dropped from sight; Scott noticed him hurry out the room a clear first, looking troubled and displeased. At end of day Scott ventured to the area of parked cars and saw broken glass at a kerb between two of them and he scraped it away with his foot. Providence was with him that day, because he was relying upon it. The thin chalk line between pupil and master, held one more time. A few days later he was facing the other flank, which could be just as difficult --

Scott could not help notice a man across from him, in the staffroom, waiting and watching. "Can I get you some coffee", he asked after starting on his own warm drink. The man shook his head gently, but began to smile; then talk openly about his long journey that morning and other schools he knew in London, places which Scott also knew.

"Are you a teacher"? Scott ventured, thinking he looked awfully like one, with comfortable suit and sensible footwear and he had an aura, like someone who had braved it before hundreds of children.

"No, not now" – he grinned sheepishly, which by then was getting all Scott's attention; it was very curious and had to be probed more, because Scott needed to know about his colleagues.

"How'd you find this school" and the man also asked for a name? It was a sudden reversal for Scott as he sat down and expired on a couch against the wall, with his first intake of coffee.

"Scott...erhmm...Mister Robinson. I am here two weeks now".

"Do you like it"?

"Well as I said...was saying...the intake is very modest, but the admin seem to be on top of things".

Scott realized he was under the spot-light and this mysterious gentleman was probing him; so held back from opinions, his usual cheeky comments and stuck to some plain facts. But he had to come up with something good because the man was waiting again and watching him closely –

"Well, I met some solid staff here and the Maths department deliver great success; the exam results I mean".

"What's your department"?

"Sorry, I forgot your name"? said Scott, trying to slow things down and parry for himself.

"Sid Baggaley" he said, shifting his weight in the opposite seat.

"It's English, actually. And erhh...I believe we're

having an inspection next month; everyone's getting very nervous". With that the man sighed a little and eased back into his own seat. He seemed to lose interest with the chat and resumed his waiting and his watching. Scott realized he had seen this man the day before, in the corridors with the Head – which meant serious business. All kinds of figures came to mind, mostly of authority and influence; but their agenda was always under-wraps and threatening to lower ranks like Scott. Of course they liked to show-up unexpected, because this was regarded as fair and honest observation. Yet without these kind of conflicts, sympathies could change; away from school new kinds of friendships were possible, even if they be fleeting and poignant.

Scott had to meet twenty 4th-Form girls at Ladbroke tube station at lunch time and escort them to an FE college for the afternoon; where staff were putting on a program about options after school and careers. He arrived at the station entrance by twelve-ten and saw the girls ahead of him at the ticket gate; but they groaned out loud to see him, definite disapproval and clear dislike of their duty teacher. It was an unpleasant start to the outing, but good escape from the pm-timetable, so he still keen on the assignment. They all got down to the platform, when Scott checked the travel diagram for a route plan, going north for half-an-hour to a new red-brick college place.

"Oh no, look at him, he doesn't know the way"! But Scott continued with his internal dialogue and signaled them to board the next train arrival. Once inside the compartment Scott searched the wall diagram again for route connections.

"See Gloria, we're lost now" – more panic from his charges as the train raced on.

"No, we're not"! Scott had to announce, in a sinister dead-pan tone, so as to make the girls more nervous; because he was beginning to enjoy seeing how uncomfortable they were.

Towards end of the journey the girls were closely round Scott; compliant to the one adult assigned to them and glad of it. All during the afternoon saw the girls vastly changed, they were happy and polite, obviously needing a known face to be close. The college was very strange for them; lots of new people and foreign parts to negotiate. Scott realized this a big departure from home turf, because they were both shy and ignorant with any kind of travel. It was only thirty-minutes ride, but for them like going to the moon. This was easy duty for a lucky teacher, so he could enjoy wandering the premises in idle thought. After some up-beat intros in the foyer, the girls were whisked away for a full session of talks, displays, tours and last refreshments when Scott joined-on. By the end of it all, he was thinking better of the girls and well cheered.

But on the way home to Ladbroke Grove, everything changed, the girls changed back. When the train returned to a familiar district, as seen by the station names, the girls became as before; cheeky, sullen and distant from Scott. So they got to their local station completely disaffected again and ran off like bugs in a yard; to leave Scott on his own at the ticket gate. It was to be expected, because colleagues reminded him the day before: "Don't be fooled Scott, back here they will revert to type; with added attitude, for letting it slip off-site". But adults did not always shy away from teenagers; though they could not be modern teachers. Scott happened upon one such adult, who did not hesitate to become dominant over kids, in full view of everyone; but it was a parent not a teacher.

The lady was about mid-thirties with a pony tail of mousy hair and hard countenance much like an angry man. She was medium built but strong enough to pull hard, pull at another pony-tail of hair; pull it from a house, through a garden and on up the street -- all the while shouting at the girl, scolding her and threatening. It was lunch time at school and Scott out

296

having a walk of air after a quick taste of food, before returning to dusty classroom service for the afternoon. He had just turned into the street on his way back, when the woman was coming through the doorway shouting about the father coming next, as approaching doom. The girl's pals were lined-up at the gateway to watch; they looked tough and savvy but helpless in the event. It was clearly parental rule to the fore, enforced without excuses or qualification. The mother was exercising a higher force that day, as she hauled her daughter out from forbidden territory, in full display of the undecided.

Scott was thinking of newspaper cartoons about 'stone-age' men hauling their women off to a cave, with animal-skin apparel and wooden club. This scene seemed to be the same kind of theatre, the same idea, a replay of primitive family struggles come through to the modern world. He was amazed and stood transfixed in his place, to savour the key scenes as much as he dare; before deciding to walk-on before he could be dragged into the action. The surprised teacher had become a bemused spectator, seeing how easily love can show as anger, when parents became frustrated and tired.

Next morning Scott was the same as everyone else in the city; getting to work on time, ready for a long day and siding with all the other wage-earners on the move. To travel like this was to join a happy work force, which met twice a day against all odds in all weathers and marched to-an-fro like it was a parade, like a crusade. One morning in October there were no buses and tube stations were gated with iron trellises; but Scott had to show at school now because he was already kitted-up with shirt-an-tie, pens, a good shave and shoe shine.

This time the 'unexpected' turned out to be from natural forces, a wind storm without precedent. Obviously there was a problem with transport, traffic and trees had something to do with it, because they were lying across the High Street blocking the way of taxis and fares. Police were in attendance at tape-barriers, turning drivers away at big oak trees fallen across the road. Scott was not deterred and decided to walk, to forget about the marvels of mechanical travel. He set off through the gates of Kensington Park, on a short-cut route down to Sloane Square, he knew from his weekend soirées.

Everyone was amazed to learn Scott had a daughter in London, it was not expected of an expatriot. Towards December she suddenly said, "tell me what you think"? It was an after-school request, which developed more thoughts about adult/child and student/teacher dynamics. His sympathies were becoming very stretched, as to make for a lonely pursuit of values and beliefs. But Scott did as requested and hit Oxford Street to see the famed lights. He started at Hyde Park Corner and crossed onto the north side, to begin his perusal of this special commercial-style advent shopping season. Clearly lots of other people thought the same that night. They swarmed over the pavement like a football crowd on Saturday afternoon; people going in all directions and taxis bumping a way through the throng strayed into their traffic lanes.

Scott was searching for a re-run of his own Christmas boyhood – snow and window lights, homely cottages and starry skies – but not to be this time. In fact it was difficult for him to find the winter themes, because Xmas had moved on; moved on from innocence to fashion, moved from children to adults, from wishes and fancies to needs and desires. Lights were hanging from high wires all down Regent Street; yet Scott failed to read the theme, could not recognize the colour patterns and did not see what they meant. In store windows too, it was confusing to watch the models and styles moving to music, or wearing bizarre outfits in a fantasy scenario. He was becoming dizzy with the impressions made upon him and the crowd kept walking into his path to elbow him in the ribs, or catch his heel from behind. Teacher as parent or parent as teacher, was proving to be a confounding pursuit of happiness. But for Scott there were going to be no second chances; no more rehearsals at his work or with his affections.

SCOTT on REVIEW

Scott Robinson was now a teacher, but his school job had devoured him. He protested and rebelled; not with acts of anger or violence, more like an 'existential' stance, neither moral nor professional. It was simply an act of 'identity' without reason or malice. The administration never wanted to understand staff like this, the kids reacted with basic instincts and some colleagues took this position to seek advantage. Because school was meant to be a working career, not an identity problem for dubious college grads; certainly not a position for fun or fulfillment. Most of all boredom was sure to get Scott kicking over the traces; he was adverse to this state more than anything else, it was entirely distasteful to him.

Scott had been flirting with two girls at school,

because he was bored and they liked the attention, it kept them quiet. He knew that girls had to like him in some way, or they would not apply themselves in class, they might even become hostile. But he got a little sloppy and overdid the attention; got too close to them after a bit of horse-play. At end of class on Friday, the girls spilled out to the corridor on their way to lunch and Scott heaved a sigh of relief, thinking his faux-pas had safely passed. But one of the girls went out last and offered a cheeky challenge through the doorway –

"We want a vodka-an-orange drink, a screwdriver – right Sir, see you tonight, okay"! She was a tall Irish girl, London Irish and last year in a girls school down at Hammersmith. Scott did not answer and watched them disappear down the hallway; then scampered off to find the staffroom, comfy and secure.

The following afternoon was uneventful, a long haul to end of day. He finished with a quick tea in the common room and went home. It was seven o'clock when he supped another tea after dinner to glance out the windows towards Bayswater at last light. Scott watched the end of a week slowly fade away, with the last commuters hurrying into a closing night. He then had the luxury of guessing about his weekend, what he might do; he enjoyed regaining his strength again after school duties. His thoughts were drifting over to Queensway thoroughfare; how it would be filling up for the evening with all kinds of people and he remembered the Ice Rink. The Ice Rink, of course – the girls were going to the rink every Friday evening, he already knew that. It was only ten minutes walk from his rooms, they would not know, so a big surprise for them. Obviously his energy was returning and his bravado – which meant mischief and guile. He had an idea -- which might work. The Ice Rink was near the tube station, so that everyone would arrive by train and walk up the road to return home. Scott knew it closed at ten o'clock, so relaxed in front of the TV after washing the dishes and checking his mail.

At nine-fortyfive Scott got a jacket on top of his street gear – jeans, runners and check shirt. He could see a good nine o'clock shadow across his face and attempted a 'James Dean' slouch towards Queensway, where he found a tree to lean against. Scott felt good with the part he played, waiting for the skaters to begin leaving and head past him to the station.

Sure enough, after a few dozen people came past he spotted his two girls. They were laughing and happy, perfectly ready for a nice surprise. When they got alongside him, at the tree, they did not see Mr. Robinson making like an alley-cat of the town; with attitude and gear and the right lines:

"Hey Sharon"! Suddenly the girls saw him and recognized the voice, if not the persona.

"Hey, what about the drink I promised"?

"What"!? They froze wide-eyed and stunned, in total shock.

"Yeah, vodka-an-tonic isn't it – great"!

"No way Sir, not tonight", as they both speeded up along the pavement; thinking to be in real peril from a deranged 'teacher man', they had mistaken for friendly staff in their other life at school.

Scott wanted to push it a little further and stepped out from the tree to shout again: "Wait a minute, maybe just orange juice, okay"! It was typical of him to go the limit, but he did not know why. The girls would be confused and fearful in a way they could not understand or admit to. But they were both well on their way to the station now and the tall one managed last words over her shoulder -- "No; we were only joking Sir; bye"!

He let the pair rush ahead, while he hung back and watched them get safely out of sight. He had his fun, it was over and went well enough for him to also go home after a satisfactory prank for the evening. But instead, he went over to a friend's place; where they enjoyed herb-tea with music from the Seventies. 'The Doors' were blasting away on the stereo, as his friend raved about Morrison and Colombian weed --

♪ Girl we couldn't get much higher; come on baby light my fire, try to set the night…♪! They stretched out infront of the home entertainment; then shouted over to each other about Saturday plans, excursions to Oxford Street for CD's and Holland Park on Sunday. ♪ You know that it would be untrue, if I was to say to you…♪!

"Hey, turn that down" came from next door, the other bed-sit room, on the same landing!

"Listen Tim, it's been a long day, I have to crash".

"Well, find me in the morning for breakfast, okay"!

Next morning Scott showed at MacDonalds in Nottinghill and sat opposite Tim at the window. They both had coffee and eggs and caught-up after a week at work. Scott did not refer to his girls at the Ice Rink the night before, because Tim was not a teacher so would not find it amusing. Instead, they talked of an execution in America they read from the Times newspaper, about an English man who was to be electrocuted.

"The Americans are insane, Hils"!

"How's that"?

"This crime was committed oven ten years ago"!

"So what's your point"?

"So, execute the same year, or forget about it. He's

a different person now; it's not that same man who committed the crime all those years ago" – only dimly aware how Scott was also a full card-carrying Yankee.

"I never thought you a humanitarian Tim, nice surprise".

"Yeah, electricity is scary stuff, man"!

"Alright, see you at Holland Park"; Scott drained his paper cup with a final tilt and stood to leave. Tim was already at the doors and glancing towards the buses passing by. "No, I will get the tube to Bond Street; then maybe walk back. Anything you want Scott; I'll look out for some 'Beach Boys' material, if you like".

"Bye Tim – till tomorrow afternoon, then". They took very different directions that day; but met on Sunday to saunter Holland Park in the general direction of the cafeteria. It was warm enough to idle the time outside, to chat about London and what came before. Tim was at Harrods store and enjoying a gentile lifestyle in Kensington; for him Scott was a Londoner too, full of angst and confusion a big city breeds. They both had salaries and white-collar jobs, to make like gents in Dicken's London of Victorian times – young blades with prospects, with wit and verve. A few men were playing chess at the café tables; older men with grey pony-tails or beards, Oxford jackets and corduroy pants. A few ladies were pulling dogs on a leash and foreign visitors were seen everywhere, happy and relaxed like it was home for them.

Tim wanted to sit and order a cup of tea. But Scott brought a flask and sat across from him at the terrace to fill the plastic top many times; while they looked around at the odd assortment gathered that day, lots of seasoned eccentrics and blue-stocking ladies. The residences nearby were exclusive and old-world, which meant remittance men and disaffected ladies; not really mobile professionals of the city. No loud happy banter round here, rather studied worn exchanges, between various middle-class has-beens.

Another Sunday Scott ventured upon his past, his own youth, in the presence of a quiet American also in London and working. This time, a chance meeting at the Round Pond, got him talking about home and the scene twenty years before on the West Coast. He was able to consider his choice of road in a wood, like the poem by Robert Frost, with no going back when one way leads into another. The young man was from San Francisco; he knew about the Vietnam Draft, music and the emerging conflicts of youth at that time. Scott felt it might be futile to explore the past from a London park, because it was years ago in far away America. But it was secure for them, to indulge in opinions and feelings not warranted much in England.

Scott took off his coat for the sun and was very free with comments on war politics, drugs and the 'counter culture'. But paranoia was still there; the colour in the man's eyes drained to a grey tint when Scott spoke, there was tension and apprehension in his countenance.

Several times Scott crossed paths with the young man and they nodded to each other without stopping; just kept on walking in a polite way and lifted an arm to wave. But Scott was clearly reminded he had a past, after his kids thought to take that away from him at school. He was not supposed have a life after school either: no sex life, no interests or quirks and no history. They had swallowed him up whole, just like a snake loosens its jaws round a prey to devour in one gulp – an unpleasant fate which could not be avoided no matter what he did. Sometimes he would take bold action, knowing defenses were not endorsed by the admin and colleagues were secretive about their own responses to hostile pupils. But Scott could never plan for trouble, because it was unpredictable and unknown; he simply played his hand when prompted, for it was their choice of ground, their weapons and kids always had the first shot --

In winter snow did not always come; but this year it came after New Year in the second term, where the playing fields were covered with a pristine white cover and blobs of flaky snow sat atop hedges or walls and such like. The lay of the land changed from a dull urban scene into a new place that shone in a white mantle, which took on a new aspect of something fresh and inviting.

The kids liked it too; they really liked the white fluffy snow on the playground and how everything changed for a while – the lessons were late, games were cancelled and buses to school slowed so much that kids had to get off and walk. Everyone had to alter their usual pace and enjoy a lot of inconveniences.

Teachers also took advantage of the upheaval, to create a little slack with the schedules, to forgo some preparation and timekeeping; the bolder ones letting classes arrive late and go off early, with arbitrary excuses. Scott was more moderate for once; he only tried for more coffee at break and bringing a last half-cup into the lesson.

Scott had to reach the East Block at break, to teach lower school classes. He had his own books to carry and a class-set of texts under his other arm; a full load for an old pro out in the elements. There was a footpath across the fields as short cut and he could still find it, because young feet had already gone before; they scuffed out a trail between the hedges and across the school gardens.

Several kids were still at play, throwing snowballs and calling out to Scott as he hurried towards the next lesson bell.

"Why you running Mister Robinson"?

"Because he's going to get hit"! -- as two or three snowballs whizzed past his ear to splatter infront of him. He was not running, but clearly in a hurry, with two arms fully occupied. He could not join the game, or defend himself from the small white missiles; but did look over his shoulder to see if he could recognize anyone, to call out some names. This was always a good strategy and kids usually knuckled under when hearing their own name called out.

When Scott turned round, they hid behind a wall, so had to continue on his way; there was no time to be distracted and get to his class in good time. This was always important, snow or no snow. The teacher had to be into the room first, before the kids arrived, to limit collateral damage inside the premises. The kids behind the wall could see Scott was at an unfair disadvantage, with his books and a classroom to find. But hard snowballs kept coming in his direction – it was very unfair, mean and spiteful.

So Scott bundled his books together under one arm and raised the other arm with hand upwards. From the same hand, he also raised the middle finger up high and steadied his pace to show calm and resolve. The attack seemed to increase, get closer to him; but his finger remained straight and high, he did not look back keeping a brave face towards an entrance in the far building. He heard young voices of frustration and confusion; still he did not glance round or show any interest what lay behind him. He made his play and followed a straight course to the objective; like a captain in the stormy sea, like a colonel on the battlefield.

It seemed a reasonable ploy from Scott on such a forgettable day and he thought no more about it, till the next day; a Deputy-Head called him to account in jaundiced terms --

"Listen Scott, you're supposed to be the adult! What were you thinking"?

"I wasn't thinking".

"Sorry, but I will have to speak to the Head about this and maybe enter something on your record".

"Well, can I go now"?

"Two of the kids saw you and rightly came to me; let's hope the parents don't hear anything".

Scott was not thinking of the Deputy infront of him, but of the malice from two kids who broke their own code of silence/honour. Of course it was kids at the wall, not the onlookers, who lost out that day and fell foul of their own cowardly prank. But this wicked follow-on to the admin was more like soured adults; it was not sporting or fair like school was supposed to be. The gap between himself and the admin became wider that day – so wide he could wave across to them like it was 'au revoir'. Scott felt this division was like a break in an ice-floe, with himself out on the piece breaking away into the bigger ocean. He became lonely, small and a little lost for the moment –

"That's all Scott, you can go now, you're late for next session".

"Right, I'm off –"

Sensing punitive action would come, Scott needed a diversion after school and sought out an unlikely friend in the movie business, an antithesis of the education business. His pal was editing film down in Wardour Street and living in a classic Bayswater bed-sit; where he indulged himself every evening with a 'mantra' of smoke, music, carbonated drinks and poignant one-liners with the visitor. Scott gained the top floor entrance to find him perched on a chair alongside the window, exactly the same as last visit.

"Far-out man; tell me some more"!

"Soren, I got school again tomorrow –"

"Just one more song. Tell me about the 'Sixties' and the 'Draft'", as he digs out another tape and cranks up the volume. It is 'Jefferson Airplane' – ♪ I see you, coming back to me...♪

"I told you before –"

"Yeah I remember, you showed us your Draft cards, A1 then 4C –"

"That's all twenty years ago..." but Scott was enjoying some sideways admiration from a Danish boy who loved music, the Sixties and dope. School was far away for an hour or so, as he recalled his army call-up in California; how he was to be a GI in the Asian forests with an M-16 and dog-tags – just simple war, youth and danger.

"Goodnight, ole chap" –

"No wait, one more – 'Country Joe and the Fish' – ♪ five, six, seven, eight, what're we fighting for; don't give a dam, in Vietnam... ♪! Soren was still toking at his joint, bobbing his head, as Scott escaped out the door into the hallway; then outside to a cold night air that was harsh and real and alive. Scott was still alive, after he got through the Vietnam War and lived to fight another kind of war, in another country.

The rest of the school year slid by without merit, without any kind of distinction – the trouble in January over snowballing fizzled into the background, the dubious report shelved for another day. Meanwhile Scott was buried in exams and marking through Easter break; it was a tacit agreement to suspend judgment and allow a new performance standard; the way of school to let things hang for a while without decision or resolution – the admin could gain considerable advantage like this. When May and June came the warm weather seemed to evaporate winter concerns and open windows let in fresh breezes for a new page to turn over, with Scott as teacher for another year. This summer he was not taking early hols, but stayed close to home to ventilate his system and oxygenate his persona one more time.

Scott was going into Kensington Park and it was July, hot and sticky. He wore shorts and T-shirt and began taking off the shirt; when he spied a known face coming towards him, along the footpath to the gate. It was Jane, a Chinese girl from his last school in Fulham, with two adults looking like parents. Scott quickly dropped his shirt back onto his shoulders and also realized he had not shaved – a bit unsightly for a teacher to meet a prize pupil. Jane was from Hong Kong and had been a top student that year; a delightful girl and astonishing athlete who won all kinds of events at sports day – altogether very impressive. Her parents came alongside to enjoy the friendly exchange with her teacher; because their English was minimum, they had to read the faces. But Scott could also read their faces to see pride and excitement, lots of promise and happiness to come. Unfortunately Scott was not showing as well and was hesitant with his responses, to appear less enthusiastic, which was confusing for the parents.

"Hello Jane, what brings you round here? I never see my kids in the park – it seems they don't like fresh-air or greenery".

"My family wanted to try walking out together and we never came here before".

"Yeah, it's a lovely evening. No books and pens for you this week, I bet"?

"Yes, I mean no; that's right Sir. How did you know"?

"Great to see you all today – *Nee how ma*", as he turned to both adults, trying to warm them.

"You know Chinese"?

"Only Mandarin, only a little. So sorry I must go now; I am jogging tonight".

"Bye Sir; bye Mister Robinson"!

"Goodnight Jane, good luck to you and best wishes for the next year"!

"Thankyou" and she walked on towards the street, attended by the two elders. Scott was already through the gate onto the lawn grass to begin running. But he hesitated and looked back to see her one last time. She was a fine girl in every way and good with her parents, good with her teachers at school and teacher man in the park. Scott never saw her again, he never heard anything more, no rumours or stories what became of her. It was a little sad for Scott having to say goodbye to the best, the brightest and not really in a satisfactory way. He had to guess what would happen and say a few words quickly, then pretend he did not think about it anymore. As it happened Scott was transferred to a primary school in September; he never knew why, but was not inclined to inquire, just glad to be working with new people in a new location --

Scott had two colleagues to chat with that day and the bus driver; during a forty minutes drive to Thorpe Park, with the kids. About thirty twelve year-olds from a deprived area of North Kensington, were enjoying some latitude on a nice bus ride, west of London; towards Oxfordshire countryside – a welcome treat for sorry souls.

By ten-o'clock the bus pulled onto a parking lot and the three teachers went up-an-down the bus to give guidelines for the day's outing. The kids were far too excited to hear, except be polite for once and wait for a signal to run-off --

"Listen class" said Scott, "meet back here for lunch, at twelve-thirty, please"!

"Away you go" said his colleague "and behave

yourselves" -- all but ignored by the kids at first words called; with adults breaking into big grins at the sight of loud happiness spilling out from a well-worn charter bus. The driver was already out and standing by the door with his cigarette also out and lit. He offered a hand-grip to the girls as they stumbled down the steps.

It was a lovely day, fair weather and good prospects -- "Okay Scott, some coffee, yes"?

"Your turn to buy, Nigel, remember"!

"No -- let me, please", a third party stepped into the fray and resolved a potential fall-out between frontline comrades early in the day. This was enough to quieten them as they headed off towards the park venues ahead.

By then the kids were out of sight, but safe in a new kind of recreation area, with large spaces of lawn infront of them; good distractions of swings, rides, climbers and slides. The three friends held their foam-cups steady and turned to look over the premises, to glimpse their charges at full pelt over the new terrain, out of ear-shot and out of range.

"Great idea, this park place"!

"Must be your first time; first time for these kids too – you can see that"!

"I never saw them like this before, so changed", said

Scott enjoying his picnic coffee; which usually tasted better outdoors, lasted longer and worked well.

The happy trio wandered round the area, not missing any part of the park, seeing everything the place had to offer. Scott was most entranced with the fortifications upon a small hill, where boys could make like knights-of-old and charge up-an-down the grassy slopes. On top were wooden ramparts, with ladders inside the mound; outside were high upright timbers fencing off the mound from hostile intent. Five of his own boys had joined forces with another school and were storming up the rise towards the fort, at full run and top voice. Two girls stood on the inside, a bit worried about the fierce attack and undecided if it was real or not. They could take no worthy action, but simply watched over the top and tried to see a familiar face, or a friendly foe; it was very unnerving for them, away from school like this.

At lunch time Scott's kids seemed to find their teachers easily, down at the kiosks, where they moved onto picnic tables to feed off sandwiches. Everyone was present and hungry and happy, like it was camping -- the afternoon same as morning; they running off in all directions, wild and free, loud and strong. One or two did appear before Scott, to ask about toilets or drinking fountain, in the most polite manner; an amazing turn-around for city kids. Otherwise he forgot all about them and completely enjoyed his colleagues for once.

Much later in the day, Nigel reluctantly recalled the group onto the parking lot by three-pm, to gather them in – "Glad to see you enjoyed yourselves! Who's been here before?... I'm sorry; we must go back to school now".

"Oh no, Sir; not yet, please"!

"Sorry, but we had an extra half-hour; we should have gone already! We're going to miss registration period".

"Yeah, great"!

Back on the coach the kids were hot and tired, starting to look sad; realizing it was a fleeting escape from school, from home and London. Oh dear, how they looked pitiful and forlorn; so that Scott felt strongly for them, was pleased to be with them and proud of his duty that day. He knew none of their parents would repeat the outing; so no better opportunities for them and no better benefits.

Back at home that night, Scott arranged a Friday drinks evening. A few friendly teachers met at a hostelry in Earls Court and began an early session. They held pints of 'amber special' and stood together in an approximate circle.

"Having a good term Scott"?

"Come on, no holding back", said the second man.

"Yeah, school is okay and boy have I some great stories to tell", said Scott raising himself up higher and pushing his face about with an empty hand.

"We depend upon it", said the third man.

"Mind you, man's stuff you understand – no women required; ha-ha"!

"What's changed, Hils" – and four middle-age white men of equal burden glanced about and at each other, waiting for the next shoe to drop.

A Life-Skills Folder

S cott Robinson had not always been a teacher; just out of school he wanted something different. When his classmates were heading off to college and defined careers, Scott left town for a working life; he yearned for travel and adventure. But what he found was dirt and toil, long hours and low pay; men without women, the have an-have nots. By the time he got to teachers college he was ready for books and libraries, co-eds in the cafes and status with his employment. But he held off a good long while, enough to separate him from the ranks of younger teachers; an exception to the rule ever after, out-of-step and inconsequential.

Scott was surprised to discover a big part of teaching as verbal efforts; most of the day he was talking and projecting to many students. He had to put authority and energy into his voice, because it was for the most part a reluctant audience, hostile sometimes. Yet his strength was improving every day and his chest/lung capacity increasing every year, without him noticing --

'Sunday observance' allowed Scott to change gears, change persona and saw him attending a local C-of-E habitat for late morning service, taking part as lowly participant. Scott started singing at the first hymn and by the second verse he was in full volume; good tonal quality and intonation too. But there was another big voice in the congregation, a few pews behind and the other man was dismayed at the competition; he was glaring at Scott as he stepped-up his performance. Scott saw the man every week, but they never talked after he heard Scott sing out, there was little chance they ever would. The man was the same sort of age as Scott and very tanned for a London person. Certain hymns did not appeal to Scott, so he wound down a little and listened to his rival; to hear a lot of power and force from the man, but not noticing any variance or interpretation in his rendition. There was another big voice in the church, in the choir this time. It was a lady, quite elderly, who seemed to have vocal training; apparently she was a music teacher. The lady could be heard above all the rest and occasionally sang a solo or featured in a choir recital. The organist directed the music and he was ambitious with choice and level of difficulty. He directed the choir from his organ seat by way of his rear-view mirror, as he played the pipes for all they were worth, clearly the instrument of his choice.

It had been like this for many years now; since Scott got into the way of teaching in London, since he was yelling and shouting at the kids in school, all day every day. It took a while for Scott to figure it; to understand how he got a surprisingly good singing voice after leaving America and taking-up favourable residence in a Royal City Borough.

In Minnesota he made the mistake of yelling and shouting at school, in anger and without control; which resulted in a lot of laryngitis on the weekends. Scott tried to project his voice more consciously, which meant no more sore throats and more success in the classroom. The larynx developed into something stronger and more lasting. By the time he got to London, it also meant his singing greatly improved. The first time he realized this, was when he sang a Christmas carol in a small gathering and someone asked if he had choral lessons. Then on Sundays in the church, he seemed to keep-up with the choir, with such ease.

Saturday was also a special day; a chance to stray out-of-bounds, to kick out and take risks. When Scott was mid-way through a weekend breakfast he got a friendly call: "Meet me at Piccadilly, so we can go shopping; you promised"!

"But that's not really a shopping place".

"All my friends go to the Trocadero. I want to find them".

"Any which way you can..."

Scott had a new kind of friend, an Italian lady, from college in Parma. She was full-blooded and keen on food. She was also interested in school and teaching, because her courses in Italy were going in the direction of education; they often talked about it.

Down at Piccadilly, they went round and round the monument looking for more Italians; like it was promenading in Spain. She never found the friends she talked of, but met new Italians and made friends with them; they could recognize each other easily and were always happy about it. For a while Scott was caught up in the euphoria and feeling like an Italian man; but by end of the evening he became very Anglo again, the pendulum swung back hard. She did not like this transference and became loud and insulting. She slapped him across the face sometimes, an open-handed blow meant to get his attention.

"You are 'gay' I told my friends; because you are too quiet and keep phoning your mother"!

"That's correct; I like to read and must call home to the US. But no, I like the ladies; especially yourself, okay".

"I don't believe you". She was getting tired and revealed this in terms of their relationship and her eyes were red, her hands hot and clammy; same as last Saturday evening – a good sign Scott learned to watch for.

The next week Scott took Claudia to his church and let his pew friends speculate on marriage or such-kind of continuation. He introduced her and enjoyed a little confusion, a little embarrassment from others. He could guess the comments made, which allowed him breathing space, as she took over the conversation and the responses. He was hiding behind a lovely coloured screen, designed and scented, accepted by others in the church; even the priest nodded and grinned for the lady. For a while Scott's weekend was a kaleidoscope of items for them and then a long flirtatious phone-call by Wednesday evening. It went on like this for months, all the way from March till summer; from short cool days all the way to summer outings and hot afternoons. He remembered it best this way; a pleasant interlude, not meant to last and not meant to spoil.

Friday was different too, Friday evening; because it was a late call on Saturday, no early rising and no rushed toiletries. He often chose to entertain at home; unwind and amuse, gossip and catch-up, eat heartily and drink merrily. The intercom sounded and Scott heard more than one voice at the other end, but one of them took control of the situation: "Hello – anyone there"?

"Who is it"?

"Jeremy and Claude, with Muriel". Scott pushed his door release inside and the front door clicked open.

"Okay; now walk straight ahead; number four"!

Scott rushed to his own door, to swing it wide open; as signal to the visitors and inviting access to his small abode. It was another dinner party for teachers and their associates, at a small flat in Nottinghill; about seven-thirty and first guests arriving laden with contributions.

"Good wine Jeremy – well done! Bread too, that's great"!

"So Scott, this is where you hide; where you crawl off to after period six. I can see you licking your wounds on that couch and refuelling for the next day".

"Quite so brother, yes, you got it right.

We can't eat till Alexander arrives, but he's coming. Here Muriel, put these nibbles on the table please".

"And let's have some wine; I can open the red".

"Excellent Claude, you'll make a good Head, with

the right priorities"!

"Quite so, colleagues, lateral thinking at it's best; eh what".

"We can see you take the correct courses, all the new education bumph and take it to heart".

"Why not, I get time off; half-days away from the chalk-face".

"It's about Miz Roberts, isn't it – to avoid a collision course with her"!

"No; Miz Roberts makes a fine deputy Head. I just don't like her hairstyle..."

"...or her new timetable; squeezing your prep time; too bad"!

Four solid teacher types milled round the living room with glasses of plonk and mouthfuls of rubbish; talking and chewing, laughing and helping, expiring and unloading. Scott usually plied his visitors with lots of boiled vegetables, pork chops from the frying pan and French bread cut-up into a table bowl.

He had the main window open wide and music coming from his tape player. The TV was left on, but the sound turned off, to allow real voices take over the evening. It was a lot of different activity for Scott, when he started the cooking and reached for necessary items to get people relaxing; to mix his friends together and check the door for last entry. It might be unsafe for Muriel to be among so much testosterone, so much ribald laughter, along with fructose alcohol and red meat. But here she was, spread out on the couch, trying to follow a TV programme and slurp the vino over her lap. She was grinning from ear to ear, pretending to hear Claude's pontifications and already beetroot red across her face. Wine on an empty stomach can take different people different ways and it unleashed the appetite from younger types. By eight o'clock Scott had a potent mix stirring in his rooms; a full spectrum of frustrations and hungers, thirst and excitement, hormones and taste-buds.

"Okay everyone, sit up please. Muriel over there next to Alex and Jeremy over here. Right; who wants potatoes"?

"Stupid question, Scott".

"Okay then, who does <u>not</u> want a nice chop"?

"More stupidity".

"Anything else"?

"Yeah, pepper-an-salt, please".

There was now a lull in the proceedings, as five adults focused on their plates before them. The verbal bantering ceased, the conversation changed; they were suddenly close together, directly facing each other over the proverbial 'food trough'. The volume went down as topics changed to serious school stuff and recent items from the staffroom; because they were still beginning careers, needing to swap information and defer to a hierarchy.

The next evening saw Scott entertaining a different clientèle; an Italian job without the heavies, without the machismo. It was 'ladies night'; usually just the one lady and she was not a teacher, not yet. Claudia asked Scott about seeing some Shakespeare theatre and picked out a performance in the 'fringe theatre' showing a new version of 'The Scottish Play'. He gladly agreed, so as to brush-up his credentials on the bard's famous tragedy and also agreed to her girl-friend coming along.

Luckily they got three seats together, very close to the front and Scott sat on their right so they could converse in Italian. They arrived on the early side and glanced at the program to see some distinguished television actors in the play. It looked like a good night for Scott and a worthwhile title for his teaching materials; good for the ladies too, to brag about a visit to the English theatre, back at home in Parma. It was fringe theatre, far from Leicester Square, but looking like a professional production.

The building was big, like it had been a school hall, or some kind of church facility in the past; an old brick structure. The music was a small ensemble to one side and the platform came out close to the front row seats. But the stage was also noisy; the wooden boards creaked and groaned at the feet of the actors when they moved across, chasing after their counterparts or dashing in from the wings. The actors wore Elizabethan gear, soft leather footwear; but the boards still sounded-out with their steps, more especially when they finally brandished swords and made hostile movements against each other.

The two Italian girls quickly noticed this unfortunate distraction, the stage noises and began to giggle. Scott did not worry too much and broke into knowing grins when he looked their way. He also spoke into the ear of Claudia: "what d'you think so far"?

"Good, but my friend thinks it funny; she does not know Shakespeare".

It was her friend who started giggling and this soon infected Claudia, so they both laughed together; trying hard to suppress outbursts with holding hands over their mouths and swallowing the laughter. But they shook violently in their seats, bent over in discomfort, because they were not successful in suppressing their amusement. This behaviour continued to the first intermission, when they all got up and walked out to the concession stand to get a soft drink and stretch their legs.

The girls chatted normally for about fifteen minutes; no mention made of any concerns with the play and went back to the stalls to sit down again. Scott thought to take preventable action; he considered sitting between the girls. But decided their giggling was a mere passing, after they appeared mature in the auditorium with their orange squash. So he resumed his place to one side of Claudia and allowed them to chat in Italian before the curtain rose.

Not long after the drama continued he heard the boards creak again, ever so softly, as if the actors were trying hard not to repeat the same soundings as before; as if they might have discussed the problem among themselves during the break. Maybe the girls were unaware and had forgotten; allowing Scott to sit back and relax in his seat to enjoy the bleak tragedy evolving. But when Macbeth leapt towards the Queen, after the banquet scene, he must have hit upon a very weak point in the stage construction and timbers beneath him squealed out; as if the nails had been dislodged, ripped from their sockets in sheer agony. It was a marked transgression to set Claudia's friend off, to trigger an adverse reaction, just like before; except this time more voluminous and more demonstrable. Very soon Claudia was reacting and together they worked up an audible consternation, upsetting the audience nearby and the actors. Yes, the actors began to notice the girls and their unseemly conduct; Macbeth and Macduff had spotted the source of the outrage and glared at the girls when going down-stage to the front; as if to shame them, to stop them. Scott's stomach was churning and his features flushed as the whole confusion went before him; a terrible embarrassment and discomfort to know they were his guests, his friends. If only it had been a comedy, a Shakespearean comedy, all would be well. But 'Macbeth' was the 'bard's' most serious play; it was very dark, near psycho serious.

By Sunday evening Scott had enough of adults, like a lot of teachers and looked forward to children again. He was ready to be with the next generation, because they did not care about money, mortgages, marriage or status. They were never snobs about theatre credit or Shakespeare knowledge.

Scott was in his favourite girls school, with his favourite girls; everything was going along swimmingly -- "What's wrong Tina"? The girl was wafting her hands and arms about, at her seat, too close for the girl next to her.

"It's a bee, Sir", someone called out! So that Scott moved closer to the commotion, but without any idea of what to do, except to shout out -- "Open the window, please, someone; the nearest one"! An old style window with small glass panes and metal frame, like a Tudor casement, was released and flung wide open. Normally the girls disliked fresh air tactics from Scott; this time he got a different response.

But Tina was still tormented by the small furry creature; she was now standing at her seat and turning this way-an-that. When someone shouted out -- "It's in your hair, Tina" -- to get the girl into full panic. She had a load of bright blond hair, normally the envy of other girls; which might attract and accommodate a lot of like-minded bees.

Unfortunately, Scott was still helpless and saw the rest of the class disrupted; the whole class were drawn into the panic, calling out, genuinely upset at being helpless, much like Scott. Altogether, this was a lot more noise than a normal lesson generates; Scott knew it would herald unwanted attention from his neighbours and the senior staff. The wrong kind of attention would not bode well for a new teacher on the block. Scott was correct, his fears were confirmed, when a deputy Head rushed into his classroom; obviously annoyed and impatient with the situation.

"What is wrong Three-C; I could hear the noise down the corridor? You're disturbing the classes next to you; very thoughtless, very disappointing"!

"It's Tina, Miss Murray, it's a bee" said Mavis at the

front.

"I can see that; but not a reason to create a scene, people have work to do"! This seemed to work in calming the girls; they quietened down and found their seats again.

"Open another window, please, see if we can persuade our 'bee' to leave. In fact, open all the windows for a moment; see if we can't give Mister Bee a broad hint" and she sent a winnowing stare round the class and across to Scott, as she took centre stage in the room. Miss Murray, or Mrs. Murray, as she really was, stood tall and straight and looked angry. She always put Scott on the defensive at chance encounters they had, with her penetrating remarks and humourless countenance. In fact, the bee got the new mood too and exited the room in a slow smooth trajectory, curling round the nearest window out to the quadrangle below. Not to return; as if it knew when the fun was over, that it was now unsafe to remain.

"Thankyou Misses Murray, he seems to have gone, glad you came by".

"She has gone, Sir; it's a 'she'".

"That's enough Mavis, you have work to do. That goes for all of you. Now get on please; everybody! Mister Robinson, can I see you outside for a moment" and together they stepped into the corridor.

"On Tuesday, you can join our Year-Ten outing, Scott; alright. I thought you'd like that. Now try to keep this group quiet please. I don't want to hear anything more from this room today; thankyou".

Scott could not reply, Mrs. Murray had spoken quickly then turned away on her heel, to move off down the corridor; not requiring an answer to her first statement or any input to the second part. He was dismayed how the need to admonish him was never satisfied; every opportunity taken to underscore his mishaps. Scott was a little nervous about seeing 3-C again; he feared more bad luck and did not relish more professional visits from Mrs. Murray. Because, blameless or not, another escapade like that would certainly be marked against him. In school, complaints and concerns were entered into a 'closed book'; it was an admin 'black list', not open or transparent and no way to address the wrongdoing. Hence the constant storms of rumour, gossip and scandal; washing over the staff and kids alike; there was no escaping for anyone.

In simple contrast, any wrongdoing with Claudia was dealt with fairly. Scott enjoyed the improved situation when she showed at his residence on the weekends.

"I want to swim, Scott; it's so hot"!

"Italy is further south, much hotter over there;

specially the southern part where you come from".

"Why do you always argue; I have to swim; people say Brighton has a good beach".

"Brighton has a good promenade, not a good beach.

Let's go to Hyde Park"!

"I am tired of the park; every Saturday you want to go there, or play the cricket game with your friends".

"The Lido is open to swim for summer; a big stretch of water on the south side and nice deck chairs too".

"I don't believe it, you always lie; you like to trick me".

But by lunchtime Scott and Claudia were walking through Kensington Gardens with picnic gear and towels to find the Lido very active in July. They paid a fee at the iron gates and went through to a large lawn area flanking the long open water. They went to the end of the compound to find a space of clean grass and spread out two bath towels. It was a nice spot with a full view of the lake. Scott liked to sit and warm-up before his first swim. He liked to get bored with his reading and contemplate how he would shame everyone with his bold dash to the waters edge, then his strong strokes out to the buoy markers. It was a long time since college days when he swam every day; a long while since he was slim-fit and youthful on the summer beaches at home in America. But he was still proud and needing to show-off for Claudia, to impress her.

The Serpentine was a famous lake in Hyde Park, artificially made hundreds of years ago by landscape gardeners; an ambitious project involving hundreds of men digging out the banks of the stream, to create a twisting shape like a snake. An underground stream, coming from the direction of Bayswater, was the source of the park stream and this water flow continued under Green Park to re-emerge into the private gardens of Buckingham Palace. Gladly for everyone, all this effort and design was still enjoyed and appreciated many years later. Again, hundreds of people gathered along the water's edge on a warm day or a sunny one; even in winter people were attracted to this segment of the park.

It was a good day out, without rancour or regret, two young people enjoying life and each other. Scott brought sandwiches and fruit in a carry bag; they also had a flask of tea and flask of milky coffee, a newspaper and weekend supplement. If the sun came out hot and bright, Scott would cover his face and prostrate himself upon the towel; but the lady continued reading with sunglasses and her chin upon her hands. This would work well for the first hour or so, then the heat would stir Scott to swim; to splash the cool water over his body and make his mark amidst the happy throng. There was every age at the water's edge; every sort of people, reduced to swim suits and naked bodies; released from weekday confines, released from decency or awkwardness. There was a psychological aspect to the bathing/swimming, that was clearly good clean therapy, healing and pleasant.

One Sunday rain came to spoil the afternoon and the temperature dropped to deter bathing. After a disappointing wait for reversal, under a canopy of trees, Scott decided they must find an alternative recreation.

"We can go over to the gallery"!

"What is it"?

"The Serpentine Gallery is only ten minutes walk; I never entered before".

"Gallery for music, you mean. I'm not in the mood".

"No art, an art gallery. It will be inside out of the rain".

After more info and debate the re-aligned pair collected their various picnic items and set off from the compound, towards a small red-brick housing on the other side of the roadway. The outer appearance was tidy and modern; inside the décor was minimal, cool-white paint with stone flagging upon the floor.

The dividing walls were full height panelling, with numerous spot-lights aimed at the exhibits. It was a painting show from a graffiti artist in New York. Scott read some bio-lit at the entrance and learned he burnt-out quickly after an exciting impact on the art world. The canvases were large and cleverly worked with city imagery, New York sky-lines, endless detail and a full presentation to art lovers and tourists alike.

"Why does it keep saying, 'tar', on each picture? I thought graffiti was bad and had to be washed off walls, cleaned off trains" --

"'Tar' is really 'art'; okay, it's an anagram. He liked to scorn his patrons and revile his admirers; also wanting to confound his audience"!

"Why he behave like that"?

"Because 'art' is not worked out in logical terms, it's not a presentation to impress. It is a dialogue with the audience, frustration and technique together, where expression and perception meet".

"Amazing really; I think I like it".

"No, you don't think about it. You feel, you find, or see something".

"Yes, of course"!

"Let's go; I had enough of New York angst and your college questions. We need some pasta tonight, after the rain-stopped-play for us".

"You want food; good; I will cook for you".

"I thought so" --

The Care Of Minors

S cott Robinson was a secondary teacher, but this position had dubious authority, unlike a policeman or parent. He needed to see how to control a class, how to exert discipline over teenagers; without using bad language or bad temper. One day Mr.Ford showed him. Scott was infront of an unruly Year-9 and sent for the Headmaster; not quite ten years on the job and still lots to learn, lots to see.

Mr.Ford arrived very soon after the call and Scott moved to one side while he took over the reins, grabbed the helm and got in the driver's seat. Evidently Mr.Ford wanted to make a favourable impression for the new teacher; still regarded as visitor, like a parent or a governor. He felt as if the school was on show and this class, that he too was on show. So he performed in a way Scott never forgot. It was remarkable for the power, the penetrating comments, the solid intent; at the same time lacking any malice, it was not rage and not dangerous.

The kids went deathly quiet and still when they realized the Head was set to give them a full measure of his wrath; it was not going to be easy to stomach and not going to be short. Scott too became cowed and a bit frightened, when Mr.Ford summoned-up his energy right on the spot without moving, without getting too loud. It was effective the way the kids recognized a solid force bearing down upon them. Just as soon as the Head saw the desired results he stepped back and beckoned Scott to join him at centre stage, to contract a promise for new behaviour and better standards of work. Just like a violent storm, it suddenly passed away and Mr.Ford was calmly heading for the doorway and gone. But the reaction lingered till end of the lesson with Scott trying to underscore the action by adding his own grave countenance; as he went to take Mr.Ford's position at front and centre to echo some of the dictates again before lesson's end.

That evening in the peaceful confines of home, Scott recalled a similar outburst years ago in America – except he at the receiving end that time. His father was upset at Scott, a college student by then and began to verbalize his anger. But it became such a torrent of abuse that hours later in bed Scott was still reeling from the assault and next morning seemed to find bruise marks on his upper body, as if he had actually been struck with a fist or weapon. He understood how a 'dressing down' would produce a headache; but this was more like actual body blows. Scott remembered the incident, to be mindful how a verbal assault could damage a pupil more than known and he tempered his outbursts with large measures of control, like an actor might pull his punches.

Obviously teaching was connected to family relationships; different sorts of parental responsibility reflected in his job. Teachers had their own school experiences to remember and parent figures lurking in the subconscious. Whereas engineers and lawyers should be free from this influence, with more objective tasks ahead of them. Scott's father lived far off in America but his influence was pervasive even is small matters --

Scott stood on the platform, left of centre in the small crowd awaiting the train; a good position to move-off from. While waiting he tried an exercise, to rise up tall, stretching high; the way his father told him years ago as a boy. Of course Scott never did what his father suggested then, but he remembered. Now Scott was on his own in the city, far from home, he recalled a lot of favourite dictates – 'always stand-up straight', 'tell the truth and shame the devil' he repeated. His father might have known, how his influence could be dormant, then would arise when the right time came. Scott could hear his voice and see the face behind it – now that his father was dead. How much like his own work at school, when the lessons would not become relevant till years later; never easy to evaluate by any Inspectorate.

Liverpool Street Station was like a cathedral place; a high glass roof over the concourse, over the stairways and escalators, the concession stores and exits. It was a homage to the transport technology; how trains came to rest at the buffers to facilitate bus connections at street level and ferry people to the tube lines below. Scott was marking his place, same as yesterday and the day before; among his fellow commuters, looking for the same train. He relaxed his stance and shook his fingers away from his pockets away from his bag; then tried the stretching again, lifting his feet arches, then his head, to grow taller; as good posture for a few minutes.

Victoria Station was another favoured site, a lot smaller, but clean and tidy; with excitement in the air, as if a theatre performance was about to ensue. It was his first station into London, forever a sentimental icon for him. The entrance from the bus ramps outside slopped down onto the concourse as if to speed-up the clients and curved round to the platform numbers and all-day convenience outlets, which made sweet aromas and tempting sights for the busy travellers and the idle ones. Above was the same kind of glass roof, a legacy from Victorian architects; it seems they were heavily influenced by all that glass at the Great Exhibition, Prince Albert's popular Crystal Palace. A continuous sound system bathed the crowd with travel information and gentle reminders. It was 'the best of all possible models'; the mass of technology interfacing with a mass of people, in an infinite continuum. Scott knew it was more than simple travelling everyday, more than clever machinery; there was an increasing pace, power developing, people benefiting, systems improving – like a hybrid machine set to grow and evolve.

Scott remembered how train carriages became smoke-free after his first arrival into London and the people responded in kind, with more hygiene, more consideration and less smoking. The grinding gears of the whole complex were self-sharpening. His father was long gone, but Scott guessed that he would approve of this 'brave new world'; it would be something he anticipated and happily accepted, if not for himself, then for his own son. But Scott's father never lived in London and was never a teacher. By this time, memories or no memories, influenced or not; Scott was on his own in the profession and alone in the staff canteen sometimes.

"Sir, over here; please join me" called out Scott as he sat infront of his lunch in the canteen. It was a big secondary school near to Holland Park and Scott's first day on the job. He knew no one and to sit-an-eat on his own own seemed to be daunting and unproductive. A maths teacher approached bearing his own tray tightly in both hands, obviously wanting a space to put it down. But he did not smile when seeing Scott, there was no facial response. "Can I help you" came a fixed reply, as if Scott was outside on the street asking directions, or like he strayed into a snooty institution and stopped by an official.

"No help needed, just wish to share my table, that's all", seemed like a reasonable request.

"That's impossible; far too many things to do I'm afraid; excuse me" and he moved off in an oblique direction to parts unknown.

A few minutes later another colleague from the same department went past and Scott tried again. He caught the man's elbow and repeated his suggestion, regarding an obvious seat across from him. But the teacher blurted out a flimsy excuse and moved on somewhere else. But seats were filling-up fast and you couldn't eat on the run or at a chair, because you had a tray which required a table. Scott could have glanced round to see where the two colleagues landed. Did they go all the way down the corridor to their department room, very unlikely; or did they join-up with a close friend already made? He decided not to look back, not look round for the consequences. Because he spotted a third colleague at the cashier's place and waited for another try at a lunchtime friend. Scott waited till the man strayed directly infront of him and his gaze flickered ahead unsuspecting towards the new teacher already seated. The man half-smiled not knowing what to expect, he seemed like a promising partner and would have to really struggle to escape from Scott's applications.

"Hey Sir, please join me; I need a lunch companion and got a nice table reserved for you". Scott really overplayed his role. He half-lifted himself from his own seat and gestured widely at the open place across from him. He swept his right hand over the position to show the opportunity and made like a trusting child, vulnerable and heartfelt. Of course others in the room were beginning to notice Scott and his dilemma, his pleading; it was almost a tragedy. Several people close to him were really watching, so that it should have been impossible for anyone to refuse such a comprehensive offer – but he did. The man did not even speak or mutter a lame apology. His half-smile moved to a grimace and he simply changed course without altering speed and went past. But the near audience enjoyed the scene; they were secretly rooting for the homeside and quickly looked at each for confirmation and got back to eating. Scott's sincere plight did not interest them, they showed no sympathy. Something else must have been on the agenda for them, to follow a different set of concerns in the staff canteen arena; perhaps long standing and more threatening. Clearly Scott was working within a difficult career, full of unanswered questions and puzzling attitudes. But on the way home he quickly learned to forget such troubling scenes and pay attention to other types of commuter in the train.

Scott was tired travelling home at evening on the Central Line going west, on-way to his hole-inth-wall at Nottinghill Gate. He was gazing round in a blank stare, switched off, systems down and running on idle; when someone caught his eye to recharge the excitement. It was an actress across from him, but he could not recall a name. She was facing him and holding onto two plastic bag-containers, clutching the tops of Harrods green with reddened fingers. Her eyes were the big give-away, large blue orbs, open and clear. She could easily see Scott looking, searching her profile for clues. But there was lots of reserve and dignity from her; a little shyness and anger at the same time. She did not want to be recognized, yet she was in central London on public transport, sitting with the oddments of a city – so it had to happen. It was the anger that made Scott try harder, until it came to him. Julie Christie the actress from 'Doctor Zhivago', was young gal up from the Sixties, a new breed of Brit for the baby-boomers. She seemed to know when he realized and squirmed/shrank in her seat, dreading him trying to talk or make eye contact. But Scott had no intent to play the silly fan and was merely satisfied his memory served him correctly.

The next day, same time, same tube line; Scott scored more points for spotting another celebrity with more current value. A hotter commodity this year, because his soccer team was surprising everyone with stellar performances on the field. It was Jackie Charlton, manager for Ireland. He sat, a big man, impassive at his place; letting his folded leg rock easily with the train's motion. Jackie was exactly like he appeared on TV, tall and unspoiled. Scott felt he was open to recognition and open to conversing normally, about football and such like. Either way, he was at ease with himself and the public and sat quietly replaying his own thoughts, as the whole world passed infront of him at rush-hour on the trains. Other people in the carriage might well have seen him like Scott, but this was London town, where even a cat can look at a queen or king and they take no mind. Occasionally Scott rode the bus to school and it was very different because his kids often travelled the same route, on the same bus.

Jimmy was skulking near the wall corner and looking round like a robbery was about to take place; because he was smoking a cigarette and Scott the hapless teacher was close-by at the bus stop. Puffs of white smoke rose above the wall, to give him away; but Scott knew how he enjoyed the risk, the cat-an-mouse game with an unsuspecting teacher in the vicinity. This scenario went on for a week and other kids waiting for the bus also noticed Jimmy at his morning habit; which forced Scott's hand as responsible teacher on duty, a known figure in jacket-an-tie with shabby brief case. But the other travelling adults would not see him like this; only his kids would recognize the persona and the routine warm-up game before school. Finally Scott asked a girl, looking concerned, what his name was; because it would not be given up voluntarily, she also gave his year group. Clearly, she was not fond of Jimmy enough to protect him like kids normally do; maybe it was not

Jimmy but the smoking that offended her.

"Thankyou, I will deal with this at school and I don't need to know your name". Scott was one place ahead of her at the metal sign pole and she nodded slightly, glad to hear Scott was mindful of her unusual assistance. It was everything he needed and he wrote Jimmy's full name into the palm of his hand to notify the Deputy Head later. Scott then climbed upstairs to the front seats, to have another short period of seclusion, before they reached a stop outside the school gates.

From the time he stepped off the bus and entered the gates, the pace began to quicken and the noise increased. Scott caught the deputy Head as she crossed his path at the main corridor junction. He quickly passed-on his complaint, not knowing if he would have a better chance that morning and continued along to the staffroom for early refreshments. The rest of the day was a full program of revolving faces, paper trails and last minute details – the metaphysics of modern mass education. He thought no more of Jimmy or his plight, because he had another hundred kids or so, coming into close range that day.

But as it turned out Jimmy was in his afternoon group, when Scott was assisting a young maths teacher. Obviously Jimmy had not forgotten like Scott had, as he kept looking over towards him instead of at the board. By the time Scott did remember, he averted his gaze in that direction to more closely follow his colleague. But this did not work as Jimmy began calling out, eluding to their earlier encounter, trying to make serious business of it. When the lady looked across for Scott at the disruption, he had to react and summoned the boy out of the room. He did not wait for compliance and went smartly ahead to the corridor, to confirm his resolve.

"Stand up straight and put the pen in your pocket – thankyou". By then Scott was directly opposite the boy, up-straight and tall; with his well-practised parade ground stance. A few minutes of preliminaries like this helped set the stage for a serious chat; it was a good prelude to the upcoming inquiry.

"Right; now what have you to tell me" and Scott waited, very still and quiet. The boy was thinking it over better now and realized he was on record, as it were. What he said next was going to count, it was important, he was important; because he was getting Scott's full undivided attention.

"I can smoke if I want; outside of school".

"But you were in uniform and the other kids too – all on our way to school. We call it 'loco parentis', the care of minors".

"So --"?

"So, if you want to smoke, do it at home, in private".

"My dad won't allow".

"Why not"?

"He's against smoking".

"I wonder why; is it because it's bad for you? What about the other kids"?

"What about them"?

"They follow the rules and I have to, so why not you"?

"I dunno".

The main thing, Scott was getting through on the boy's terms, using his frame of reference and his kind of straight talk. The boy was becoming aware of what was wrong and how others were involved. He was getting the broader picture and seeing Scott's point of view.

"We have rules in school for the benefit of kids, like better health; okay. We're not making things up. We also have rules about homework, punctuality and behaviour; or it would be chaos, right"?

"I suppose so". He was looking sheepish now, with his face turned down. The boy got more than he bargained for; he wished to be back with his friends in the classroom. He was missing out and the teacher seemed to have all the answers, seemed to be enjoying this time out in the empty corridor.

"I'm not stopping you smoking; but please do it in private not at the bus stop, okay; is that fair"?

"Yes, alright".

"Now before you go back inside, anything more to say, anything else to tell me"?

"No, not really". By now the boy had enough, the whole interview was overwhelming, tedious and humourless – no fun at all. He just wanted to get away from Scott's prying stare, the teacher taller and straighter as if threatening him. Scott knew about all this going-on inside the boy, because he was replaying an old familiar drama of reflecting behaviour back onto the pupil, without threats or blame.

"Alright, go in please" and he gestured openly to the door as Jimmy gladly took the chance to end their conflict and return to the lesson, return to his own private thoughts again. The teacher got too close for comfort and seemed to be digging into his head. It was very unpleasant for a fourteen year old boy like this and he didn't enjoy the cigarettes that much anyway.

But Scott's attention was easily diverted; embroiled with a particular pupil one day and next session involved with the machinations of staff management. This was a worthwhile skill for any teacher, wanting to go the full distance in the job. He was in the office and overheard an exchange between the Head and a Year Head; it was loud enough not to be private, he could not help overhearing:

"I wonder if you might do the school a special favour, Miss White"?

"Yes, fine"--

"We are having an extra half-day off next week; I need to know which day..."

"I see"--

"Could you poll the staff and let me know by tomorrow"?

"I already have a staff list to check off with about forty names – not too arduous"! She laughed a little to make it easy for them both.

"Yes, of course; you're very helpful. Thankyou". Both the Head and the lady then spun off in opposite directions after the happy deal was struck and the Head took Scott's query next.

"Sorry Scott, not now. See me by Friday". But he took the report folders from him and sighed at the number of them, "can't do anything today" and went into his office to shelve them on any flat surface available. It was all very convincing, the way the Head spoke to three or four staff in the time Scott was around and also directing secretaries about phone calls. He was on top form and enjoying the swirl around him, the continual activity he redirected. Scott was the proverbial 'fly-onth-wall', confirming his low status. He did not have a preference for the half-day, so forgot about what he heard and resumed his routines. Yet he was impressed the way the Year Head took this task without thinking; because it might be quite a chore to canvass every staff member so quickly and they being so contrary over such matters. At such a time he was glad to be on 'scale one' pay rate, at the bottom.

In the staffroom, the new gossip was this half-day and when it might be. A small table in the room created a 'sub-set' of teachers; men gathered together because of football and a need for free laughter, like they were back in the pub. But they could be a strong influence and played with a lot of jokes at every break they sat together. One of the group was a confident Scotsman who tempered an acceptable disdain for the English in London. His right-hand man was also from the outer territories, a more congenial Irishman who smoked cigarettes with tea, or cigarettes with coffee. It was a tight group and any comments towards one was regarded by all of them. They heard about Miss White at her poll but were keen to speak their own preferences right there-an-then to each other and anyone else in earshot. They were not worried about a Year Head, or any kind of admin, because they were regarded as seasoned regulars. Their club confidence and jocular assurance was formidable to some members of staff and Scott was inclined to steer clear of their table and their influence; not to take a chance, he was usually prudent and cautious with other staff at school.

At afternoon break there was more buzz than usual; along with the intake of tea and cake. Scott managed to grab a slice of shortbread and went to a section along the wall; where he knew a place was waiting for him and turned to face the front. The Head was near the hot water urn, a pivotal position in the room and waving a prop in his hand, a roll of papers appearing to be relevant for today. "I think everyone is here. Right" as the Head unrolled the papers to show -- "you all heard, by now, about an extra half-day, the Governors have..."

"Yeah – it's Thursday-pm" came from the Irishman at the table.

"What's that"?!

The men at the table consolidated this remark with lots of nodding towards their colleague and a chorus of guttural assonance directed at the Head.

"We talked it over this morning" said the Scotsman.

Scott was alarmed to see the Head take this comment on board so easily so quickly. Miss White was nowhere to be seen, she had not yet arrived. But maybe her results were in the papers Mr Ford held. The attention from other teachers in the room was mixed and two at Scott's elbow were still looking down at their own papers, to glance up only occasionally. The cranky dramas of a staff meeting were nothing to them, as they continually ploughed on with book items, registers and grades.

Suddenly Miss White arrived, rushing through the door and gushing over to Mr. Ford, "So sorry to be late". She found a space opening between two lady friends at the front and happily squashed between them.

"Glad to see you Miss White" but he continued with the table crowd, "well, that's settled; anyone object to Thursday? Right, any other business, no; thankyou". He rolled up his papers again and joined the discourse nearest to him, then disappeared, firmly rejecting any offers of sustenance.

Meanwhile Scott was dismayed how Miss White had been treated, how all her efforts were for nought. Because Scott was the only teacher privy to Miss White's original instructions, he omitted to confer with his neighbours, it seemed futile. But the whole sorry production sat with him for days, as he saw the lady dashing everywhere as usual. Luckily she was very young and needing to shine out, whether it was of any consequence or not. Results did not matter as much as impressing the right people with enthusiasm and possible sincerity. Either way it did not impress Scott and he determined to stay clear of school ambitions, rankings or promotion. He wanted to parlay the idea of honest work for honest wages, into secure employment. But it was a hopeless gambit; an out-of-date reaction in reconciling the loose ends of public service through government service.

New Lesson Material

I t was safe to say that Scott often played the teacher role better out of the classroom, such as when at home on his doorstep talking with youngsters next door. His kids in the classroom were convinced he was a fraud masquerading as pedagogue, that he was an officious crank wasting their time and patience. So they set to trip him up, unmask him and denounce – as learned from their comic fiction. Foreign students and foreign neighbours said he would be titled 'professor' in their own country; he was good as a doctor, a farmer or a priest – worthy and elevated. In London, where Scott Robinson lived, there were many foreign nationals from every place on earth; a whole coalition of diversity domiciled within reach of his jurisdiction, in attendance with his prologues and epilogues. Inside school Scott was a nonentity, regarded as a sidesman, strictly on the reserve team when approaching his superiors for an upgrade --

"Let me have your CV Scott, let's see what you got, what these colleges in Minnesota offer" --

"Traditional English Lit – you'd be surprised – very little US Lit and I never took the Can-Lit options".

"Sounds safe, but can you teach Fitzgerald; we have the 'Gatsby' novel on our exams again?

Scott was warming-up to Mr. Harrowby, as head of English. It began with a friendly intro meant to be funny and endearing, at morning break in the English department rooms. Two other teachers were enjoying the esoterics, checking books on wall shelves and penciling into the record book lying on a desk. It was busy and engaging for Scott, as long-time pundit for literature and language. His dress was suitably workman-like and convincing; a modest Oxford jacket with light-blue shirt and two pens in his breast-pocket, red and black. Today he sported his old college tie fresh from the cleaners and his shoes were like new. He was in top form and seeking better duty with sixth-form work, where he could talk more about literature and less about behaviour; altogether a more appealing task. He might get to talk about his favourite authors and Fitzgerald was already one of them, yet he never

warmed to 'The Great Gatsby' like he should have –
all the consideration to the idle wealthy and Gatsby's
romance/courtship coloured in terms of prestige and
income status. He found it disdainful and depressing;
obviously not a problem for the author, who sought no
other social situation except to fill-up on alcohol.

Mr. Harrowby seemed keen to learn about his staff
and their strengths and appeared to relax with Scott
in the very centre of the English rooms. So much so,
Scott declined to visit the main staffroom at any break,
to grab a hot drink and sustenance at the canteen and
negotiate a safe trail back to the department rooms
along two busy corridors. Maybe at this school he
could move-up a little, make a career change and leave
the lower forms behind. After leaving college Scott was
wanton to pursue only one sort of promotion, head of
English; not head of school, not year head or anything
else – just head of department, to become stuffy and
eccentric like a college teacher; amiable and pedantic,
guileless and humorous.

One such visit to his habitual enclave Scott was
on-hand to overhear a short exchange between Mr.
Harrowby and next-in-line, Mr. Swan. Mr. Swan also
looked like an English teacher, except he chose to wear
a Norfolk jacket and county shirt of heavy off-white
cotton with feint check lines. He was a Cambridge man

and of course came with a recognizable aura; he gave the room a certain distinction with his ready laughter and good cheer. Mr. Harrowby was a London-U man and displayed a different presence, altogether more pragmatic; his dress sense had no style, no appeal, it was merely functional and his repartee was practical and serious. But the two men could influence each other with style and attitude.

"So, where you off to" he said to his boss?

"The new learning centre, by Portobello Road".

"It should be diverting -- used to live in digs round the corner. I knew the place from before; great London scenes".

"The fish shop was a real treasure on Friday night, after a bit of ale at the tavern".

"And your Sixth-form group, this afternoon"?

"Oh, they've already gone. I let them go early".

Scott was incredulous as to what he heard; he tried to rewind the conversation, see if he heard correctly; but instead he simply listened to more of the exchange, from where he sat to one side, at a marking assignment.

"Caught them at lunch to give a homework essay and said they could leave school early; I had no one to teach their time-slot".

Scott stood up and without thinking joined the pair of staff standing on the nice floor mat they acquired.

"Mister Harrowby…"

"Yes Scott, hope we didn't disturb your marking down there, very bad form for us".

"About the Sixth-form class, you know I can take the lesson. Remember, we talked about the books last week. I am keen to do it".

"Oh yes, by jove, you like our Fitzgerald book – smashing! But that is next session, this week it is poetry; Pope's 'Rape of the…"

"I like poems too, you should read mine".

"But you have Year-Nine's".

"Not today".

"Listen, I must away; the 'beak' needs me at a HOD conflab"!

Scott was very wounded, though he did confront Mr. Harrowby, fully as possible; but it was no use. He could not decide if it was forgetful oversight, or lack of confidence, which kept him from his big opportunity. If he had been a fateful man, then this would not be unexpected; but Mr. Harrowby gave him lots of hope that Scott would be destined to rise-up and lecture to the matriculation class, to find a new slot in the department ranks and flourish in the realms of literati. It was not only women who kept hitting the 'glass ceiling', men too could be thwarted and disappointed countless times during a working life, where it seemed nothing he could do or say would allow him to succeed. He was to be forever with Year-8's or Year-9's and the menial duties of a relegated professional.

As it happens Scott was assigned a small 6th form group the following term, if only by default; pregnancy leave was often sudden and unexpected. It was the first year of Lit 'A' levels and deemed safe from exam stuff in the second year. Just before lunch Scott got a nice classroom upstairs, overlooking a pronounced view of an old style cemetery; where he could savour the ironies of mortality and destiny, fate and sorrow -- written in stone above the burial plots. He was always the first to see his cues/reminders out the window, he took as omens of tragedy; a somber backdrop to many poems and narratives they tackled together. Scott knew plenty of notable verses were written in a country churchyard, not unlike this one – a heart-felt epitaph appeared on another headstone, in Italy; but the poet was English and his career brief. Death and dying can be romantic, mysterious and compelling for the young; like those found in classrooms at seventeen years old --

"There are four kisses in this line; why four, is there anything happening"?

"Oh yeah; he got carried away".

"But kissing like this was standard form, way back when..."

"I think he fancies her".

"Yes, very good – well done"!

Scott was leading a discussion with his Tuesday group and as luck would have it, talking about 'La belle dame sans merci' – one of his early favourites. It was always good to talk about Keats with young people, because he was their first rebel, the first with youthful angst; a tortured romantic, happy friend and faithful suitor. This was the first reading of the poem, but the class already heard of John Keats; the eighteenth century poet dying overseas at an early age, so that he always belonged to the young.

The boy with the answer took heart over Scot's comments to enter a new level of competence; he was drawn into the literary world of pastoral lyrics, good opinions of teachers and the favour of his classmates. Scott was keen to capture his interest, to wrestle the attention away from physics or mathematics. Scott knew about the competition from other departments and had no compunction to sway his students, to persuade/direct them towards literature and the success of language, the problem of love and images of humanity. In this way, Scott was never feint-hearted, coy or ambiguous. In fact it was the only activity he was sure of, the only thing he believed and trusted, was prepared to work at. This was top of the mountain for him, the cherry on top; a splendid journey for himself and for those he loved.

"The knight's feelings have changed towards her". The boy was hunched over the text and reaching for more credit.

"Let's read it again, Ivor; please start from the beginning".

The boy took a deep breath and did a good job with a spoken language that was long gone, almost dead and buried. The phraseology appeared very obtuse and awkward for a sixteen year-old in West London, but he made some sense of it. Old language and romantic themes were far off for modern kids, a long distance away from their post-modern world.

Vietnam was also far from the UK as you can get; but sooner or later every nationality appeared in foggy London town. Scott knew of the troubled nation from America, because of the military action taken against communists. A lot of his friends were called-up to enlist and fight. Little did he know the Bac Viets would become his neighbours, right here in Kensington; though he avoided going over to their country all those years ago.

Phong was about thirteen years old; a special age for any girl, when they are at a crossroads in adolescence and specially vulnerable to impressions. She was from

Saigon, a refugee with the boat people, by-way of an internment camp in Hong Kong; very quiet in the class and distant in her dealings with others. So much that Scott noticed her straight away; he was intrigued by her stoicism, dignity, her Asian mystique.

Surprisingly, the girls were very loud and excited that day, requiring Scott to get angry and stop the lesson. A short condemnation was called for, to restore a sense of purpose in the lesson. He looked across the rows of faces to admonish and saw that Phong was missing; yet she had been present at the beginning and was not normally tardy or absent from school. But her place was now conspicuously empty.

"Where is Phong; I thought..."

"She is under her desk, Sir".

"Really..."

In disbelief Scott treaded a few steps forward from his own desk at the front and peered at her place to see a crouching figure upon the floor, just as he was told. He declined to comment or look more closely, to avoid further embarrassment for the girl; a special kind of disgrace and estrangement loomed ahead for her. But Phong was down there squatting on the floor and no one knew why or what to make of it, what to think. It was something new for everybody, something distinctly different and no one understood what her action really meant. Scott could only think of it as shame; an eastern response to misbehaviour and old style respect for elders. He decided to step back and leave her alone; there was nothing to say and nothing more to do. Phong had served an object lesson to everyone and her classmates; because of a rowdy start to the Humanities lesson, she reacted in a singular way to remember her by.

Two days later Scott enjoyed a very different world, a far cry from disturbed teens in a city jungle. It was Sunday and he was hosting a very English event; a quintessential test for English gents at the home of a newly made-over resident. They were gathered round the table like characters from a Lewis Carroll story.

"Alright, we have one boiled egg each – well, two if need be; but I don't recommend the cholesterol"!

"Great idea, this tea-party, Scott. We went in the park before and --"

"Got a good appetite; you can have extra toast".

"Lovely egg cups, Scott".

"Got them from 'Woolies', you know, the great proletariat store. I saw Tony Benn in there last week, stocking up on batteries; like he was fore-warned"!

"Buying votes more like it; not goods and services, come on".

"No, he's long past votes; he's looking for kudos,

you know".

The men sat with open shirts and summer slacks – it was meant to be a brief interlude in late afternoon – then out to the happy throng in the park again, or traipsing the tired streets to go off home. Their chat was short and breezy, with upbeat moods and diverse topics, a ready mix of fun and info.

"Very small, this place – how'd'you live here"?

"Well – each piece of furniture has three tasks or it goes out".

"What about this stool"?

"You can sit upon it, stand on it to reach the top shelves, or it serves as end-table for the couch".

"Anything else"?

"Yeah, sit this way for dining, then turn your chair to face the TV".

"More jam, please and more tea – vicar".

"Oh dear, we forgot to say 'Grace'"!

"For what we're about to receive --"

"-- is totally unexpected".

"and very under-priced".

"Ever get any girl-friends in here Scott; to sleep over I mean? How can you"?

"Our host does very well for himself; that's enough heckling, just shut-up and chow-down"!

Two young teachers sat with Scott and his church

pal, round a nice pinewood table to relish a small repast at about four-thirty-pm. The sun spilled from the main sash window, to remind them it was mid-summer, just as much fun outside; still glorious light out there in the royal borough west of the main city. He forgot about Phong and what she might be doing away from school; he forgot about Vietnam and Hong Kong, for a while. But he was to meet another Asian student in North Kensington, the next term; this time it was to be a boy. Yet like the girl, he too was estranged and plaintive --

It was lunch hour and Scott drew supervision duty for the week, which allowed him a complimentary lunch for the week following. He had to head out to the playground at sound of the second bell, straight from the lesson and eat a sandwich on his rounds of the yards and corridors. This boys school also had a garden area of sorts in the main yard, where a few scraggly trees covered rough ground meant to sport green grass cover. But the boys never allowed this to happen, because they constantly scampered over it with balls and rough footwear.

It was Spring and Scott was enjoying his duty that warm day as he sauntered round to the main gates to return by the bike sheds, scouting for any kind of misbehaviour or unwanted visitors at the front. The local neighbourhood was tough working class and often rough youths were at the main entrance, appearing uncouth and suspicious. Scott could guess at all kinds of foolish connections between the lads outside and the silly ones inside school – it was a niggling worry for the admin and teachers with pastoral duties. He saw two teens outside with cigarettes, leaning against an adjacent wall and enjoying the idea of annoying Scott, embarrassing him infront of his school kids. He was not angry, he was only bored with this repeating scenario; but took a look at the faces in case it became necessary to remember them. One of them was a regular nuisance with his black bomber jacket, the smoking and dropping butt-ends to the ground around his feet.

However, Scott was not to be distracted and continued his patrol of likely trouble spots, the bike stands and dark corners in the school corridors. He stepped past the garden patch and noticed a figure under the biggest tree bush. It was a boy, one of his own boys in Year-Nine, Trinh from Vietnam. Scott stopped his trek and looked harder, to be sure. It was Trinh and he comfortably squatting on the ground against the trunk upright, blowing into a long pipe. There was a feint sound like woodwind, coming from the tree – a surprising touch of Zen in a London playground. It looked like he had been there awhile and intending to remain; but he appeared content, at peace with his new world far from home. Eventually, he noticed Scott and lowered his head, not inclined to talk or explain himself. The music continued; it was a foreign sound, unlike any western melodies, strangely dissonant; probably a Vietnamese piece to remind him of somewhere, something he had to leave behind.

Scott was intrigued but remained put to be sure the boy was safe and untroubled. Then he stepped back to show respect and empathy; he had chanced upon something very new for a London teacher and was trying to discern it, to realize clearly the boy should be left alone. The other boys at play were also ignoring Trinh, the way he wished, though they must have seen him. Scott thought it a happy event at lunch break if the others did not mind, if the sun shone from above and the boy did not forget about his bamboo pipe.

The next posting for Scott was out towards Kent, a long rail journey and miles away from new immigrants. These kids were distinctly Anglo, with red hair and freckles, chalky white complexions and strong identities --

"Mister Robinson, this is Misses Gordon; my daughter, Anne, is in your class".

"Yes, Nine-C, I think it is. In fact, I had the class today". But Scott had a difficult time hearing.

"That's what I wanted to talk about"!

The class were attempting a grammar comprehension exercise and Anne always sat in the back row with two friends. But they chatted constantly and loud too; it was a continual disruption. And today he acted upon it; he moved Anne forward directly infront of Scott. She was middle of the three, to create a space between the other two. Immediately the lesson became easier and more pleasant for Scott. He did the right thing and thought no more about it.

Scott was on his mobile phone, walking across open ground on way to the train station; going home at end of day, all the way from the south-east outskirts of London into Kensington.

The mother was talking, obviously irate and stubborn: "Why punish Anne like that; she wasn't doing anything wrong"!?

"I did not punish her".

"You forced her to the front row".

"I really had no choice".

"And left her friends, said nothing to them. It's not fair"!

"She is doing better at the front; it's not punishment".

"What about the other two"?

"They had to be separated".

"But why move Anne"?

"It was arbitrary".

"What does that mean; are you trying to be rude"!?

It was a fine afternoon and a welcome breeze blew across Scott's face. His tie was loosened and the top button of his shirt opened – he needed air and space. When the phone first rang Scott was mid-field behind the school; he could see a clump of oak trees by the station; there were wildflowers following the pathway and rocks strewn over the open area, making it difficult to care for. It was rough ground, free from cultivation or design, to allow a weary teacher a place to breathe and come alive again. But the phone call spoiled everything, because the exchange ended badly, with anger and threats coming from the other end.

Some kids from the same school were also enjoying the parkland, two or three at a stone wall, clambering over it and yelling out. One of them stood up and waved two arms high above her head.

"Mister Robinson; goodnight, goodbye"! It was a girl, about fourteen and distinguished by her blazer badge. She seemed to be unworried, happy to be free after school and pleased to see Scott out on the common.

It was Anne; yes, the same girl from Nine-C,

Scott had moved to the front; the same girl whose mother had taken a grievance against. But he waved anyway. Scott held up his right arm/hand; more of a signal than a greeting to say 'Alright, you got me, I see you'. It dawned on Scott the girl talked to her mother earlier; how could she not know about the phone call. Would Anne guess what her mother might do; should she be glad to see Scott take the heat at an awkward moment!?

Back at home it was still sunny enough to sit outside before thinking of bedtime. He nursed a large mug of herb tea at his front porch to catch the last rays of sun warming his doorway for another half-hour. Where he finally met a whole family of Asian people, right on his own doorstep in middle Kensington; Vietnam people in the house next to Scott. They were veterans of the US intervention and refugees of the aftermath. One of the girls spoke of going to college and meeting British students --

"My friends keep asking about boyfriends; they want my advice. But I never had a boyfriend, my parents will not allow, till I get married". She was a lovely twenty-four year old, giving Scott an account of her dilemma. They often sat on the stone steps together at the front door, watching the youngest sister play with a small tricycle.

"At home in my village you get married in one day –
just go to the next village to meet his parents, where we
eat food and sit quietly with the elders. Then I go off to
his hut and leave my parents behind. But I'm not ready,
you must be ready, no one will force me. Everything is
different here and I don't understand".

Scott was looking into a broad open face. It was
honest and fearful of the future; worried about menfolk
and leaving her parents, her sisters – because they were
happy and ignorant of a world outside the family.
Pham had no brothers, only a father figure who was
thin and quiet, always smiling; smiling when he was
glad and when he was sad, when he was excited and
when he was scared. She knew he was not like other
men she encountered in London, nothing like the men
girls talked about.

The little girl infront was very silent but full of
activity with her trike. She rode round and round in a
small circle and kept getting off, then back on again. A
lot of work for a four-year old, a lot of love for the pink
plaything she had. She bit her lip and stuck out her
tummy with sheer pride and determination, because
her sister was sitting with a stranger and they were
watching. But Scott was no less foreign; he too was far
from America, with little opportunity to return while he
held a job and kept a home. Scott and the family next

door, Phong and Trinh, were found to be cohabiting an inner city core. They were the new material required of a living centre in a modern age; where differences like age, race or colour seemed not to matter – yet these things did matter.

Afterword

Of course London has changed since 1980 to 2000; but I purposely stayed within these confines, when cell-phones and the Internet were still in their infancy. The population is also changing; new immigrants arriving, students and celebrities; along with new programs from the Ministry of Education. I tried to maintain the milleur of the place and keep the details factual/ correct, for my years of residence. At the same time, to touch upon poignant things about children, parents and teachers (just about all of us). Lastly, I wanted to show modern London with all its anomalies and surprises. There are many things to think/talk about in the city, for interest far and wide; because it is a popular destination for more visitors than ever and not without good reasons – it is both dynamic and diverse, also historic.

Hoping you enjoyed these people and their stories; the schools stuff and a special location that has spawned lots of good authors and their own tales. I think it fitting that London has loads of kids cohabiting the popular sites, behind the adult activities like commerce and government – because there is vitality/fun in these children that is infectious and pervasive...

—

I was born in the North-East of England and attended school there; but first went into farm work, then to the Royal Agricultural College in Gloucestershire. Shortly after I went to Canada and then onto California, where I worked at many diverse jobs; finally ending up at university in Vancouver, to study English and Education. So far I have written five books of poetry and short articles on current events for 'Mensa' (joining in 1997). I trained to be a secondary English teacher, but taught lots of different subjects and primary schools, all over central London and sometimes in the outskirts (such as Ealing). Truly, my experience was very comprehensive – church schools, lower income and middle income, high achievers and low achievers...